**Marine-Terrace, Saint-Hélier, Jersey, Sept. 29, 1854.
'Death' speaks to Victor Hugo through the tables:**

"May your posthumous work be still a living thing, so that, at certain intervals, it will be able to talk to posterity and tell it unknown things which will have had time to ripen in the grave. What is impossible today is necessary tomorrow. In your Last Will and Testament, space out your posthumous works, one every ten years, one every five years. Can you not see the greatness of a tomb which, from time to time, in periods of human crisis, when some shadow passes over progress, when clouds blot out the ideal, suddenly opens its lips of stone and speaks?

"Christ was resurrected only once; you can fill your grave with resurrections; you can, if my advice seems good to you, have an extraordinary death; you would say while dying: You will awaken me in 1920; you will awaken me in 1940; you will awaken me in 1960; you will awaken me in 1980; you will awaken me in the year 2000."

Original transcript page, in the handwriting of Victor Hugo, from a turning table seance held at Marine-Terrace, Jersey island. Named as present are Victor Hugo, Mme. Adèle Hugo, their daughter, Adèle, and Auguste Vacquerie. Date unknown, probably autumn, 1853. Discovered only recently, this page is not included in the edition of the transcripts in Volume IX of <u>The Complete Works of Victor Hugo</u>, *ed. Jean Massin, Le Club Français du Livre, Paris, 1967-1969. Reproduced with the kind permission of Frédéric Castaing, Autographes et Documents Historiques, 13 rue Chapon 75003, Paris, France.*

De nous quatre, qui est ce qui a le plus de fluide?
Adèle
la mère ou la fille? la fille
Après elle? Auguste
Après lui? Victor
Qui es tu? Tu es un rouge
Je méprise la France
Continue. A battre murs
Ton nom? La délivrance.
C'est une abstraction la délivrance mais ton nom?
La foi.
Donne-nous d'autres synonymes de toi.
- [Rature en forme d'X surmonté d'une croix chrétienne] Homme, fi, tu es un sujet rare.
Qu'entends-tu par sujet rare?
D'ou es-tu sorti corromps
Toujours ton nom?
La femme de la multitude.

Of us four, who has the most fluid?
Adèle
mother or daughter? Daughter
After her? Auguste
After him? Victor
Who are you? You are a red
I hold France in contempt
Continue. Knock down walls.
Your name? Deliverance.
'Deliverance' is an abstraction.
What's your name?
Faith.
Give us other synonyms for yourself.
- [Erasure in the form of an X with a Christian cross on top.]
Man, for shame, you are a rare subject.
What do you mean by rare subject?
From whence did you emerge corrupt?
We're still asking for your name?
The woman of the multitude.

See Verso

Je vous, quatre, qui es que a le plus
de plus ? — Août.

Le mieux ou la fille ? — la fille.

après elle ? — Auguste.

après lui ? — Victor.

qui es-tu ? — Tu es un rouge.

Je méprise la France

Baptême. — Dans abattre

mur.

Ton nom ? — La Délivrance.

... obstruction les oiseaux
... toi-même ? — la foi.

Que ... nous ... d'aussi ...

à toi. — L'homme, fils tu es

un ~~...~~ sujet rare

... tu ... ?

— D'où es-tu sorti corrompis

... ton nom ? — De femme

de la multitude.

CONVERSATIONS WITH ETERNITY

THE FORGOTTEN MASTERPIECE OF VICTOR HUGO

TRANSLATED WITH A COMMENTARY BY
JOHN CHAMBERS

WITH AN INTRODUCTION BY
MARTIN EBON

BOCA RATON

NEW
PARADIGM
BOOKS

1998

NEW PARADIGM BOOKS
22783 South State Road 7
Suite 97
Boca Raton, FL 33428
The New Paradigm Books Web Site address is:
http://www.newpara.com

CONVERSATIONS WITH ETERNITY:
THE FORGOTTEN MASTERPIECE OF VICTOR HUGO
Copyright © 1998 by New Paradigm Books
Translation © 1998 by John Chambers
Cover design and illustrations by Knockout Design
Map Created by Peri Poloni

The publisher wishes to thank the Bibliothèque Nationale of Paris for permission
to reproduce artist's renderings of seven channeled drawings communicated to
Victor Hugo and now in the possession of the Bibliothèque Nationale. It wishes
to thank Alfred A. Knopf, the publisher, for permission to reprint selected passages
from *The Changing Light at Sandover* by James Merrill, Copyright © 1980, 1982
by James Merrill; to thank Beyond Words, the publisher, for permission to reprint
selected passages from *Songs of the Arcturians* by Patricia Pereira, Copyright ©
1996 by Patricia L. Pereira; and to thank New Solutions, the publisher, for
permission to reprint selected passages from *Bashar: Blueprint for Change. A
Message from Our Future* by Darryl Anka, Bashar material Copyright © by Darryl
Anka, compilation, *Bashar: Blueprint for Change*, Copyright © 1990 by Luana
Ewing.

First New Paradigm Books Quality Paperback Edition: November 1998
New Paradigm Books ISBN No. 1-8921138-01-8
Library of Congress Preassigned Catalog No. 98-065689

10 9 8 7 6 5 4 3 2 1

THE FORGOTTEN MASTERPIECE OF VICTOR HUGO

This book is dedicated to the memory of my father-in-law

Morris "Mike" Tarnpoll

1913-1996

CONTENTS

THE NON-LIVING DRAMATIS PERSONAE (HISTORICAL AND ABSTRACT) OF THE *CONVERSATIONS WITH ETERNITY*: The Names of the Spirits who Spoke through the Turning Tables, in Alphabetical Order and with the Number of Appearances.

Abel (1)
Aeschylus (4)
Aesop (1)
Alexander (1)
Amelia (a fairy) (1)
Amuca (Babac) (1)
Anacreon (1)
Andre (Pinson's Brother) (1)
Apuleus (1)
Archangel Love, The (1)
Aristophanes (1)
Aristotle (1)
Ass of Balaam, The (1)
Being Speaking Latin (1)
Being, A (1)
Bonnivard (1)
Byron (1)
Cagliostro (1)
Cain (1)
Cerpola the Shepherd (1)
Cesarion (1)
Charlet (1)
Chateaubriand (1)
Chenier, Andre (7)
Cimarosa (1)
Civilization (1)
Comedy (1)
Comet, A (1)
Corday, Charlotte (1)
Criticism (2)
Damianiels (1)
Dante (1)
Death (7)
Delorme, Marion (1)
Diderot (1)
Diogenes (1)
Drama, The (16)

Finger of Death, The (1)
Flamel, Nicholas (1)
Galileo (2)
Glory (1)
Grim Gatekeeper, The (1)
Hannibal (1)
Happiness (1)
Haynau (1)
Idea, The (6)
India (1)
Inspiration (1)
Iron Mask, The (1)
Isaac Laquedem (1)
Isaiah (1)
Jacob (1)
Jesus Christ (6)
Joan of Arc (1)
Joshua (3)
Judas (1)
Lady in White, The (3)
Lais (1)
Latude (1)
Leonidas (1)
Lion of Androcles, The (18)
Lion of Florence, The (1)
Lope de Vega (1)
Louis-Philippe (1)
Luther (2)
Machiavelli (1)
Marat (1)
Marie-Blanche (1)
Metempsychosis (1)
Mohammed (1)
Molière (11)
Moses (1)
Mother, Durrieu's (1)
Mozart (3)

Napoleon I (The Great) (1)
Napoleon III (Louis Bonaparte) (1)
Novel, The (3)
Ocean, The (2)
Plato (1)
Poetry (1)
Prayer (1)
Racine (1)
Raphael (1)
Reverie (1)
Robespierre (1)
Roothan (1)
Rousseau, Jean-Jacques (2)
Russia (1)
Sappho (1)
Sesostris (1)
Shadow of the Sepulcher, The (9)
Shakespeare (11)
Sister Soul (Ame Soror) (1)
Socrates (2)
Spirits, Assorted (7)
Table draws a series of pictures (2)
Tragedy (1)
Tyatafia (from Jupiter) (1)
Tertius (1)
Vestra (1)
Vestris (1)
Voltaire (2)
Vulcan (1)
Vux (1)
Walter Scott, Sir (1)
White Wing, The (1)
Wind of the Sea, The (1)
Z (2)
Zoile (1)

WHAT THE TURNING TABLES TOLD

THE WORLDS OF REWARD

THE PUNITARY WORLDS

The Imprisoned Souls of the World of Mankind

of the World of Animals

The Imprisoned Souls

ENGLISH CHANNEL

The Imprisoned Souls of the World of Plants

GUERNSEY

CHANNEL ISLANDS

SAINT-HÉLIER

JERSEY

The Imprisoned Souls of the World of Stones

FRANCE

THE MANY WORLDS OF VICTOR HUGO

As Communicated to the Exiled Poet on the Channel island of Jersey September, 1853, to October, 1855

Saint-Hélier to London
188 miles/300 km

Saint-Hélier to Paris
200 miles/320 km

Acknowledgements

I would first of all like to express my profound gratitude to Martin Ebon, dean of writers on the Paranormal (and many other subjects as well) in the United States, without whose extremely gracious and extraordinarily generous support this project could never have been completed. It is an honor that *Conversations with Eternity: The Forgotten Masterpiece of Victor Hugo* should begin with his Introduction.

My heartfelt thanks also to Guyon Neutze, Senior Lecturer, Educational Development Department, Wellington Polytechnic, New Zealand, one of the few philosophers willing and able to grapple with the complex problems of channeling, and whose comments and suggestions have been invaluable throughout. Thanks also to the ever-generous Marilyn Raphael, whose world-class classes in channeling provided me with precious insight into that most mysterious of processes.

For their help and support, I would also like to thank: my mother-in-law, Grace Tarnpoll; Patricia Pereira; Julia Jones; William Blaine Hill; Joseph Rowe; Alan Annand; Laura Fenoglio; Barbara Norcross and Diana Neutze.

And thank you, also, to Judy, without whom, as always, not a single word of this would ever have been written.

Introduction

VICTOR THE GRANDIOSE

By Martin Ebon

In the fall of 1950, I was sitting in a half-empty office at the "Voice of America," surrounded by books, files and clippings on the subject of Indochina. I had just been appointed to direct the newly-established Vietnamese Unit of the United States' short-wave and medium-wave broadcasts to Viet Nam, having previously served as head of the information agency's broadcasts to Indonesia. (Later, I would take over the Hindi and Urdu units, transmitting to India and Pakistan.) Now, I had to immerse myself in the political-economic and religio-cultural milieu of a new target area: Viet Nam. Remember, this was years before the United States became involved in the Viet Nam War; at that time, the armed struggle was for the future of Korea.

All went smoothly, until I came to the religious orientations of the Vietnamese people, and read that the third-largest religious movement, after Roman Catholicism and Buddhism, was a denomination known as the Cao Dai. I read that this was, broadly speaking, an amalgam of Eastern and Western faiths—and that one of its three major saints was the French poet-novelist-playwright and politically volatile persona, Victor Hugo (1802-1885). I had a fairly good idea of Hugo as a commanding literary figure in Europe of the nineteenth century; but, aware of his controversial life style, I had never thought of him as a saint of anything, anywhere, at any time. And what, exactly, was the Cao Dai?

Bear with me for a minute! Caodaism considers itself, "The Third Alliance between God and Man." Its actual founder was Ngo Minh Chieu, born in 1878, a civil servant for a short time in Saigon, who, in 1902, underwent the spiritistic experience that literally "inspired" him to found this all-encompassing religion. Thus the movement's belief-system was rooted in the region's deep spiritistic traditions; with followers numbering in excess of two million today, it represents God's third attempt to convey His Ultimate Truths to humanity. In November, 1926, Chieu revealed the conclusions of his four years of mediumistic contacts with the dead, many of them distinguished and prominent.

Chieu regarded the first attempt at conveying the divine message as coinciding with the emergence of Buddhism, Confucianism and Taoism; the second contact was personified by Moses and Jesus; and the third attempt centered on the Middle Buddha. (Buddhism went through a variety of stages and regional adaptations). As an amalgam of Eastern and Western religious principles, Caodaism embraces universal ethical standards, and has widely adopted vegetarianism. "Cao Dai" may be translated as "Tower of the Highest," a metaphor for God. The religion's unique characteristic lies in its combination of traditional, actually pre-historic, ancestor-worship, its rituals that closely resemble such spiritistic techniques as trance mediumship, and so-called automatic writing.

One Cao Dai link to Victor Hugo appears to be his own voluminous spirit communications, detailed in this volume, while his family was in exile on the Channel island of Jersey. In fact, the wide-ranging messages from prominent personalities, collected by Caodaism, closely resemble the astonishing number of alleged historic spirit entities who manifested at the Jersey seances. The Hugo sittings, as far as we can tell, centered on the spiritistic rapping movements of a table leg, or actual table-turning.

Initially, Caodaist spirit communications were undertaken by table-turning. When participants complained that this was an extremely time-consuming technique, the entities suggested what appears to be a very sophisticated variation of traditional spiritistic automatic writing. The central device was a wicker basket shaped like a crow. Four ropes were attached to the basket, which was known as a *corbeille à bec*. Each rope was held by a different medium, so that no single personality would, in any way, be the sole instrument of communication. The basket was positioned in such a way that the "beak" of its crow-shape made contact with flat, fine sand beneath; thus, the writings were visible in the sand.

The Cao Dai spirit of Victor Hugo evolved from communications originating with an entity who initially called itself Nguyet Tam Chon Nhon, but later stated that it was, in fact, the spirit of the famous Victor Hugo. Adherents have meticulously recorded that the first, momentous encounter with this spirit took place on April 20, 1930, at 1:00 a.m., the earthly interviewer being one Ho-Phap. A bit later, the entity said that one prominent Caodaist, Tran quang Vinh, was, actually, a reincarnation of the French poet's third son, François-Victor Hugo (1828-1873). Tran later became head of the Cao Dai Army, and eventually Minister of Defense (1948-1951) in the ill-fated government of Bao Dai. During a session of the Cao Dai's legislative body, Victor Hugo was appointed titular head of the movement's "Foreign Missions."

One of many messages received by the Caodaists from the alleged spirit of Victor Hugo speaks eloquently of Beauty, Divine Peace and Harmony, Science and Wisdom, as well as of the spirit's perception that "within the infinite, countless universes exist," whose inhabitants "do not know the word War," and in whom "the spirit supersedes mortal frailties." The entity also communicated that, "Death is overcome through high consciousness; death and life are but the same..."

Now, back to the flesh-and-blood Victor Hugo, whose extraordinary prominence evolved within a very specific psycho-cultural and religio-political framework of nineteenth century France, and, specifically, within the highly politicized literary society of Paris. To say that Victor Hugo, throughout his life, was a man of multiple contradictions, comes close to understatement.

Victor was the third son of a brash, self-centered father, ultimately General Joseph-Léopold-Sigisbert Hugo (1773-1828), who served in the army of Napoleon Bonaparte, or Emperor Napoleon I (1769-1821). General Hugo was intermittently stationed abroad, including Italy and Spain, and his family accompanied him on occasion. While Victor's father was, at least by reasons of career, a monarchist, his mother, Sophie, was, by private sentiment and conviction, republican and, therefore, anti-monarchist. Father and mother managed to get along by a mixture of mutual disregard and opportunistic tolerance.

Victor Hugo himself remained a monarchistic republican and a republicanistic monarchist, a liberal and a conservative, an elitist and a populist, for most of his contradictory life. It is difficult to imagine, in retrospect, the impact of a literary colossus such as Victor Hugo during the century that his life spanned. No matter how eccentric or volatile his beliefs might have been, at any given time he was capable of expressing them in such prose or poetry that he could provoke the roaring cheers of the Parisian masses as well as the jealousy-tainted approval of his peers and rivals.

What was he, then? Well, what was he not?

The term, "mad genius," has pretty well gone out of fashion. But it certainly applied to Victor Hugo. With due respect for exact clinical terminology, one might well generalize that he fitted, at one time or another, the categories of egomaniac, mythomaniac, and, quite possibly, manic-depressive. His hunger for admiration could never be stilled. He was eager for honors and

4

awards, such as membership in the Académie Française. He was elected to parliament, where he made long, provocative, and at times barely coherent speeches. But even if readers found it difficult to comprehend the "deeper meaning" of one of his long, metaphor-ridden poems, they might still be pulled along by the soaring rhythm of his words. Listeners, in turn, could be carried away by the fire of his passion, by his rousing, lyrical oratorical fireworks. The fierce power behind it all was not only the fire of Hugo's genius, but also the unquenchable thirst to be admired, loved, and even worshipped.

The French Empire, under Napoleon the Great, the Corsican Joseph Bonaparte (1769-1821)— who had placed the royal crown on his own head at the Cathedral of Notre Dame on December 2, 1804—spread all over Europe. One conquest demanded yet another, and still another. And all this neo-monarchistic expansionism happened, we must remember, after the bloody, history-making, anti-monarchist French Revolution of 1789.

Napoleon's armies swept on. Most of Europe was overrun. As the grand conquests continued, the apparently invincible Emperor was hugely popular throughout France, and aroused admiration, sincere or opportunistic, within much of Europe. Yet, England and Russia eluded him. Eventually, grossly over-extended, Napoleon had to retreat from Moscow in 1812. With this, he seemed to retreat from history as well.

Victor Marie Hugo was born at Besançon, on February 16, 1802. So, when Napoleon resigned, on April 11, 1814, little Hugo was twelve years old. Napoleon was exiled to the Island of Elba, and a member of the royal Bourbon family, Louis XVIII, took over the reign of the disillusioned nation. But, with surprising speed and daring, Napoleon made his stunning come-back. On March 15, 1815, he arrived at France's Mediterranean coast with an army of 1,000 men. They rapidly marched up to Paris; Napoleon re-conquered an unresisting France in three weeks. The masses, fickle and frightened, re-embraced the man whom they had reviled as a monster only months before.

But this Grand Illusion was quickly followed by Total Disillusion: Napoleon's effort to re-conquer Europe ended with his ultimate defeat on June 18 at the Battle of Waterloo. He abdicated a second time. Napoleon was taken into exile once more and died on the Island of Saint Helena, on May 5, 1816; he was 52 years old.

The end of the Napoleonic Era also marked the end of the profitable military career of General Hugo. Son Victor had accompanied his father, briefly, to Italy when he was five years old. By the time he was eleven, the Hugo family had settled comfortably in occupied Spain, where Victor was fascinated by the exotic scenery, and picked up some of the Spanish language. He had also learned Latin.

The Hugo family, like much of the society that had allied itself with Napoleon, fell on relatively hard times. Little Hugo received a rather scrappy education. Beginning in 1815, he lived at the Pension Cordier and attended lectures at Louis-le-Grand College. His literary fascinations burgeoned. He had always admired the work of Voltaire (1694-1778), perhaps the leading figure of the eighteenth century "Enlightenment" movement. Now Victor read voraciously. He also did quite well in philosophy, geometry and physics.

Soon, his volcanic literary talents began to erupt, and he wrote a string of verses, odes, satires, acrostics, riddles, epics and madrigals. Victor's older brother, Joseph-Abel, edited a journal, *Le Conservateur Littéraire*. Victor contributed a horror novel, *Bug-Jargal*, to the short-lived periodical, but also a great deal of quite marginal writings. In his mid-teens, he had all the makings of a hack writer. *Bug-Jargal* was a bloody, highly-charged terror yarn about a violent rebellion in Santo Domingo.

That, in later years, Victor Hugo achieved a wide popular readership might well be attributed to elements of horror and the macabre in much of his writings. Today's audiences of the musical based on *Les Misérables* miss much of the stench, sadism and plain cruelty contained in the original novel. And those who have seen the Disney cartoon version of Hugo's melodrama, known in its English version as *The Hunchback of Notre-Dame*, are deprived of the ultimate macabre scene, which shows the skeletons of the Hunchback and his much-pursued lady love in a final, mortal embrace.

Victor's mother died in June, 1821. He refused money from his father. And, secretly engaged to his childhood sweetheart, Adèle Foucher, Victor Hugo spent a year sweating it out on the fringes of poverty. His observations during this period would later provide material for his hugely successful novel, *Les Misérables*, melodramatically embroidered with cruel incidents. The universally successful musical, based on this novel of the poor, maltreated and deprived, greatly softens Hugo's ultimate macabre touch.

Hugo could not have written in his uninhibited style had the traditional, so-called "classical" literary style continued to prevail. Victor Hugo, who sometimes composed full-length poems virtually in his sleep, refused to be confined to a literary straight jacket he regarded as outdated and essentially meaningless. He thus became the most prominent spokesman of a literary approach which, for much of the century, flourished under the benign label of "Romanticism."

But Romanticism, in that period's literary sense, does not correspond to our popular and contemporary meaning of the term. Today, Romanticism is commonly identified with the purely erotic: the Romance Novel, Romantic Love, and the word "Romance" as indicating a love affair. Consequently, dictionary definitions of

7

"Romanticism" are forced to cite disparate interpretations. One that would apply to the Hugo period describes "Romanticism" as a "literary and artistic movement, originating in Europe toward the end of the 18th century, that sought to assert the validity of subjective experience and to escape from the prevailing subordination of content and feeling to classical forms" (*The American Heritage Dictionary of the English Language*, New York: American Heritage Publishing Co., Inc., 1969). Of course, Romanticism included, in its emphasis on "the validity of subjective experience," the specifically erotic, possibly the most subjective of all human experiences.

Victor Hugo had entered the Parisian literary-political scene at ramming-speed. He quickly perfected the game of sending groveling letters of thanks to his teachers and other betters, often by writing odes in their praise. Graham Robb, in his comprehensive biography, Victor Hugo, states that his "most successful ode was the poetic begging bowl held out to M. le Compte François de Neufchateau, of l'Académie Française. It earned Hugo a powerful patron." It also revealed his early understanding, and skillful manipulation, of the powerful, the rich and the decision-makers, both in literary and political affairs. Among other deals, Hugo became Neufchateau's secret ghost-writer. His new mentor later arranged a royal pension for the sixteen-year-old poet. All his life, Victor Hugo's letters could deliver the most obsequious and flattering hyperbole, as well as the most vicious contempt, denunciation and accusation—all in his poetic or pseudo-poetic melodramatic vernacular, frequently exceeding the boundaries of the rational, or even of his own true convictions.

Victor's career-building-by-ingratiation accelerated as he entered his twenties. He targeted the French Court, and specifically the person of Louis XVIII. His device was a volume of verses, *Odes et Poésies Diverses*, which contained the appropriate number of love poems for his fiancée, Adèle Foucher, but was clearly designed to attract the sentimental attention of Louis XVIII. In fact, Hugo's elegy in memory of the Duc de Berry is said to have brought tears to the eyes of the monarch. He gave young Victor a pension from the privy purse. This was in 1822, and Hugo was just twenty years old. The following year, the pension was doubled.

With money in his pocket, he heightened his courtship of Adèle, and the two were married on October 14, 1822. The great and lasting family tragedy was that Victor's brother, Eugène Hugo, was passionately in love with Adèle; but Eugène had shown signs of mental imbalance from time to time. If we can trust melodramatic records, he went mad on the day of the wedding, and ultimately had to be committed to an asylum where he died in 1837.

Professionally, Victor Hugo continued his output of prose and poetry. He wrote another popular horror novel, *Han d'Islande*. He had, of course, never been to Iceland, and this novelistic fantasy featured Hugo's first disfigured protagonist (in the vein of Quasimodo), Han, a red-haired dwarf. Robb summarizes the plot with as much detachment as seems possible:

"The novel opens promisingly, in the morgue at Trondheim. Bodies have been torn to shreds as if by a long-haired beast. Meanwhile, among the icy crags to the north lurks a weird, red-haired dwarf, the son of a witch and the last descendant of Ingulphus the Exterminator. Abandoned in Iceland, the hideous infant, Han, was taken in by a saintly bishop (a forerunner of Bishop Myriel in *Les Misérables*). Immune to Christian charity, he torches the bishop's palace and sets sail by the light of the flames on a tree trunk, bound for Norway. There, he incinerates Trondheim cathedral, whose flying buttresses now resemble the rib-cage of a mammoth's carcass. He slaughters regiments, hurls mountains down on villages, extinguishes beacons with a single breath, carries a stone axe, and rides a polar bear called 'Friend.' He also provides a tenuous link with the rest of the novel by stealing the casket which contains proof of the father's innocence."

Considering that not only Broadway, but Hollywood, have discovered Victor Hugo's works, this horror fantasy might yet find a fresh market, either as a sex-and-violence motion picture (with earlier episodes on television), or as a musical melodrama. Robb comments that the horror play and Victor's letters to Adèle "spanned two years of unrequited lust, and formed a ramshackle bridge over the abyss opened by his mothers death" on June 21, 1821.

In order to be able to marry Adèle, Victor applied to the King for yet another pension. He managed to get it, and so the two were married on October 12, 1822. His prominence increased, while he maintained a delicate balance between his neo-monarchist conservatism and the emerging literary revolution. He received the Legion of Honor, as well as a personal invitation to the coronation of Charles X at Rheims.

The next decades re-enforced his position as France's outstanding progressive literary figure. Novels, poems and plays flowed from his pen. Their content and form reflected a spirit of emotional liberation which, inevitably, put him once again at odds with monarchistic paternalism. The symbol of this literary-political conflict was Hugo's play, *Hernani*, which he wanted to be performed at that center of French theatrical arts, the Comédie Française. On the surface, this was just another exotic, fanciful melodrama, set in Spain. It centers on the fate of a beautiful young girl, in love with a handsome persecuted hero, who seeks to rebuff the advances of several repulsive old men—one of whom is a royal personality, a lustful sovereign called, of all things, Charles. The opening night of the play became the scene of a war of generations, with teenagers in open revolt against social restrictions. On the afternoon of Thursday, February 25, 1830, a huge line began to form outside the theater, clogging up the Rue Richelieu.

During the performance, rowdy applause followed particularly outrageous lines—as when the young hero tells pretty Doña Sol's lecherous guardian, "Go, get yourself measured for a coffin, old man." Satire became standard tragedy, as, in the final act, Hernani and Doña Sol die in each other's arms. According to Graham Robb, the audience erupted into "simultaneous booing and cheering, fisticuffs and arrests." It was, Robb adds, prophetic "enactment—even, in some minds, a direct cause—of what was to happen in the streets."

With success came prosperity. The Hugo family moved to new quarters, a comfortable apartment on Rue Jean-Goujon, surrounded by fresh air, trees and a lawn. Victor and Adèle Hugo had three children by then: Léopoldine, Charles and François-Victor, soon to be joined by a fourth, conveniently called Adèle II. But success took an emotional toll. Victor Hugo became more and more autocratic, egocentric, and eccentric. His literary output was, if anything, exceeded by his conveyor belt of sexual liaisons. He had become, in current terms, a stud, and women yielded to or pursued him like groupies. Meanwhile, his wife, Adèle, had formed a tentative liaison with Hugo's old friend, the respected literary critic, Charles-Augustin Sainte-Beuve (1804-1869). Dramatically, Sainte-Beuve used to sneak into the Hugo apartment when Victor was elsewhere, disguised as a nun. The affair ended when Sainte-Beuve, rather abjectly, confessed his love for Adèle to Hugo.

Meanwhile, on the streets of Paris, history caught up with Hugo's revolutionary play, *Hernani*. On July 25, 1830, Charles X dissolved parliament and abolished freedom of the press. A bloody three-day uprising followed (July 27-29), and Louis-Philippe was crowned "King of the French." Monarchy was back in full force. It was also a new disaster. But Hugo was undeterred in his creative energies: In April, 1831, he published Notre Dame de Paris, which, as *The Hunchback of Notre Dame*, achieved lasting world-wide fame.

But first, on the see-saw between public life and sex, back to sex! On February 2, 1833, Hugo's latest play, *Lucrezia Borgia*, was being cast. The part of Princess Negroni was given to a young, beautiful actress, Juliette Drouet. She quickly became Hugo's Number One Mistress, and remained—always, discreetly, a few houses removed—his very close friend for half a century.

Some of Hugo's finest love lyrics were addressed to Juliette. And, tragically, some of his most memorable verses of grief and mourning were prompted by the drowning death of his daughter, Léopoldine, in early September, 1843. Hearing the news of this tragedy, and in an oddly self-centered note to Adèle, his wife, Victor wrote, "My God, what have I done to you?"

If we glance forward, to the dramatic seances to which this book is devoted, we may view the death of Léopoldine as the central emotional core in Victor Hugo's dramatic dialogue with death, and its implied assurance of eternal life.

Poetry moved into the background when, in 1845, Hugo was elected a member of the House of Peers. His often contradictory but always dramatic verbiage did not fit into the traditions of the House. At Hugo's home, an atmosphere of fearful strain developed. The man himself, who wore the banner of a realistic atheist, seemed to fear a vengeful, malevolent God. Both he and Adèle turned to the erotic as an antidote to death, or to the fear of it. Adèle's friendships with the men in her crowd took on a flirtatious note. And Victor Hugo flung himself into a new infatuation, Léonie Biard. Later on, Léonie sent a batch of Victor's exuberant love letters to Juliette, presumably in order to break her relation with Victor; but Juliette had put up with too much of that sort of thing to be manipulated by yet another temporary rival.

Juliette, not lacking in either candor or humor, complained at one point that her cat, Fouyou, spent more time in bed with her than Hugo. As if it were not enough to have exhausted himself in a day's writing—he was then working hard on what was to become *Les Misérables*—Victor Hugo also kept an erotic diary, in code! The indomitable Juliette came across it, decoded most of it, and even asked a friend to translate the occasional Spanish phrases. Lively trans-Channel gossip kept the London literary scene up-to-date on Hugo's activities. One British writer, who, regrettably but understandably, remains anonymous, observed, "It would appear that, alternately, M. Hugo's pen and penis overflow."

Victor Hugo's multifarious pursuits came to a temporary halt due to the revolution he had anticipated, feared and favored. On February 12, 1848, Paris awoke to the sight of barricades everywhere. Louis-Philippe fled to England and settled in Surrey as 'Mr. Smith.' Hugo himself achieved a quite uncomfortable image as a Messiah of the Revolution. He was elected to the new National Assembly. But the Assembly wanted the rebels to halt the destruction of the city. This was the same "rabble who followed Jesus Christ," as Hugo had put it earlier. Which side was he on? He didn't really know himself.

Reprisals were fierce and chaotic. Government troops began to round up "suspects," four of them hidden by Juliette, who managed to talk her way out of the chaos. Hugo suffered from psychosomatic symptoms, including intermittent loss of his voice. The Assembly ended martial law on November 4, 1848, and placed executive power in the hands of a single head of state. Six days later, a president was elected whose name was Louis Napoleon Bonaparte, a nephew of the Great Napoleon. He was an odd bird, hesitant, reluctant, indecisive—the makings of a weak tyrant. Hugo described him later as "a man of weary gestures and a glazed expression," who "walks with an absent-minded air amidst the horrible things he does, like a sinister sleepwalker."

Before the election that brought him to power, the new Napoleon visited Hugo in his apartment. Sitting on a packing crate in the poet's front room, the new ruler pledged that he would not "copy" Napoleon, but seek to "imitate Washington." It was all quite humble, cozy, and falsely reassuring. Napoleon and the Assembly resorted to a frightened and frightening tyranny almost immediately. Victor Hugo found himself in the middle, orating fiercely, and profoundly challenged in his self-esteem.

It was then that the members of his household turned to the occult, a rehearsal for the day-and-night seances during their later exile on the Channel island of Jersey. One visitor, Georges Guenot, reported on a variety of apparent psychic phenomena at the Hugo apartment between the end of July and mid-November, 1851. The phenomena included alleged contact with the spirit world, and it is notable that, during this period, a variety of "progressive" movements, ranging from Socialism to Feminism, tended to run parallel with Spiritualism (Spiritisme, or Spiritism, in France). Contact with a spirit world was said to underscore the essential equality of all worlds, a unity of creation. Adèle Hugo sought the help of a "somnambulist," or "psychic," to contact relatives in Normandy. Rather questionable phenomena, such as reading words through a closed envelope, were reported, and participants attempted to or completely succeeded in pushing needles painlessly through their hands. Robb, somewhat obscurely, writes that "even the ghosts of Hugo's verse began to take on a more ectoplasmic consistency, long before the orgy of communication with the spirit world which is usually associated with the years in exile." This could mean that one or the other in the group went into a mediumistic trance, with the result that real or imaginary personages from Victor Hugo's poems manifested to the assembled group. If this interpretation is correct, there existed an emotional and practical basis for the more extensive spiritualistic phenomena on the Island of Jersey later on.

In any event, exile was just ahead. After successive efforts to come to terms with the increasingly tyrannical regime of Napoleon III, and under actual threat of arrest, Victor Hugo decided that his family was no longer safe in Paris, or anywhere else in France. On December 14, 1851, he escaped to Brussels, by train, in disguise. His family followed him, first to the Belgian capital, and eventually to the Channel island of Jersey, where they settled in a large house called Marine-Terrace.

Two exceedingly influential opposition writings were the product of these years. The first, written in one month, was *Napoléon-le-Petit*, which, published in England under the title of *Napoleon the Small*, became an underground weapon. Hugo had written a 600-page volume in record time, with his usual flowing, literary style which could be read like a novel. With all the skill of a twentieth century narcotics smuggler, the author had the book smuggled into France, in mini-editions, printed on thin paper. Even plaster busts of Napoleon III himself were used to sneak the banned volume into French territory; additional copies were carried by balloon. The first printing of his super-pamphlet appeared in Brussels two days after Hugo arrived on Jersey, where the family spent the first three years of its ultimately 19 years in exile. The remaining years were spent on the island of Guernsey, at a residence called Hauteville-House.

Exile enabled Victor Hugo to jettison Léonie Biard, but he refused Adèle's subtle urgings to let go of Juliette as well; she, too, settled in exile, not far from the Hugo family. A book of Hugo's politico-ideological poems, *Châtiments (Punishments)*, may well have been the seed for the Cao Dai movement, described earlier. These poems—part political, part philosophical—carried the message of a future faith that would not replace, but would supersede, the world's major religions.

At this point, the Hugo clan was, in a contradictory fashion, both at the center of a new revolutionary storm and in total isolation. None of them were any good at English, least of all the master of the house, who looked upon the French language as something like a divine gift. Jersey had a French exile community, but Hugo did not take to it, and tended to look upon most of its members with elitist contempt. Who, then, could represent a vast new audience for Hugo's thoughts and ideas? Who might stand well above the Paris literati or the Paris bourgeoisie or the Paris political establishment? Well, of course, a higher dimension of existence, the world of the spirits, the world of great minds, and of even greater superhuman concepts! It was at this very moment of isolation and frustrated emotional energies, in September, 1853, that Hugo's old friend, Delphine de Girardin, introduced the family to the latest "American" device for spirit contact, the turning table, capable of tapping out messages from the dead by knocking a table leg on the floor.

The book for which this is the Introduction, *Conversations with Eternity*, consisting of the most important of the transcripts of these seances, is the first account in the English language of Victor Hugo's encounters with the spirits. This emotional experience lasted for over two years, and the record of its strange and exalted nights and days is certainly a unique document, as well as a glimpse into the subconscious of an egocentric, frustrated genius, seeking to crash through the barriers of human communications, and exploding like a volcano of yearning, fear, madness and creativity. And—who knows?—it may even be that Hugo succeeded at moments in crashing through those barriers, and in communing with worlds beyond our human realm; there is much to startle, and even to transfix, the attentive reader of this amazing document. Long after the last rap of the last spirit had died away—after 18 years of exile on the Channel islands of Jersey and Guernsey—Hugo was able to return, in triumph, to Paris, as the Republic succeeded the reign of Napoleon III.

The final years of Victor Hugo's life were overshadowed by the decision of his wife, Adèle, to leave him and move to Brussels, where she died on August 27, 1868. Their daughter, Adèle, fell, literally, "madly" in love with a British officer, Albert Pinson, and followed him to Canada. Emotionally disturbed, she hoped that he might marry her. Disappointed, she settled in the Caribbean, eventually returning to Paris, where she was permanently hospitalized. Adèle II died in 1878. Juliette Drouet, who had spent fifty years both at Hugo's side and at a distance, died on May 11, 1883.

Victor Hugo died on May 31, 1885. The mass of mourners, moving through the streets toward the Pantheon, where he was interred, was estimated at two million, more than the actual population of Paris at the time. Although, in his lifetime, Hugo had been an outspoken, and even flamboyant, spokesman of the Paris underclass, in poetry, prose, plays and speeches, he left only one percent of his fortune to the "poor." On the other hand, and always conscious of grand symbolism, he had ordered that, at the funeral, his body be carried in a simple, black "pauper's coffin." Of course, the coffin was at the center of a vast state parade, complete with uniformed marchers, funereal music, and appropriately gaudy floral decorations. Thus, in a final irony, Victor Hugo's funeral procession symbolized his life's ultimate contradiction.

Hugo's last will reflected his belief, or certainty, that there was life after death. He also had a brief, self-assured message for those who came after him: "I have tried to introduce moral and human questions into what is known as politics....I have spoken out for the oppressed of all lands, and of all parties. I believe I have done well. My conscience tells me I am right. And if the future proves me wrong, I am sorry for the future."

Chapter One

LÉOPOLDINE BECKONS

On Aug. 5, 1853, Victor Hugo arrived on the island of Jersey with his wife, Adèle, his sons and daughter, and his mistress Juliette Drouet disembarking discretely sometime afterward. Glancing around, Hugo could scarcely have imagined that he had come to a place where he would spend hundreds of days and nights in the company of the departed souls of some of the most interesting people who had ever lived.

Jersey is a stark, bare island of 51 square miles, a British possession lying in the English Channel only 25 miles from France, but 188 miles from London and 200 miles from Paris. Even today, the almost wholly French-speaking population of the island doesn't exceed 100,000. The capital, Saint-Hélier—on whose outskirts Victor Hugo would live in a house called Marine-Terrace—was, in the poet's day, an unprepossessing hole whose saving graces were mainly a theatre and a library.

The average temperature of Jersey island is 51 degrees Fahrenheit, and the weather is usually overcast. The greater part of the time, wind, rain and sudden squalls vie with each other under a glowering sky as to which will bring the greatest despair to the hearts of those whom fate has brought to this place against their will. On every beach, in every cove, white-capped waves, often whipped to a frenzy, scud across jagged upthrust rocks.

The island, though, has scenes of great natural beauty, and plenty of history, and these two factors, combined with the ubiquitous, eternally-whispering sea, were often to bring peace to the turbulent heart of Victor Hugo. There were intricate grottos hollowed out through the millennia by the sea. There was the occasional castle, or its splendid ruin, harking back to the Middle Ages. Scattered here and there were mysterious dolmens and menhirs— huge, columnar, polished stones often laid out in the enigmatic circular shape of a cromlech. These ancient monuments were thought to have been erected by a Druidic people; they were associated in the minds of the nineteenth-century islanders with barbaric rituals of blood-letting; and, mostly for these reasons, it was believed that ghosts were on the loose everywhere: Druidic priestesses in white or black, men carrying their heads under their arms, blackbirds screeching as if possessed. None of this would be lost on the endlessly active imagination of Victor Hugo.

There was also on Jersey at this time a ragtag collection of political exiles, some 300 in all, mostly from France, but also from other parts of Europe, men of integrity and intelligence for the most part but now seething with bitter frustration. The majority of them, Hugo was to treat at best with a benign aloofness; some, whose liveliness of mind or compatible views caught the poet's attention, he would single out as friends; a few, such as the hunchbacked, poverty-stricken Hennet de Kesler, he would treat with enormous generosity, providing the little French teacher with room and board for the last two years of his life. All in all, the intelligent attentiveness of these fellow exiles would help make the poet's life a little easier.

Still, for a man of Victor Hugo's huge talents and restless energy, the island must have seemed at first like hell on earth. It's likely that, in those first weeks, his mind, depressed, cut off from its habitual pursuits—cruelly prompted by the surrounding sea—

must have gone back to the appalling, unthinkable death by drowning of his eldest daughter, Léopoldine, with her husband of ten months, Charles Vacquerie, on September 4, 1843.

Not only had Victor Hugo not been at home at the time, but he had been returning from a trip to Spain with his mistress, Juliette Drouet. The couple had stopped off at Bordeaux to visit the famous charnel-house of Saint-Michael's Church with its 70 mummified bodies. The sight of all this death had made Victor Hugo peculiarly gloomy; it had filled him with a presentiment of some oncoming disaster. Continuing on their way, the poet and his mistress had arrived at the village of Soubise, and sat down to rest for a few minutes in a local café, the Europe. They glanced desultorily at two newspapers that lay on the table, Juliette Drouet at the *Charivari*, and Victor Hugo at *The Century*. In the most shocking moment of his life, Hugo read the headlines:

The sinister report of an appalling incident which will cast a pall over a family held dear by the world of French letters has this morning afflicted the inhabitants of our town...

M.P. Vacquerie...took with him in his yacht...his nephew M. Ch. Vacquerie and the young wife of the latter, who is, as everyone knows, the daugher of M. Victor Hugo...

In December, 1842, Léopoldine had married Charles Vacquerie, brother of Auguste Vacquerie, the journalist who would share most of Victor Hugo's years in exile with him. On a bright, cold September day only ten months later, Léopoldine and Charles, and Charles's Uncle Pierre and his Cousin Arthus, had boarded a small yacht at Villequier on the Seine. They had set out on a day trip across the river which flowed with particular swiftness at that point. The vessel was slightly top-heavy with sail. Though Uncle Pierre was an experienced sea-captain, the craft had capsized. Everyone on board had drowned.

The first reports claimed that the bodies of Léopoldine and Charles had been found clasped in each other's arms in a final embrace. It later emerged that Léopoldine had drowned clinging to the boat, while Charles's body had been washed much farther downstream.

Léopoldine was 19 years old and three months pregnant. Didine, as her father called her, had been his favorite child. A stunned and terribly grieving Hugo arrived back in Paris only in time for the funeral. Some months later, he would write:

I've lost you, O precious daughter
Thou who fills, O my pride
My whole destiny with
The light of your coffin

Nothing in his life would ever wound him again quite so deeply as the unexpected death of his young, vibrant, beloved daughter. Guilt would also hound him to the end of his days; despite his sturdy rationalism, in his worst moments he would wonder if God had punished him for his philandering ways.

To what extent this horrendous, never-to-be-accepted, never-to-be-forgotten tragedy weighed on Hugo's mind during his first weeks on Jersey island, we can never know. But something was about to happen which would precipitate him into the occult world of the Spiritists, and drive him to indulge whatever longing he might have to converse with the souls of the dead. On September 6, there arrived at the Port of Saint-Hélier his childhood friend, Delphine de Girardin, journalist, member of the tout-Paris—the high society of Paris—and wife of Hugo's close friend Emile de Girardin, the publisher of *La Presse* and the man who had introduced advertising into the newspapers of France. Delphine came bubbling over with news of the latest craze to seize the attention of the upper crust of Paris: talking to the dead through the agency of tapping, turning tables.

This was a phenomenon that had mushroomed from almost nothing into a world-wide fad in only six years. In Hydesville, New York, in 1847, three Fox sisters had heard loud raps which they were certain signaled messages from the dead. In the months and years that followed, they had communed with the spirit world by means of raps—often, but not always, created by tapping table legs—in front of increasingly large audiences seeking, and sometimes finding, assurances that there was a life beyond this one.

The Fox sister seances, however controversial, had been the match that had lit the powder keg that exploded into the Spiritualist movement in the United States. In 1910, Sir Arthur Conan Doyle estimated that there were 10,000 practicing mediums in America in 1850 (the country's total population was 23 million at the time). The craze had leapt across the Atlantic, where it was appropriated by one Hippolyte-Léon Dénizart-Rival—later to be anointed (by his own rapping spirits!) Alan Kardec—into a burgeoning movement called Spiritism. Spiritualism had affirmed the existence of the spirits of the dead, and of their readiness to communicate with the living; Spiritism would do the same, with the addition of just one or two provocative concepts, in particular metempsychosis, a type of reincarnation which incorporated living lives as animals.

The new religio-occult movement took the upper crust of French society by storm. Eighteen fifty-three, the year Hugo moved to Jersey, was the *annus mirabilis* of Spiritism. Grasset, in *The Marvels Beyond Science*, quotes Bersot's account of "these heroic ages of turning tables:"

"'It was a passion and everything was forgotten. In an intellectual country whose drawing-rooms were generally famed for the lively conversations held therein, one saw, during several months, Frenchmen and Frenchwomen, who have so often been accused of being light-headed, sitting for hours around a table, stern, motionless and dumb; their fingers stretched out, their eyes obstinately staring at the same spot, and their minds stubbornly engrossed by the same idea, in a state of anxious expectation, sometimes standing up when exhausted by useless trials, sometimes, if there was a motion or a creaking, disturbed and put out of themselves while chasing a piece of furniture that moved away. During the whole winter, there was no other social occupation or topic. It was a beautiful period, a period of first enthusiasm, of trust and ardor that would lead to success. How triumphant with modesty those who had the 'fluid'! What a shame it was to those who had it not! What a power it became to spread the new religion! What a love existed between adepts! What wrath prevailed against unbelievers!'"

One indication of the success of Spiritism was that the Roman Catholic clergy inveighed against it from the pulpit. The Bishop of Viviers, later to be Archbishop of Paris, forbade practicing Catholics on pain of hell from consorting with the tables; no one paid any attention. At the same time, the government of Napoleon III, happy to see this new fad diverting attention from its own misdeeds, encouraged interest in what the great cartoonist Daumier later scornfully called "fluidomania" (a kind of astral "fluid," flowing through the body of the medium, was thought to be the animating power behind the tables). For whatever reasons, talking with the turning tables became the pastime of preference for the idle and the not-so-idle rich of Paris, and indeed of much of Europe.

An interest in Spiritism had preceded the Hugos to Jersey island. Among the exiles were those who had been infected by the mania, and who had acquired beliefs in past lives and other realities. The Saint-Simonian Pierre Leroux believed that the human race could not fail to go on forever since its members were endlessly reincarnated in lifetime after lifetime. His disciple, the exile Philippe Faure, was convinced he had been present in a previous lifetime at the crucifixion of Christ. And Jules Allix, scion of an old, established Jersey family, believed that if particular groups of crawling snails were observed closely, their motions could be seen to be spelling out messages from the dead (those with eyes to see should have read trouble in this unusually weird conviction; it was Jules Allix who, in the throes of a nervous breakdown, would wave a revolver in front of the Hugos' seance participants in the autumn of 1855 and help bring the gatherings to an end.).

All this would be brought to Hugo's attention—he had long been interested in the occult, but had not taken much interest in the tables—when, on the day of Delphine de Girardin's arrival, after the obligatory exchanges and usual gossip, Delphine brought the conversation around to the burning question of the day. "Do you do the tables?" she asked them.

They confessed to only a slight interest in the subject. They wondered, exactly how was it done in Paris? Delphine quickly filled them in. The medium or mediums—those with the psychic gift—placed their hands lightly on the top of the table. When the piece of furniture was ready, it raised one leg, or even two, and tapped out the message on the floor. Sometimes the table, though it moved, did not tap; the rappings seemed to come from nowhere. The procedure took a long time, since the table leg, along with communicating 'Yes' with one tap and 'No' with two, was obliged to tap out the number of taps corresponding to the place of the letter in the alphabet; one tap, for example, meant 'A,' while 26 meant 'Z.' The phenomenon was unpredictable; sometimes, the table leg remained poised in the air for whole minutes without tapping; other times, the table would levitate entirely, even rising up to the ceiling; it often shook, and even shook violently sometimes; occasionally, it slid right across the floor while turning around on itself.

Hugo was sternly skeptical, while his wife, Adèle, known for her good sense, smiled benignly. The Hugos pointed to a small table in the corner of the drawing room; they had to confess to Delphine that they had spent an hour or so trying to make that table move themselves—though they hadn't really known how to go about it!

Jean de Mutigny recreates the scene in his informative *Victor Hugo and Spiritism*: "Not even waiting for dessert, Delphine de Girardin asked to see the table...It was a little, square four-legged table. Delphine burst out laughing: 'It's not surprising that the spirits haven't manifested! You need a little round table. Otherwise, the phenomena can't possibly appear.' Unfortunately, there was no piece of furniture of this sort at Marine-Terrace, this location not having been furnished by those specializing in the occult. So this situation wouldn't endure indefinitely, Delphine—who, once she got an idea into her head, wouldn't let it go—went into Saint-Hélier that same afternoon and did the rounds of the furniture stores..."

Delphine quickly found a small, round pedestal table, the single leg of which ended in three golden claws. She brought it back to Marine-Terrace under her arm, and placed it on top of the larger table. That same evening, profiting from Delphine's extensive experience, the Hugo family tried to make the tables turn. Delphine and Mme. Hugo "held the table;" they acted as mediums. The group spent considerable time shifting the position of the large square table and the small round pedestal table around in relation to one another. But, despite their efforts, particularly those of Delphine, nothing happened. They tried again the next day, with the same lack of success. Sometimes Auguste Vacquerie, sometimes General Adolphe Le Flô and his wife, sometimes Sandor Téléki joined in. For four more days, the group periodically labored away at the tables under the enthusiastic direction of Delphine.

During this time, Victor Hugo took almost no interest. He did not sit at the table, nor even near the table; sometimes he sat in the far corner of the drawing room doing something else.

Suddenly, on Sunday, Sept. 11, 1853, an event took place which had all the force of a grenade being thrown into the center of the group, though the effect was entirely positive, especially for Victor Hugo.

That afternoon the poet had joined the seance for the first time. Vacquerie and Mme. de Girardin sat at the table; the remainder of the group included Mme. Hugo, sons Charles and Victor-François, General Le Flô, and Pierre de Treveneuc.

For the first time, the table had begun falteringly to tap out words. The group had succeeded in calling up the spirits! For the first while, the messages were brief, scattered, fragmentary—almost incoherent. The participants acted like children at play, asking the table to guess what they thinking.

The defining moment came: Auguste Vacquerie asked the table, "Guess what word I'm thinking."

The table tapped out:

Suffering.

This wasn't his word, said Vacquerie; he had been thinking of love. But, over the next few minutes, they observed that the motion of the table had stiffened a little, become almost abrupt and willful, as if it were about to give some order.

"Are you still the same spirit who was there?" asked Delphine de Girardin, sensing the change.

The table tapped twice: **No.**

"Who are you?" asked Victor Hugo.

The reply came: **Dead girl.**

"Your name?" asked Hugo.

The table tapped out:

L.E.O.P.O.L.D.I.N.E.

The group felt as if some large supernatural anguish were weighing upon them. Victor Hugo went pale with emotion. Adèle Hugo collapsed in sobs. Charles Hugo maintained his self-control enough to ask his sister:

"Where are you? Are you happy? Do you still love us?'

The reply came: **Of God.**

"Sweet soul, are you happy?" asked Victor Hugo.

Yes.

"Where are you?"

Light.

"What do we have to do to go to you?"

To love.

The table was tapping out words without hesitation, as if the presence felt it were being understood.

"You were sent by whom?" asked Delphine.

The Good Lord.

"Is there something you want to tell us?"

Yes.

"What?"

Suffer for the other world.

"Do you see the suffering of those who love you?" asked Victor Hugo.

Yes.

"Will they suffer for some time to come?" asked Delphine.

Yes.

"Will they return to France soon?"

The table did not respond.

"Are you happy when I mix your name with my prayers?" asked Victor Hugo.

Yes.

"Are you always near those who love you? Do you watch over them?"

Yes.

"Does it depend on them whether you return?"

No.

"But will you return?"

Yes.

"Soon?"

Yes.

And then the spirit was gone.

Victor Hugo was hooked. He would be intimately involved with the turning tables for the next two years and more.

Chapter Two

TWO VOYAGES TO THE AFTERWORLD

The words tapped out apparently by the spirit of Léopoldine had spoken to Victor Hugo's heart, and drawn him into the magical circle of the seances. But this encounter had been more in the nature of a profound psychodrama experience for him; he did not believe that he had necessarily spoken to the spirit of Léopoldine, or that he was necessarily speaking to the spirits of the dead. At first, he thought he must be talking to his son, Charles, who seemed to have a gift for mediumship. On September 21, Hugo told Charles: "It's quite simply your intelligence multiplied five times by the magnetism [the psychic "'fluid" in Charles] that makes the table act, and makes it tell you what you have in your thoughts."

But, a week or two later, we find Hugo deciding that, while spirits might actually be involved, these spirits were not necessarily the ones they said they were. "It's possible that this is a spirit who assumes these names in order to catch our interest," he told a friend at the end of September.

During the first autumn, and well into 1854, he tried in every way he could to find out if these were really spirits from the afterworld. He asked them to provide him with specific information—how to cure madness or rabies, how to steer a balloon, how to find gold in Australia. He sent the answers to the French Academy of Sciences for verification; we have no record of what their answers were.

In January, 1854, he asked the spirits, in effect: 'Why is it that you, who, if you are who you say you are, have access to all the resources of the universe, cannot come up with a way of demonstrating to us that you really exist?' They replied that to doubt was an unalterable part of the human condition (their response was considerably more complicated than that, and became a topic of discussion that ran from beginning to end of the turning table experience). Hugo's ultimate position seems to have been that the spirits did exist--even though they might all be facets of one single, overriding entity, possibly, he thought, the Shadow of the Sepulcher. He never ceased to be fascinated by the rich, occult content of the communications, even suggesting, in September, 1854, that the transcripts of the seances might well become one of the "Bibles of the future."

Throughout October, the participants met almost daily; throughout the entire experience, they rarely met less than once a week. Sometimes, bizarre and flighty communications came through. But, as the weeks went by, the communications became more and more meaty, original and revelatory—even sensationally so. There seemed to be two types of spirits: Those who seemed never to have taken life in this world, and the shades of historical figures of major importance. The most powerful of the former, the Shadow of the Sepulcher, introduced himself at the seance immediately following the one at which Léopoldine had appeared. Though he didn't reveal his full name at the time—and certainly not the giant role he was to play—this entity's appearance brought to the seances the first hints of the vast and benign uncanniness which would often characterize them.

The initial encounter with the Shadow of the Sepulcher took place on Tuesday, September 13, 1853, beginning at 9:30 p.m. In attendance were the entire Hugo family; Delphine de Girardin (who would leave to return to Paris in a few days); and General Le Flô with Mme. Le Flô. At first, Charles Hugo and Téléki sat at the table; partway through, General Le Flô took over from Téléki.

After a few brief, preliminary exchanges, Victor Hugo asked the table who was speaking.

The Shadow.

"The shadow of someone who lived?"

No.

"It it necessary for you to live?"

No.

"Are you an angel?"

Yes.

"The angel of death?"

Yes.

"Why have you come? Call you tell us?"

To chat with life.

"What do you wish to tell us?"

 Believe.

"In what?"

In the unknown.

"Is the world you belong to a continuation of this life?"

Death is the balloon that takes the soul to heaven.

"And what is it that you have to say to life?"

Spirits, come, here there be seers.

"Are we the spirits you're addressing?"

No.

"You mean we're the seers?"

Yes.

"Can you see us?"

No.

"Have the spirits you've just summoned lived life as we live it?"

The table said nothing.

"Are you able to reply?"

No. The table shook.

"Is there any way I can calm you down?"

No.

"Are you a happy spirit?"

Happiness is only a human phenomenon, since it cannot exist without unhappiness.

"Do you speak this way because you're in the void?"

Yes.

"Talk about yourself."

Infinity is an emptiness packed full.

"Do you mean by that that what we call the void is filled with the world of spirits?

My goodness!

"So, Shadow, you're capable of a good belly laugh?"

No.

"Talk to us."

Use your body to search out your soul.

"Are you the only spirit here?"

I am everything and I am everywhere.

"Do you want me to continue questioning you?"

Yes. You hold the key to a door that has been closed.

"Are you aware of the vision I had yesterday?"

I know not yesterdays.

"Can we be certain of seeing you after we die?"

You're only wearing glasses.

[Ed.: *The Shadow of the Sepulcher may be suggesting that "seeing" on earth is a matter of "wearing glasses." When we die, we will no longer wear these glasses, so that "seeing" will becomes an irrelevant concept.*]

"If we behave well in this lifetime, can we hope for a better life?"

Yes.

"If we behave badly, will we have a more painful one?"

Yes.

"Are the souls of the dead with you?"

Under me.

"You say that you are everything and everywhere. Are you God?"

Over me.

"Are you nearer to souls than to God?"

For me there is neither near nor far.

"Tell me, are worlds other than earth inhabited?"

Yes.

"By beings like us in body and soul?"

Some, yes; others, no.

"After death, do the souls of those who have done good deeds find themselves in regions of light, or do they end up inhabiting other worlds?"

Light.

And then the table was still. The Shadow of the Sepulcher had gone. He would return many times.

The responses of the Shadow of the Sepulcher had been mysterious and bewildering. Perhaps, the seance-goers speculated, a being who apparently had never lived away from the plane of the afterworld couldn't be expected to present an intelligible picture of that realm to living human beings. They could only hope that a dead and articulate human would come along and fill them in.

Their wishes were granted in the form of the shade of the eighteenth century Swiss social reformer Jean-Jacques Rousseau. In the first of two formidable table-turning sessions—whose exact dates are unknown, but which took place between September 19 and December 6, 1853—this agreeable spirit engaged them in a highly technical discussion of French politics in the eighteenth century. In the second, the shade relaxed a bit, holding forth on subjects of interest to all humans: Not only did he describe his personal experience of heaven in eloquent detail, but he expressed his views about getting there by committing suicide.

In real life, Jean-Jacques Rousseau (1712-1778) had believed that man was born good and that only social institutions made him bad, or evil—institutions which, wittingly or unwittingly, were designed to bring him under control and even to enslave him. Rousseau had written *Emile* (1762), a book which urged that children be educated in a natural setting wholly in accordance with the entirely good instincts with which they had been born—even, preferably, on a one-to-one basis in a forest with one teacher! This was a very original, very radical approach to education; the book created a sensation, winning Rousseau many friends (and enemies) and launching a number of fads among the aristocracy, including daily walks in the forest and, for mothers who up till then had disdained the task, the breast-feeding of their babies. This latter change in behavior in particular had a far-reaching effect on all social classes of Europe. Rousseau wrote an equally radical and equally influential book on political science, *The Social Contract* (1762).

The Swiss philosopher was thus a most interesting and sympathetic figure (notwithstanding that in life he had been extremely moody and difficult, even succumbing to flat-out paranoia in his final years); the participants at the seance were delighted to be able to talk to him—they seem to have had no difficulty believing it was him!—and they showed their delight. Early on in the second session, Xavier Durrieu addressed him as follows: "You suffered greatly and you loved greatly, and that's why we're deeply sympathetic to you. You've been reproached for being prideful, but that pridefulness was dominated by a love for humanity. You made mistakes, but you confessed them, and, by the tone of your confession [Rousseau's autobiography, *The Confessions*], we feel that your repentance was a genuine one." Durrieu then asked Rousseau, straightforwardly, "What is heaven like?"

Day and night are synonymous. Heaven and God are the same word. Night and Earth are synonymous; man and doubt are the same word. Genius is dawn, grave and twilight; the resurrection is light. Alive, I desired God; resurrected, I behold Him. God is the love star radiating out into infinity and visible to the eyes of the soul. The eyes of the body are condemned to see only the physical stars. The eye of the soul alone can contemplate the suns of intelligence. God is the planet of the tomb's night; I have been its Herschel [the eighteenth century English astronomer].

Durrieu asked: "Can you make comprehensible, to us whose eyes can only see the physical stars, that vision of God which you now can see through the eyes of the soul?"

Yes.

"Tell us."

I see in the infinite depths before me a dazzling abyss which seems to draw me toward it ceaselessly. I am carried away by the irresistible attraction of that radiance. I am always in flight, and never do I arrive to where I may alight. I am plunged in infinity for an eternity. I am dizzy with God.

"Are you totally happy?"

My happiness is like a perfume. I am forever inhaling it, and it is forever eluding me. It is a ceaselessly-renewed intoxication, a never-satisfied intoxication. I have the fullness of happiness and the desire for happiness.

"Among human feelings, is there one that can give us a remote idea of this happiness?"

Yes.

"Which one?"

Love.

Charles Hugo objected, "But your happiness is insatiable in itself, and human love always leads to satiety."

Imagine my happiness as a bath in an ocean of beams of light. Human love has something of these light beams, but there must also be lightning bolts therein.

Leguéval asked: "What do you think about suicide now, after what you've written?" [Ed.: *In his writings, Rousseau approves of suicide under some circumstances.*]

Suicide is the act of a traveler who has eternity to travel in and who is afraid of being late. To commit suicide is to advance the hour-hand of the watch of your life.

"Do we have the right to commit suicide?"

No.

"Is it the act of a madman?" Charles Hugo inquired.

No.

Charles opined that he thought it was; Durrieu continued, "Why do men fear death? Seeing as life where you are is so happy, why does nature want men to fear death?"

God wants man to live, and therefore hides the nature of death from him.

Durrieu asked: "Now that man is in possession of this revelation, isn't it to be feared that he will no longer fear death, and that he will be tempted to commit suicide?"

If he commits suicide, he discovers what his own Paradise is. [Ed.: *And perhaps he discovers that it is not Paradise.*]

Durrieu commented: "But at least, if he lives the whole time he has to live, he will no longer be afraid of death?"

No.

And that was the end of the seance, which had been, at the

very least, provocative enough to make the Jersey island exiles want to come back for more. Looming on the horizon were figures at least as substantial as Rousseau, and more substantial, and whose comings and goings—the participants would realize long afterward—were soon to begin to fit into a larger pattern, one hospitable to the revelation of many truths.

Among those figures was the mighty one of Hannibal of Carthage.

Chapter Three

HANNIBAL STORMS
THE TURNING TABLES

With Steven Spielberg's brilliant 1998 movie *Saving Private Ryan*, and its merciless depiction of the D-Day landing at Omaha Beach, few can still doubt that war is hell.

For millennia, though, men not only believed that war was necessary, but that it was glorious and heroic—an essential part of a young man's education.

This belief was delivered a mortal blow by the blood-baths of the Napoleonic era. But it lingered on through the nineteenth century, not the least in the form of an abiding interest in the exploits of great military leaders. The band of political exiles gathered around Hugo on Jersey island shared these interests, with the most interested of all being Hugo. After all, the poet's own father, "Brutus" Hugo, had been a successful general under Napoleon. And Victor Hugo himself was often called the "Napoleon of Letters."

Given this climate of interest, it's perhaps not surprising that, on the evening of December 8, 1853, one of the greatest military leaders of all time, Hannibal of Carthage, came tapping through the turning table.

In 218-201 B.C., Hannibal came close to bringing the mighty Roman Empire to its knees. Carthage was a great city-state located across the Mediterranean Sea from Italy, on the coast of what is now Tunisia, in North Africa. At the age of 25, Hannibal, already a general, had launched an attack on Rome by way of Spain and France, which were Roman colonies. He did not go directly to Italy, but instead crossed the Mediterranean and advanced northward toward the Alps over these Roman territories. The youthful Carthaginian general won skirmish after skirmish, ingeniously outmaneuvering the Roman soldiers.

Hannibal's army consisted not only of 40,000 soldiers but of numerous elephants. In one of the most daring military exploits in all of history, he led this extraordinary band up over the Alps and across and down into Italy. No one knows what route he took. But we do know that he lost half his soldiers and a good portion of his elephants during this unheard-of, freezing, food-shy crossing of the formidable mountain range.

However decimated his forces, Hannibal arrived in one piece on the plains of Italy. For 15 years he waged war against the Romans on their own soil. Winning subjugated peoples within Italy, and even Romans, over to his side, he won battle after battle with stratagems of amazing originality. He almost conquered Rome; eventually, though, he was narrowly defeated and driven back to Carthage.

According to the Jersey island transcripts, this man who was prepared to storm his way through anything—one of his favorite maxims was, "I will find a way, or make one"— stormed his way over 2,000 years later through the tapping table into Victor Hugo's drawing room at Marine-Terrace.

Some of the discussion that ensued isn't of compelling interest to those of us who are not history buffs. Hugo told Hannibal that Napoleon had considered him to be the greatest military leader in antiquity because Hannibal had sacrificed half his army just to arrive on the battlefield, and had stayed there, far from home, for 15 years. Hugo wondered what Hannibal thought of Napoleon?

The Carthaginian shade replied—in Latin, of which Victor Hugo and the seance participants had an excellent knowledge—that Napoleon had been the greatest of military leaders in victory, but the worst in defeat.

What did this mean? wondered Victor Hugo. Hadn't Napoleon, in the course of his long retreat through Russia—where it had been the winter, and not the Russians, that had defeated him—kept his composure admirably, and, once back in France, managed to put together a whole new army?

Dixi ducem, non virum. Victus a hyeme, dux magnus non fugit, moritur. Mors suprema victoria, replied the tapping table. [I said the worst of leaders in defeat, not the worst of men. Defeated by winter, the greatest of leaders does not flee; he dies. Death is the supreme victor.] Asked to repeat this in French, Hannibal explained: **A defeated Napoleon is a selfish Napoleon. Conqueror, he thinks of France; conquered, he thinks of himself....A defeated Napoleon is a fleeing genius who takes refuge under a crown instead of abdicating under a halo. That abdication is death.**

Hannibal meant that the honorable thing for Napoleon to have done, as a military leader, would be to stay and fight the Russians in winter, even if that meant death. The participants at the seance weren't so sure they agreed with him. Hugo asked the general if he recalled the names of the Roman legions he had defeated at Cannes, in France, near the beginning of his campaign. **Faith, Vengeance, Native Land:** Hannibal tapped out the names in Latin. Did he remember the names of the Carthaginian legions that had fought in that engagement? Hannibal spelled those out, too.

There was an exchange between Charles Hugo and the discarnate general about Napoleon III, Hannibal communicating his contempt for the French dictator. Then Victor Hugo asked a question which would have seized the attention of today's "New

Agers," avid as they are for information about vanished civilizations and ancient, inscrutable monuments: Would Hannibal describe the vanished city of Carthage for them?

Carthage became a "vanished" city in 146 B.C., when the Romans, after defeating the Carthaginians once and for all, razed the celebrated city to the ground, ploughed over the ruins, and sowed salt in the furrows. Carthage was soon rebuilt as a Roman colony, and fragmentary descriptions of the original city have come down to us from antiquity—but historians are by no means certain just what this throbbing empire/metropolis of Carthage actually looked like.

Could it possibly have resembled the magnificent and magical city that Hannibal now described?

It was a giant city. It had 60 leagues of towers and 6,000 temples, 3,000 of which were made of marble, 2,000 of porphyry, 600 of alabaster, 300 of jasper, 50 of stucco, 45 of ivory, four of silver and one of gold. The streets were 300 feet wide, and were paved with marble and covered in silver tile. Along the entire length of the houses, perfumed lamps burned, and white elephants swaying beneath towers brushed against the singers and dancers in the streets. The air was so scented and melodious that flowers and birds never died there. Carthage had 30,000 vessels, 600 fortresses, 100,000 horses, 12,000 elephants, 100,000 talents a year and Hannibal.

'The air was so scented and so melodious that flowers and birds never died there'? This sentence, with its fantastical details, didn't put off Victor Hugo, perhaps because it was beautiful, and perhaps because (as we will see in later chapters) Hugo regarded all plants and animals as creatures with souls. Now he asked Hannibal: "Would you like to tell us the names of the four silver tempes and the golden temple?"

Yes.

"First, tell us the Carthaginian names, then translate them one by one into Latin. First, the names of the silver temples."

Hannibal performed this task with apparent ease: **First temple, in Carthaginian, Bocamar, in Latin** *Sol* [sun]. **- Second temple, Derimos, in Latin** *Luna* [moon]. **- Third, Jarimus, in Latin** *Dies* [days]. **- Fourth, Mossomba, in Latin** *Nox* [night].

"Now, tell us the name of the golden temple."

In Carthaginian: Illisaga; in Latin, *Lux* [light].

Hugo's next question is another tidbit for modern-day Atlantis buffs who believe that the Basque country was settled by survivors of Atlantis, and that the Basque language is related to 'Atlantean':

"We find lines in Punic [the Carthaginian language] in [the Roman] Plautus. The scholar Abbe Elicagaray claimed that these lines had close ties to Basque. Are the Punic and Basque languages basically the same?"

Yes.

"So it's certain that Basque derives from Carthaginian?"

Yes.

And on that note—which may suggest to some that the Carthaginians were descended from the survivors of Atlantis, though according to recorded history Carthage was ounded by the Phoenicians!—Hannibal took his leave.

Was Victor Hugo really talking to the shade of the great Carthaginian general? Though some knowledge of "Carthaginian," or Punic has come down to us, Hugo and the group could hardly have had much knowledge of that language. Nor did these seance attendees, learned as they were, necessarily know the names of the Roman and Carthaginian legions that fought at Cannes.

And what about the peculiar fashion (apart from the exotic details) in which Hannibal described Carthage? With his dry and meticulous enumeration of the numbers of towers, temples, elephants, and so forth, and what they were made of, he sounded hardly like a poet, but more like an engineer—or like a general enumerating the types and dispositions of his troops.

The seance goers would soon surmise that the coming of Hannibal—or whatever strange concatenation of the warrior energies of our species that he represented—had not been entirely accidental. By bringing to the forefront the fierce, bloody and endlessly warring nature of mankind, it helped set the stage for the disturbing message that an entity called Balaam's Ass would deliver to the seance habitues only a little later that same month.

Chapter Four

GOD'S CONVICT

On Tuesday night, December 27, 1853, the messages of the spirits took on a somber, sorrowful note. One Balaam's Ass, appeared, and began methodically to lay out a whole new, strange way of looking at the universe. One of the two principal pillars in this cosmological edifice was the Spiritist belief in metempsychosis: that we reincarnate through lifetime after lifetime, in the earlier stages as animals, along a Great Chain of Being which can take us up to angelhood. The metempsychosis of the Jersey island spirits differed from that of the Kardecists in two important respects, however: Whereas the Spiritists believed that we progressed more or less steadily up the Great Chain—if delayed a bit at certain points by bad behaviour—the spirits who spoke to Hugo and Company cautioned that we could backslide badly between lives, even tumbling back down into a 'lower' species. And those 'lower species' were far more extensive than for the Kardecists: They included reincarnations as plants and as stones.

The other principal pillar of this startling cosmology was the awful truth that Balaam's Ass would unveil to the guests this evening: Not only did every particle of matter in our physical universe contain living, conscious spirit; not only did every stone, plant, animal and human being on our earth have a living, conscious soul; but every one of those souls had come to earth solely to expiate a wrong committed in a previous existence.

Our entire physical universe was a prison. As Hugo was to express it in the coming year in his poem, *What the Shadow's Mouth Says*, every human being was God's convict.

Why had a spirit with the name of 'Balaam's Ass' been entrusted with the task of delivering this news to the seance enthusiasts at Marine-Terrace on the night of December 27th, 1853?

In Verses 22-31, the *Book of Numbers* of the Bible tells the story of how Balaam, the holy man of the Moabites—who was able to speak directly to God—was asked by Balak, the King of Moab, to intercede with God and ask Him to give Balak the strength to drive away the Israelites who had encamped on the borders of Moab. When Balaam asked this of the Lord, He declined to give his help to Balak, explaining that the Israelites were a blessed people. Balak persuaded Balaam to ask again; God refused again, but this time said that Balaam could go to the capital of Moab and speak with Balak, if he asked God's permission.

Balaam set out for the capital on the back of his ass. At this, God became angry with Balaam, since he had not asked for His specific permission. Three times, an Angel of the Lord with a flaming sword showed itself to Balaam's ass; twice the ass dutifully moved off the road; the third time, having no more room, it lay down.

Angered, Balaam proceeded to beat the ass. God enabled the creature to speak, allowing it to demand of Balaam why he had struck it three times? The ass added that, though Balaam had ridden it all the days of his life, it had never struck him. Now the Angel of the Lord appeared to Balaam, explaining that God had not given him His specific permission to go to the capital of Moab, but that now he could, though he must reply no firmly to Balak. Chagrined and humbled, Balaam continued on his way.

Such personifications of beasts who had helped man—other

examples are the Lion of Androcles and the Dove of Noah's Ark—
were to come regularly through the turning tables. They seem to
have been important in the pantheon of the spirits because they
were imprisoned souls who had reached up from a lower echelon
of the Great Chain of Being to successfully help souls imprisoned
on a higher; in so doing, they exemplified, it seemed, the kind of
transcendent, loving action that was the most conducive to helping a soul along the path toward deliverance from imprisonment
in our physical universe. But such revelations—as well as others
having to do with the special nature of animals—were still in the
future for the seance-goers at Marine-Terrace. On this December
night two days after Christmas, Balaam's Ass, who could see things
from the animal's point of view, and who had in real life inter-
ceded between species, took the first, dramatic step of explaining
to them that our physical universe was nothing but a cosmic penitentiary.

We have no record of who was present that night, or when the
seance began. When the table began to move, Auguste Vacquerie
asked: "Who's there?"

The reply came: **Balaam's Ass.**

For the first little while, Vacquerie was the sole questioner:
"Well, if you're a spirit in the afterworld, you who have been a
beast in this one, you are better equipped than anyone to answer a
question we've often asked: Do animals have souls?"

Yes.

"Talk to us about that."

**Mankind is the minimum security prison of the soul, the
animal its maximum security prison.**

"So, life is truly a punishment?"

Yes.

"Explain how."

The created being passes through creation as a bird passes

through a tree, alighting on every branch. Man flies through infinity alighting on every world. You inhabit a world of suffering and punishment. We inhabit a star of light and reward. Man, being born into life on this earth, comes here to expiate a guilty past, and the animal comes here to expiate a monstrous past. Man does not know what his error was, nor the animal what his crime was. If they did know, they would be happy. Punishment would no longer be anything more than suffering that said to itself: I committed such and such an injustice. I'm certain what it was; I'm in no doubt about that.

Now, it is in the having doubts that the punishment lies. For man to know his error would be for him to know his judge, would be for him to know God. And the certainty of God's existence makes for Paradise on earth....In order to punish, divine justice puts on a mask. Punishment consists in seeing only the mask of the judge. The reward is seeing the face of God.

"Come down a step in the ladder for us: Do plants have souls?"
Yes.

"Then, do plants suffer greatly? For, if the essence of punishment lies in not being able to see God, the plant is blinder than the animal. Are you asserting that man in effect is in a minimum security prison, the animal in a maximum security prison, and the plant in solitary confinement, for all their lives?"

[Ed.: *The terms used by Balaam's Ass roughly translate as "prison," "galleys" and "dungeon." Modern terms have been substituted.*]

If the plant suffers, then it has deserved to suffer. Undeserved suffering, be it in a single atom, would be sufficient to make the heavens collapse. Trees would fall, terror-stricken worlds would sink into the abyss, and infinity would cease to radiate always outward, if the rose were oppressed or the daisy victimized. Suffering necessarily entails a weakening. The plant is the grimmest of the soul's prisons. The lily is sheer hell.

"So you are asserting that animals suffer more than men, and plants suffer more than animals?"

Yes.

"How is that possible? Aren't pangs of conscience the worst of all? Don't you suffer all the more when you live according to the dictates of your soul? Do you really expect us to believe that a blade of grass feels less happiness than a dog? Or that a creature that can't think suffers more than one that does? I grant you that there might be some truth in this if [the souls within] plants and animals were aware of their former greatness. But even man himself has only retained a twilight gleam of his true nature. For the brute animal, that gleam is merely a shadow; for the vegetal being, it's pitch-black night. How can something be a punishment if you can't even feel it? Are you trying to tell us that a horse that is perfectly happy with a single bale of hay is more harshly punished than man with his unquenchable thirst for the ideal?"

The horse is more harshly punished because it is more deeply plunged in matter. The plant is even more harshly punished because it is rooted in the soil. The ladder of punishment has three rungs: the body of the human, the hide of the beast and the root of the plant. The soul imprisoned within the plant has two rungs to climb, the soul within the animal has only one, to attain to the level of man. The soul's punishment begins in the animal and vegetal worlds with material suffering and is completed in the world of man with moral suffering; and by that time it has become almost a deliverance, since to suffer in the mind only is to be halfway to freedom already. In man, the soul breathes; in the plant, it suffocates. The eyes of man are skylights which open out upon a higher life; the prisoner-soul in the human brain peers out at heaven through these skylights.

"You say that, for the vegetal world, punishment lies in its complete ignorance of its true nature, and for man, in his doubts about his true nature. You also seem to be saying that the pain resulting from complete ignorance, or from being in doubt, would cease the moment we found out who we really were. And then you go ahead and tell us who we really are! If what you're telling us is true, then, if we accept what you're saying, our punishment will cease. And it follows from that that our lives will cease, since the only reason we have been born at all is to be punished. The very world itself would cease to be, if our punishments vanished by virtue of our having had our true natures revealed to us! You tell us that we are sentenced to doubt, and then you reveal that truth to us!"

I said, to be in doubt about one's true nature is the punishment. I affirm the truth of this proposition, whereas you are doing no more now than doubting your doubt. Therefore, your punishment continues.

Victor Hugo entered into the discussion: "In regard to these truths you are affirming, for some time now I, Victor Hugo, who am speaking to you, have believed in exactly what you say. If one has to doubt these things in order to be punished, then, tell me: Why has an exception has been made for me?"

If you're so sure of yourself, then tell me what punishment is meted out to the soul of an ox?

"You didn't understand my question. I'm telling you that I've glimpsed some of the truths you've just revealed to us, that those touching upon the human soul and its punishment in our world are at the level of a certitude for me, and have been for some time. On this point I'm not in a state of doubt, and yet I'm punished. I ask you, then: What special category am I in?"

The proof that you doubt is that you have merely glimpsed. As for myself, I affirm these truths. You believe what your thoughts tell you, and you doubt what our revelations tell you. Your thought is merely human; ours is divine. The thoughts of

even the greatest mind always wear a blindfold over one eye. That blindfold is life. You are a living, and therefore fallible, genius. I will spell out to the dead Victor Hugo the errors of the living Victor Hugo. Truth awaits you at the door of the tomb. You take God for a child's book that can be read in a flash!

God is infinite, and what is infinite cannot be known. Death will astonish you. Death is always astonishing. When he emerged from the tomb, Moses exclaimed: 'How splendid it all is!' Socrates ran about everywhere in heaven and cried out: 'How ravishing it all is!' Jesus fell to his knees. Mohammed covered his face with his hands and did not dare look.

Mme. Victor Hugo joined in: "For a long time now, my husband has been reflecting on and talking about the destiny of man in the way you have just described it to us—except for the animals and plants, in the souls of which he does not believe. He had thought these things out long before you revealed them to us tonight."

He has expressed only a one-millionth part of the truth concerning your humanity. As proof, I give you, from a million examples, this one: He doesn't know that your globe contains another globe inside it, like a pit, or a stone, in a fruit. Volcanoes are the mouths this inner world breathes through. That world is your Hell. Punished souls inhabit it, not in the midst of flame, but in the midst of shadow.

Balaam's Ass now described in detail how the damned soul sank down through the ground from its tomb until it reached this interior globe which was Hell, and how, if the soul was pardoned, it was ejected up out of this inner Hell by the eruption of a volcano. He explained how the soul, if not forgiven, could rise up through the earth and be imprisoned in a plant or animal. He described how the souls in this interior Hell were partly punished by continually hearing their misdeeds eloquently described by living members of society.

But Auguste Vacquerie's mind was still on the bewildering revelations that had preceded this description. He burst out:

"Is mankind to be forever in a minimum security prison, the animal to be forever in a maximum security prison, the plant to be forever in solitary confinement? Is the world always so condemned? Is the earth really, from the root of the oak to the brow of the genius, nothing but a vile morass where the dirty linen of the higher worlds is washed throughout eternity? Everything that thinks, everything that walks, everything that vegetates—everything is punished? What? Woman, virgin, baby being born—they're all guilty? The adoring dog, the hovering bird, the rose giving off its glorious scent—these are all criminals? Is there not a single blade of grass that's innocent?"

You all come here guilty.

"Repeat that for me: Everything on earth is expiating a fault committed elsewhere."

Yes.

Balaam's Ass made some final comments to the effect that the soul damned to Hell in the center of the earth hears forever words and sounds connected with the crime he has commited. The session ended. The spirits had introduced a major theme into the seance. It would be energetically pursued for the next two years—with Auguste Vacquerie tenaciously fighting the spirits every inch of the way.

Chapter Five

ANDRÉ CHÉNIER LOSES HIS HEAD BUT ENDS UP KEEPING IT

Were the comings and goings of the various spirits really as arbitrary as all that? A week or so before Balaam's Ass appeared with his grim revelations about our prison universe, the shade of the French poet André Chénier had dropped by. Mostly, he had discussed the politics of the French revolution.

Then—the day after Balaam's Ass's visit—André Chénier came again, this time to tell his own story. It was one that would bear out Balaam's Ass's assertion that man was indeed God's convict.

Many writers suffer from writer's block. That is nothing compared to the troubles of André Chénier. This French poet had his head chopped off before he could complete his final poem.

Chénier was born in Constantinople in 1762, the son of a French businessman/diplomat and a Turkish mother. The poet's father brought the family to Paris when André was three. His mixed blood proved a potent brew. The young Chénier was a brilliant student, a fine poet (who kept very quiet about his poetry), an ambassadorial secretary and a journalist—and an indefatigable sexual adventurer who sowed his wild oats all across Europe.

André was 27 when the French Revolution swept through France. He was a moderate liberal, happy that the power of the nobles had been broken, but inclined to favor the royal family.

This respect for royalty would cost him his head. In 1793, Robespierre came to power. The dreadful period in French history known as the Terror began. Already, on Jan. 21, Louis XVI had been guillotined. Now, hundreds of prominent people not completely anti-Royalist were rounded up and executed. Bloody repression was enforced throughout the country. Though he had tried to keep out of the public eye, André Chénier was arrested and thrown in the prison of Saint-Lazare on March 7, 1794.

Desperately, André continued to write his poetry. Before, he had written gentle love poems in the classical manner of ancient Greece and Rome. Now, his verses, written on small strips of paper and smuggled out of prison in his laundry baskets, took on a bitter, contemporary note.

July 25, 1794, dawned clear and cool. André Chénier was taken from his cell in Saint-Lazare and marched through the winding streets of Paris to the guillotine. He mounted the scaffold and was forced to kneel. His head was buckled into an iron collar. He looked down in horror. A slop basket swayed a foot beneath his face. It was half-filled with blood, some of it fresh, some of it in coagulated globs. André was staring into the blood of those who had been guillotined before him, some that very morning.

He had little time to experience his own revulsion. Suddenly, the crowd was silent. There was an odd creaking sound above his head. He had the sensation that his head was being hurled downward, toward the bloody slops in the basket.

Abruptly, he was far above his body, which was slumping, headless, onto the floor of the platform . He was being enveloped in a diaphanous sheath. What was being enveloped in the diaphanous sheath was his soul. He looked up at the glittering, azure sky. The sky had become a mirror, and in that mirror he saw himself. He was 20 years old again. His face was fresh and sunny, full of hope. As he gazed, he felt as if he were being kissed slowly, adoringly, from head to foot, with a kiss in which he felt not only the presence of his mother but that of every woman he had ever loved.

The face in the mirror in the sky was connected to a body. Where the guillotine had sliced through André Chénier's neck, there was now only a pulsing, luminous line...

How do we know what happened to André Chénier after he was guillotined?

It would seem—and Victor Hugo believed it—that the spirit of the beheaded poet came tapping through the turning tables on Jersey island.

Beginning on Dec. 9, 1853, André Chénier not only told the participants at the seance about his afterlife experiences. He also tapped out the remainder of the poem he had been working on just before he was taken out to be guillotined.

This posthumous performance of André Chénier has confounded skeptics of the Paranormal. Not only was this poetry, tapped out by the "spirit" of André Chénier, of the highest literary merit, but it was in exactly the same style as the work of the living Chénier.

These skeptics can hardly argue that this poetry allegedly from the afterworld was the unconscious work of Victor Hugo. Hugo wasn't even at the seance that night.

Here's how Claudius Grillet, in his *Victor Hugo, Spiritist*, tells the story.

"Friday evening, Dec. 9, 1853, we [Grillet writes as though he were present, though he was not] saw what amounted to a renewal on Jersey of the experience of [the early 14th century Pope] Julius II (an enthusiastic user of the turning tables, by all accounts), who persuaded the spirit of Homer to pick up the lyre again and add a verse to the *Iliad*. The seance took place at Leguéval's house, and not at Marine-Terrace. Victor Hugo was not in attendance.

"At the start, Socrates occupied the tripod table for a few minutes. Then, suddenly, an abnormally strong shaking of the table alerted the assembled host that something unexpected was about to happen.

"'Who's there?' inquired Charles Hugo. The reply was: 'André Chénier.'

"We know that numerous works of this poet remained incomplete," Grillet goes on, using the present tense for emphasis. "Durrieu, one of the exiles who is at the seance, finds that this is an excellent opportunity, since we have Chénier in our hands, for asking him to complete several interrupted poems. And so it is that, solicited to complete the fragment of *Idyll XII* that begins, *Come running, young Chromis, I love you and I am beautiful...*, he replies with a declamation in fact greatly resembling his style:

Neere is swift-footed, but Chromis is agile,
Woods in which Amaryllis is the bird in Virgil...

"Six stanzas follow. Other participants, their appetites whetted, also express their wishes. All the questions fuse into one. At the request of Guérin, Chénier is made to complete his final poem which was interrupted by the executioner. He is also made to produce new sections joining together a number of the poems he wrote while he was alive."

Grillet concludes: "Without losing his head, the glorious decapitee lent himself with perfect good grace to these various requests."

It's not easy for us citizens of the sound-byte world of late twentieth century America to take an interest in the poetry of late eighteenth century France—even when it's ostensibly dictated by a discarnate entity doing a perfect imitation of a late, great poet's style.

It's easier for us to read—because it is morbidly fascinating—an account, allegedly by a dead man, of his own beheading and what came after.

Here, as tapped through the table by, ostensibly, the obliging spirit of André Chénier himself, is the full story of his decapitation and its aftermath.

The man climbs up on the scaffold. The executioner attaches him to the platform. The half-moon closes around his neck. The souls of those who have been guillotined take flight in this iron collar. Then the man has a terrible moment. He opens his eyes and sees below him a basket full of reddish mud. It lies in the gutter at the bottom of the scaffold; and his head tells him: 'I'm going to be there.' 'No,' replies his soul.

The scene has just changed. Instead of mud, he sees an ocean; instead of blood he sees light. He has entered the sky by way of that gutter. O, terror! O, joy! O, awakening! O, tremendous kiss! O, falling to one's knees! O, soaring! The soul takes flight, yet remains on its knees. It remains a child, yet becomes a bird.

But O, surprise! It feels itself being slowly enveloped in a diaphanous sheath. The sky changes into a mirror. The soul sees itself. It is beautiful. It is 20 years old. The body no longer hides the soul; it reflects it. The soul is no longer enclosed in matter. Beauty is no longer a matter of flesh. The soul has released from this corpse being dragged to the charnel-house all that was precious in it: its smile, its glance, its sunniness, love's first kiss still lingering on the lips of the severed head, a forgotten sigh, a song of an autumn evening, the perfume of an April's early morning, the tiny little fast-subsiding outburst of a dove, the words: 'I love you;' and it has carried all that away into the sky.

I recognize myself, and yet I no longer have my senses about me. I'm alive, and yet I no longer carry the weight of my life. It pulsates through the light in my transparent veins. I drink infinity through all my pores. An invisible mouth covers me with a long kiss in which I sense my mother, in which I recognize my mistress, and which gives forth one after the other the perfume of all my lovers.

A luminous line separates my head from my body. It is an alive and feeling wound, which is receiving the kiss of God. Death appears to me simultaneously on the earth and in the sky; while my body, transfigured by the tomb, plunges deep into the beatitudes of eternity, I see, at an immense distance below me, my other body which the executioner is throwing to the worms, my head rolling in the gutter, my wound gushing blood, my guillotine blade being washed, my scalp hanging at the end of a stick, and my name being execrated by the crowd.

Then I hear a voice crying, "Glory to Chénier!" and I see a halo descending from the heights of the sky down to my forehead. The basket into which my head had rolled has ended up becoming an annunciation of God. The guillotine has ended up blazing forth in beams of light. The executioner has discovered his own wholeness in God. The sower of death has harvested immortality.

I am reborn in a huge cradle. I emerge alive from the shadows, as pink as a lily in springtime. Every soul is a flower growing out of the dirt of its tomb. Heaven is a bouquet. The scent of cemeteries is the softest scent. God will always inhale the odor of a rose that grows out of death. Prayer plucks the rose for God. Prayer is the bouquet-maker of Heaven.

All of a sudden, I hear voices in the infinite, one saying, "O, my poet, my name is Neere. I am sad; my crown is incomplete.

Your verses abandoned me. I died while being born. O, my poet, make me live again. Look once more upon my Idyll. Let me rejoin Chromis." The other says, "O, my lover, I am Camille; you made me love you, you made me sing. Give your love back to me, and take up my song once more. O my love, enable me to find Chénier again." The other says, with a grim and plaintive note of mockery: "O, revenger, I am Louis Sixteenth. You hold in your hand anger's whip. You're on a first-name basis with thunder. Seize the lightning lines of poetry and avenge me. Make the scaffold wilt--

We will not linger longer with André Chénier, for now his channeled utterances begin to be those which will interest only close students of French literature and history. André apparently meets in the afterworld those figures he created in his poetry but was not able to develop thoroughly because he was executed, but which he will now complete by making use of the turning table. And he meets the King of France, whom he defended, and is about to meet Robespierre, also in the afterworld, who executed Chénier, and whom Chénier will forgive...

It's all quite improbable. And quite amazing. Perhaps it is time to begin to look a little more critically at all these channeled revelations. Were these spirits really who they said they were? What were they, anyway?

Before anything else, though, we must meet and talk with Metempsychosis.

Chapter Six

METEMPSYCHOSIS SPEAKS

The universe as prison and all life as punishment: That was one of the two principal tenets of the strange and disturbing cosmology presented by the spirit world in the person of Balaam's Ass to the seance-goers at Marine-Terrace.

The other tenet, inextricably intertwined with the first, consisted of the Spiritist doctrine of reincarnation—or, metempsychosis, which included reincarnational lives in the bodies of animals. According to Alan Kardec's spirits, metempsychosis was a slow and steady process, a progressive movement up the Great Chain of Being to the areas of Angelhood.

To hear the spirits of Marine-Terrace tell it, the process was a whole lot more bumpy. It wasn't just that you also reincarnated in stones and plants; it was that you could backslid horribly while on you way up the Great Chain of Being. If the deed you committed was horrible enough, you could even tumble back downfrom the world of humans all the way to the world of stones—in a single reincarnation.

Cleopatra—was she really that evil?— had become a worm!

Here's how Claudius Grillet sums up what he calls the Hugolian belief system of "metempsychosis applied to a doctrine of universal redemption:"

"Souls survive bodies, but take on a new material form. It's a sort of generalized purgatory. Souls survive bodies, but reintegrate matter around themselves anew. They plunge into inferior forms of being (animal, mineral), or they mount up toward the more perfect form of man or of angel, according to whether their present existence has merited reward or punishment.

"Everything that is, is also conscious and alive to varying degrees.

"Beyond the impassive, unmoving and speechless appearance of things, the Spiritist eye saw a nature that was all aquiver with life, that bled, and that suffered for being contained in the blind horror of matter or in the punished flesh of animals—that purified itself and that sang on the heights of the spirit.

"In this system, there is no eternal punishment. But there are penalties.

"In awaiting their re-entry into grace, all criminals suffer, in their prison of matter, a punishment proportionate to their crime. From the pebble in the road to the stars in the sky, the entire universe is alive.

"But universal burial in matter is the sentence imposed on those who are guilty—and also the means by which they expiate their sins."

Cleopatra had become a worm!

Hugo used this image in *What the Shadow's Mouth Says*, the more-than-600-line-long poem he wrote, late in 1854, at the urging of the spirits, basing it almost entirely on the communications from the turning tables. Hugo is on record as saying that this one line, and the overall concept of a progression up a Great Chain of Being with includes lives as rocks and plants, are the only ideas he ever borrowed from the turning tables and incorporated into his poetry; everything else, he said, came from him.

Hugo spoke very differently to his fellow seance-goers on Jersey island, and wrote quite different comments in his journals, than he made to his professional colleagues about the extent to which he adopted the spirits' words. Hugo was always a master of public relations, and he well knew how ridiculous a public profession of faith in the tables would made him look, and how much it would open him to attacks from his enemies.

But it's likely that this ultimately highly secretive man borrowed more than a single image from the turning tables (of course, the skeptics argue that the turning tables borrowed all of their images from *him*, and from his friends; but that is not the direction of the argument of this book). Since fully three-thirds of the transcripts have been lost from sight, it's difficult to find out what the truth is. Let's glance briefly at the metempsychosical, plant- and stone-inhabited- universe images in some of the rest of his poetry. Many of them likely did come from the turning tables; and a quick look at them will help us greatly in filling in the picture of this strange and rather merciless form of reincarnation.

Psychoanalyst Charles Baudouin summed up metempsychosis as seen in Victor Hugo's later poetry in his 1943 work, *Psychanalyse de Victor Hugo* (Baudouin regards this imagery as issuing not from the afterworld but from Hugo's earliest, ambivalence-and-fear-creating, relationships with his mother, his father and his brothers).

Baudouin sees five basic premises as underlying the Hugolian metempsychosical universe. In setting them forth, he illustrates each one with examples from Hugo's poetry:

1) The universe is peopled with souls that move upward from echelon to echelon, as a function of their moral worth, and continuously. This is a creation

Which goes from rock to tree and tree to beast
And from the tree to you mounts imperceptibly,

But, far from stopping at mankind,
Enters the invisible and the unfathomable,
Filling the blue sky endless
With beings neighbor to man, and others far away...
This is the sublime ascension of the starry ladder.

On the other hand, the beings, in function of how much merit they have earned, transfer in death and reincarnation from one echelon to another, mounting or descending and taking on, according to a law of moral equilibrium, the form that corresponds to their degree of merit.

Everything lives. Creation hatches forth metempsychosis.

2) This continuous ladder of beings goes right up to the archangels, and in the upper reaches vanishes in God, while at the other end the ladder plunges straight down into absolute evil, the image of which is almost a negative of God:

A dreadful black sun from which radiates the night!

3) *God made the universe; the universe made itself.* It is on account of original sin that the soul has fallen down through the various stages of matter. From now on, the world on which it lives is *the punishment-world.*

In the monster, it expiates; in man, it repairs...
Yes, your untamed universe is God's convict.

4) For man, the reward is to ascend, in dying, to the level of pure spirit; while the punishment is to fall to the level of animal, of plant, and of stone.

All who misbehave
Cause to be born, in dying, the monster of their life
Which [in the next lifetime] seizes hold of them.

The monster-animal and the monster-stone are described in Hugo with some partiality. For the animal:

Pity the bird of crime and beast of prey.
That which Domitian
[one of the most tyrannical of the Roman emperors],
Caesar did with joy,
The tiger carries on with untold horror.

The ultimate jail is in the interior of stones:

The stone is a cave wherein a criminal muses.

The nameless cry of pain of the condemned soul is "walled up in the stone."

O! What eyes fixed wide open
In the depths of the pebbles, secret dungeons of souls!

This vision of the stone-dark cell haunted Hugo:

Man, captive spirit, listens to them (the magi)
While in his brain, doubt,
A beast blind to gleams from heaven,
So as to transport there the indignant soul
Suspends its spider's web
Down from the skull,

Down from the dark cell's ceiling.

5) The images of punishment which Hugo presents in his later poetry are especially those of the punishment of kings, emperors, men in "purple" (the higher-ups of the Roman Catholic Church) and tyrants from every century. He imagines the more tyrannical Caesars of ancient Rome as reincarnating as "birds of crime and beasts of prey," and, even worse:

Tiberius in a rock, Sejanus in a serpent.

In *Night Weepings*, Hugo even has the souls of the very worst tyrants of all—Nero, Caligula, Louis XI and the like—reincarnating in huge tomb-stones above rotting, half-opened graves!

In Hugo's later poetry, the revenge of metempsychosis is great indeed!

What would Metempsychosis itself have made of all this?

To jump ahead of our narrative by a year, on Dec 17, 1854, the personification of metempsychosis—an entity calling itself 'Metempsychosis'—paid a visit to the turning tables.

This visit wasn't long; just long enough for that entity to dictate fourteen mainly short sentences, each one of them summing up the nature of metempsychosis.

These fourteen sentences stand as a monument to the utterly mysterious occasional brilliance of material allegedly channeled from the spirit world.

Each one encapsulates the entire essence of metempsychosis. A few are quite plain; others express the nature of metempsychosis with an astonishing pithiness combined with metaphorical richness.

Here they are, with commentary when deemed necessary. No

comments from the evening's seance participants have been preserved:

I am the eternal idea. I am the real.

Only I complete myself by the I.

I take man and I wrest him into thingness.

I am the slope of the soul between infinity and the finite.

I am the shortest path from pebble to God. [Ed.: *The soul must pass through every echelon of being in the shortest time possible.*]

I am immensity's arm bearing the grain of sand and mixing it with the seed of fire.

I am the corridor leading you to secret doors.

I am the staircase of Babel climbed by Jacob and leading to the unknown ceiling.

I have a countenance fashioned out of the creation; my eyes are stars, my ears are wind, my mouth is the abyss, my skin is the sky, my hair the forest's branches.

I am the mysterious portrait hanging on the wall of the terrible house.

[Ed.: *This single sentence could be an entire short story by Kafka (but without the other-dimensional realities). The sentence evokes a picture of a human being in a single incarnation living in a house which is rent by every sort of catastrophe, in which the one stable element is the portrait of an unknown personage hanging on the wall (in this context, 'house of holy terror' might be a better translation for maison terrible). Now and then, in the course of living his or her lifetime in this house, the human being, in the midst of every sort of difficulty, happens, in passing by the portrait, to glance up at it. It is always unchanged, this portrait of—he or she doesn't know whom, in this house constantly rent by the thunder and lightning of terrible events.*

This unchanging portrait is the portrait of the unchanging, eternal self of the human being; the Oversoul, so to speak, which contains within and as itself the ' soul' of each individual lifetime, in dynamic interrelatedness, and in such a way that the Oversoul, as an entity, remains essentially unchanged throughout each lifetime. The portrait is always mysteriously present for the occupant of the terrible house— though he or she scarcely ever has the time to even look at it. The occupant cannot know the identity of the personage until, in death— between lives—he or she knows that it is their own self-portrait.]

I am the formidable atom seed of man.

I am the root of the flower, the foundation of the rock, the insect's tendril, the convict's ball-and-chain, the angel's wing.

I am that which enchains and that which unchains.

I am the archangel-jailer, and I shine forth in the immensity like a sun in the shape of an iron collar.

Chapter Seven

THE COSTUME BOX

Is our entire physical universe really nothing but a prison?

Did all of us take life on penitentiary earth solely to expiate a mistake made in a previous lifetime?

How seriously should we take a talking table, anyway?

The third question is the one we have to deal with first. And, to answer it, we have to grapple with the central conundrum of channeling, which is (as seen from the perspective of Victor Hugo's experiences) as follows:

If energies from the beyond truly came through the turning tables at Marine-Terrace, they must, by definition, have existed outside of conventional space and time. They must have been, when they came to Hugo's house, not only invisible, but also completely naked, so to speak, in terms of any of the physical or mental accoutrements of time and space as we know them.

To communicate their ideas at all, the spirits would have had to make use of the words and concepts and images and memories that they found in the minds of the human participants at the seance.

Fortunately, this difficult idea has been brilliantly set forth for us by one of the most distinguished masters of channeling that has ever lived, the Pulitzer Prize-winning American poet James Merrill. The undisputed masterpiece of Merrill—who died in 1995 at age

68—was the 500-page poem *The Changing Light at Sandover* (published in 1982, but issued in three separate volumes before that), which was written largely under the guidance of, ostensibly, a host of spirits speaking through a Ouija board.

Over the almost 40 years that he 'channeled entities,' James Merrill was never able to make up his mind whether the spirits existed as such or not. This brilliant, urbane and learned man, who was awarded the Pulitzer Prize for the first book of *Sandover* and received two National Book awards, one for the second book of *Sandover*, knew that most of what came through the Ouija board had not been in his head beforehand. He knew himself well enough to know that these strange, esoteric concepts—involving reincarnation, Akhnaton, Atlantis, an upcoming new species of mankind, and much else—had not been buried in his unconscious before they were swiftly spelled out by the marker. In *The Changing Light at Sandover*, he had had the courage to put in block letters what came unbidden and unexpected from his guides, which was close to half of that immensely lengthy poem.

But, if Merrill was, as he often said, obliged to maintain an attitude of "perfect ambivalence" toward his spirit guides, this did not stop him from giving serious thought to the phenomenon. In a landmark interview in *The Paris Review*, Summer, 1982, the distinguished American poet disclosed that he believed both that the spirits had a measure of objective reality, and that they were dependent for the expression of their truths on pictures and ideas created by the mind of man.

Merrill set forth his belief that, in whatever realms of cosmic forces or elemental processes are in existence, human language "doesn't exist—except perhaps as vast mathematical or chemical formulas—which we then personify, or tame if you like, through the imagination [when we "channel"]. So, in a sense, all these figures are our creation, or mankind's.

"But," added the poet carefully, "the powers they represent are real—as, say, gravity is 'real'—but they [these powers] would be invisible, inconceivable, if they'd never passed through our heads and clothed themselves out of the costume box they found there. How they appear depends on us, on the imaginer, and would have to vary wildly from culture to culture, or even temperament to temperament....A process that Einstein would entertain as a formula might be described by an African witch doctor as a crocodile."

As late as 1994, a year before his death, Merrill suggested to critic Helen Vendler that many of the entities in occult, channeled works were personifications. "There are forces in the world that it is convenient for us to personify," he explained, using the gods and goddesses in Homer's *Iliad* as an example; in the modern era, "the new angels ought to be things like electricity and gravity; they too would lend themselves to personification."

With Merrill's description of the channeling process in mind, let's return to that extraordinary vision of a prison/convict universe which was communicated to Victor Hugo and Company by the Jersey island spirits. Let's ask ourselves: Assuming that they had any objective reality at all, would these other-worldly energies, when they passed through the heads of the seance-goers at Marine-Terrace and sought to cloth their thoughts and concepts out of the costume boxes they found there, really have foundonly costumes consisting mostly of prison uniforms, balls and chains?

The answer is an emphatic: Yes.

Victor Hugo and his family, and the people who surrounded them on Jersey island, were quite literally prisoners. As we learned from Martin Ebon's Introduction, Hugo had been driven from France in 1852, in the aftermath of the coup d'état of Emperor Napoleon III. The other members of Hugo's circle on the island were also either political exiles from France, or, like Sandor Téléki, of Hungary, 'proscripts' from the failed revolutions of other countries.

All of them were prisoners chained to the rocky, barren surface of Jersey island, which was separated by 25 miles of cold and windswept waters from the coast of France.

In the mid-nineteenth century, the best minds of the time were awakening to a horrified awareness of the extent to which Western society had been a punishment/prison culture. The greatest men and women of the day were passionately campaigning against capital punishment. As early as 1829, Hugo himself had written the fiercely polemical *The Last Day of a Condemned Man*, and on Jersey island he had sent a letter to Lord Palmerston (one that moved that English statesman to action), describing in vivid detail a particularly brutal hanging on the neighboring island of Guernsey. In Russia, Leo Tolstoy—forever traumatized by a public execution he had witnessed in Paris in his youth—would soon begin to meditate on the principles of passive resistance, and Dostoevsky's chronicles of the horrors of the prison camps of Siberia were not far in the future.

There were few French nationals who did not remember, or had not been told by their fathers, of the bloodshed of the French Revolution, in particular the Terror of 1793, when hundreds of distinguished citizens were summarily guillotined. Hugo's own father, Joseph-Léopold-Sigisbert Hugo (1773-1828), had been, as we learned in the Introduction, a general serving under Napoleon.

Every educated Frenchman or woman knew of the tyranny and brutality that the French Revolution itself had overthrown. They knew also that, during the Middle Ages, 95 percent of the population of France—and of other European countries as well—were, effectively, prisoners, their lands and every moment of their lives owned by a feudal lord.

70

The political exiles on Jersey island lived and breathed the notion of the universe as a prison. These were the concepts and images—typical of their age—that the spirits, seeking human words and concepts and images and memories with which to clothe their own words and concepts—and themselves—would have found inside the costume boxes in their heads.

If, from the vantage point of the late twentieth century, we strip away some of the prison garb from this grim mid-nineteenth century vision of reality—for, in our time, things seem to be a little better—what vision are we left with?

We are left with one of a physical universe that is entirely permeated with soul, and that is made up of a series of levels of reality, the densest of which is composed of rock. The levels composed of plant and animal matter are progressively less dense, and that of man the least dense of all—at least in terms of our material planet. For the very coming of the spirits suggests that, elsewhere—among the stars and planets? in other dimensions?—there are other, completely ethereal species of being, whose modes of existence we might do well to try to emulate.

This vision of the universe which we are left with, stripped of the grim fetters of mid-nineteenth century Europe, is one where reincarnation is a reality, and one where we are admonished to strive—not only in terms of lifetime to lifetime, but in this particular lifetime as well—to improve ourselves by working toward a more spiritual kind of existence.

Remarkably, this is exactly the sort of universe presented to us by the channeled entities of today.

It is, with numerous variations in fine detail, the universe of the spirit guides of James Merrill in *The Changing Light at Sandover*. In that poem, we are told that the universe consists of ten levels of reality, only the first of which, our earth, is physical. All of the rest come after death; only the most elite of the souls can finally attain to the highest rung, from which most of their soul matter is usually distributed back among living geniuses on earth.

Reincarnation is also a fact of life—or of 'lives'—in *Sandover*, and it's striking to note that Merrill's guides tell him that human souls reincarnate from time to time in the plant and mineral worlds (though not exactly in the animal). This kind of reincarnation isn't the result of having commited a heinous crime in a human lifetime; rather, it seems to be a knowledge-acquiring adventure taken on by hardier and more gifted souls. Merrill's guides even tell him the soul of W.H. Auden has lately reincarnated as a mineral deposit! They also inform him that there is a sense in which plant souls reincarnate in humans, since plants possess a quality called *shooting* which is sometimes inseminated into a human soul before birth; Luther Burbank is an example of a human born with a vigorous supply of shooting.

In a later chapter, we'll take up in more detail the theme of reincarnation as it appears in modern-day channeled literature. But, a universe of ascending levels of refinement, only the earliest of which consist of matter, through which the human soul moves progressively, is a staple of such literature today. According to the spirit guides who dictate *Songs of the Arcturians* to Patricia Pereira, our universe is comprised of 13 "densities" or "dimensions" (the terms seem interchangeable). Earth is only a third-density world, with our afterlife being a fourth. Pereira's guides, allegedly from the Blue Crystal Planet revolving around the star Arcturus—itself a fifth- and sixth-dimensional system (and therefore a completely ethereal one)—tell her that in mankind's universe "for every physical planet there are at least four or five light-substance planets."

In Darryl Anka's *Bashar: Blueprint for Change. A Message from our Future*, the extraterrestrial Bashar channeled by Anka comes from the planet Essassani ("Place of Living Light"), which revolves around the star Sha 500 light-years from earth, in the direction of the constellation Orion. Essassani is a fourth-density world evolving into a fifth-density one. Bashar explains that he has come to earth as an emissary from his world to help us evolve from our third-density experience into a fourth-density one--an evolution which he says it is essential that we accomplish. Bashar makes fourth density existence sound attractive, and certainly more refined than the kind of living we are involved in here: "You will be living in the moment and truly understanding that every single moment of time is literally a new moment....You will begin to truly see through the illusion of physical reality as your own projection. You will be able to come and go, in and out of your body at will."

We could go on at some length about the many volumes of 'channeled' literature which have appeared over the past 20-30 years, and which paint a picture of our universe consistent with the universe of Hugo's spirits when more or less stripped of its ball-and-chain elements. This is not to say that these books, where they are actually channeled from other-dimensional beings, express a 'true' picture of the cosmos. This is merely to say that they express a picture of the cosmos which is cobbled together from the words and concepts and images and memories in the costume boxes in *our* heads—the heads of late twentieth century human beings. That vision is no more nor less true for us than was the vision of the Jersey island spirits for Victor Hugo and his fellow exiles; it is simply one that makes more sense to us, since it is, necessarily, partly created by us.

Perhaps it would not hurt for us to remain open-minded to the notion that, behind both mid-nineteenth century and late twentieth century versions of reality, there just may move objectively-real energies seeking to make their presence known; or, perhaps, somehow just simply being picked up at propitious times by people of certain talents. But so essentially different are these spirits/energies/presences from time- and space-bound humankind that our apprehension of them is thoroughly garbled by our own preconceptions. Is there any way of arriving at a single objective truth behind all of these subjectivities masquerading as the truth? In our day and age, many would say there is not even such a thing. But, for those who still have hope, one method might be to try to see what remains after the more obviously time-and space-related elements are removed. That is a method that really needs to be applied to the whole history of channeled literature going back to the beginnings of mankind; but, in these *Conversations with Eternity*, we can at least try to keep a sharp eye out for those elements which seem particularly capable of standing alone—of wearing only a fig leaf or two from the mid-nineteenth century costume boxes that the spirits have had to dip into.

Let's look at a final example, in a different realm, of making use of the costume box. In "Deep Inside the Patmos Cave" (in *Doomsday! How the World Will End—and Why*, edited by Martin Ebon), James R. Wolfe provides us with a fascinating account of why one of humankind's greatest religious visions—the Apocalyptic *Revelations* of St. John—may have taken the form it did. Wolfe suggests that, given the essentially indescribable, transcendent experience which John was trying to describe, he would have been forced to unconsciously search through all of his own experiences in order to find even minimal time-space terms with which to describe his titanic four-day experience of the Word of the Lord. He would have had to ransack his own costume boxes! Wolfe believes that John's memory of the eruption of an underwater volcano near Thera, which he could have seen from Patmos; and of the canopic jars topped with bizarre animals heads which stood at the four corners of the crypts in Egyptian tombs—of which John would also have known—along with much else, could have provided him with a great deal of the imagery he needed to dress up and make manifest his essentially inexpressible experience.

The Book of Revelations of John, then, contain truth—but it is a transcendent truth necessarily dressed up in the time-and-space accoutrements of John's time, and therefore enormously distorted in its expression.

As we will see in the final chapter of this book, Victor Hugo believed that he was the reincarnation of John of Patmos (along with a number of other religious prophets); perhaps the poet had some intuition of the similarities in their essential nature of the revelations of John and the revelations of his turning tables. On that note, let us turn to Victor Hugo and those revelations—for they have only just begun!

Chapter Eight

ENG. LIT. 1000: SHAKESPEARE HOLDS FORTH AND BYRON AND SIR WALTER SCOTT NOD DISTANTLY

Not long after the arrival of the Hugo family on Jersey island, François-Victor had begun to translate the complete works of William Shakespeare. Eventually, he would produce an admired and definitive French version of all the plays. Victor Hugo would write the introduction to his son's work, and not long afterward expand his introduction into an entire book on Shakespeare's life and artistic genius in general. Thus, interest in Shakespeare was already high in the Hugo household when this greatest of all English dramatists and poets, if not the greatest in the world, born in 1564 and died in 1616, first came tapping through the turning table, on January 13, 1854.

Victor Hugo and Auguste Vacquerie were present at this first seance, with Mme. Hugo and Charles "holding" the table. Once the identity of the illustrious shade had been established, Victor Hugo put the first question:

"As you know, for us you are one of the four or five greatest creators of all mankind. Would you like to tell us what happened in the tomb and what encounter took place on April 23, 1616?"

I kissed Corneille, just then being born. [Ed.: *Pierre Corneille was a French dramatist who lived from 1606 to 1684.*]

Victor Hugo corrected Shakespeare: "I didn't say 1606, but 1616. Gather together your thoughts, and consider whether that day Shakespeare did not meet another great representative of human thought."

No.

"However, on April 23, 1616, Cervantes [,the author of Don Quixote,] died—the same day, almost the same hour, as yourself. Didn't you meet him? Would you care to answer that?"

No.

Hugo explored this: "Do you mean, you wouldn't care to answer, or that you didn't meet Cervantes?"

Cervantes did not die at the same time as I.

"But he died the same day. You must have met him in the place you both went to. Two geniuses like yourselves must have had things to say to each other. What did you say?"

When you die, you straightaway take on the age of all those who have died—that is, of eternity. In heaven, there is neither a first nor a last to arrive. Everyone has a single second of life, and that second lasts a hundred thousand years. Asking a dead person, 'How long have you been in heaven?' is like asking a sunbeam, 'How long have you been a part of the sun?' A soul is a sister who has no older sister. Infinity is not the elder sibling of love, nor eternity that of genius. All great minds are twinned together....Ideas have brothers—but never little brothers. If you question the sunbeam about its age, it will reply, 'Ask the lightning bolt.'... We [artists] write the drama; God produces it. Behold heaven: It is the final act of the drama. The tomb that yawns open to receive our souls is the curtain that goes up on this final act. Applaud, Cervantes! Applaud, Molière! Applaud, Shakespeare! Enter God.

Hugo had another question:

"When you were on earth, you created— you created in imitation of God. Now that you've left earth and are living the true life, living in the light, what is your genius doing with itself? You,

Shakespeare, lived, and you created; and for you these two ideas cannot be separated: For Shakespeare, to live was to create. So are you continuing to create? Are you continuing your work? If you're getting on with your creative work—if it still comes welling out of you—then this must also be true of all the other geniuses in heaven. So that, running parallel with the primary creation of God, there must also be what we could call secondary creation—that is, God's creation through the agency of great minds.

"This opens up vast new horizons! If you're [continuing your work], are you doing so with reference to the world of men that you lived in, or with reference to the world of souls in which your being now dwells? Has your work undergone the same transformation as yourself? Do you now write—if the word write is applicable—in a language that is new to us, that men would not understand, in a language appropriate only to heaven? What are you writing: dramas? What passions are you describing? What worlds? What ideas? If these dramas were translated for us, would they be accessible to our human intellect at all? In a word: What is the connection between the work you are now doing in heaven, and the work you did on earth?"

Human life has human creators. Celestial life has the divine creator. Creating is work; contemplation is work's reward. On earth, great minds create in order to point out morals; but, in heaven, everything is moral, everything is good, everything is just, everything is beautiful. I could only create something here if heaven were incomplete; but, as it is, I dwell in a masterpiece, I now have my being in perfection. I who was admired, am condemned to admire. I am lost in a crowd of spectators, I who was the creator of the spectacle.

God has fashioned for himself an orchestra pit composed of demigods: Orpheus, Tyrteus, Homer, Aeschylus, Sophocles, Euripides, Moses, Ezekiel, Isaiah, Daniel, Aesop, Dante, Rabelais,

Cervantes, Molière, Shakespeare, and others whom I can but dimly glimpse in the depths of infinity without quite seeing who they are. We sit pensively before the Light of Eternity. Jesus is on His knees. The Light illuminates us; it bedazzles us. Life ravishes us and flows over us; and if you saw all the prophets and all the magi and all the poets and all the geniuses who are seated in a circle before God, you would not ask me if I created.

No; I look. No; I listen. No; I am no more than an attentive atom before the face of immensity. I am a great man abdicating before infinity. I fall from archangelhood. I get down from my pedestal as inconspicuously as possible, and I throw away my halo. I am a dream the awakening from which is death. That which, for me, in life was art, has been, for me, transfigured in death into love. My creations have left their wings behind in the tomb. As I have become what I now am, so has my art been resurrected in the forms of love. Art walks to heaven's door, but only love may enter. Happiness is an eternal Mecca toward which art makes its way as a pilgrim, but for which love is the angel.

Shakespeare would quickly become a regular at the table. He would be the only English-language regular! But, six months later, two other greats of English literature would come dropping by. They would have virtually nothing to say; just a word or two each. But their impact on the seance attendees—particularly one young Englishman—would be enormous.

That young Englishman was Albert Pinson, a British naval Lieutenant.

A few years later, Lieutenant Pinson would play a strange and painful role in the history of the Hugo family. While he and the family were together on Jersey island, Victor Hugo's other daughter, Adèle, would fall in love with the youthful officer, and become convinced that he had fallen in love with her. Tragically, in 1863, she would follow him, first, to Halifax, Nova Scotia, Canada, then to Barbados. During this period she would live alone, almost never seeing Pinson—and then only from a distance—while he consistently ignored her. It would eventually become apparent that her feeling that he loved her was a delusion, a symptom of schizophrenia. In 1872, Adèle would return to Paris, eventually to be confined to a mental asylum, where she died in 1915.

On Wednesday, June 7, 1854, none of this was apparent. Pinson and Adèle were merely engaged in a mild flirtation.

Pinson had come to the seance partly to show the others the foolishness of these table-turning experiments. He had an idea about how he could do this. He would only ask the spirits questions in English, and insist that they only answer him in English. This shouldn't be a problem for them, if they were who they said they were, and had the world of the supernatural at their fingertips. But Pinson was sure they weren't who they said they were, and that they wouldn't be able to respond—since nobody in Victor Hugo's seance-loving group knew much English at all (François-Victor, who was hard at work translating Shakespeare, spoke the language poorly, and rarely attended the seances).

We don't know if Pinson thought that any of the seance-mavens at Marine-Terrace were consciously perpetrating a fraud. But he was certain that, at the very least, they were unconsciously and innocently transmitting the information to the table themselves.

Present at the seance that night was a large and varied crew: Pinson, Mlle. Adèle Hugo, Victor Hugo, Guérin, Téléki, Charles Hugo, Vacquerie, and Kesler.

Pinson held the table with Charles Hugo and asked if he could put questions to the spirits in English. The group had no objections—nor, apparently, did the table. It began to move. Charles asked who was there.

The table responded, in Latin: *Frater Tuus [Your brother]*.

"You aren't my brother," said Charles Hugo. "Are you Mr. Pinson's?"

Yes, Andre.

This created a sensation. Lieutenant Pinson confessed that he did indeed have a brother. No one around the table had known this. Pinson explained that this brother had disappeared some twelve years before, and that his family had no idea what had become of him.

Pinson now proceeded to ask a question in English. The table responded in English. Pinson asked a second question in English. A second reply came in English.

It's not clear from the records whether the other members of the group had any idea what was being said, or if Pinson reported it to them.

We do know that the English Lieutenant was visibly shaken by what had occurred. He stood up, deeply moved.

He told the group that personal, family matters had been involved in the questioning. He asked them that, for this reason, they not put on record anything that had been said.

However remarkable all this was, what was to happen in five days would be much more remarkable.

On Monday, June 12, 1854, at 10:15 a.m., the same group met around the table again. Charles Hugo and Lieutenant Pinson held the table.

After a minute or two, the piece of furniture began to move.

After a brief exchange of commonplaces, Pinson asked: "Who's there?"

The table answered:

Byron.

"Is Montague Helt alive or dead?" Pinson asked in English:

The table tapped out, in English, **Alive.**

Guérin put a question to Byron: "Can you formulate a complete thought in several lines of verse? We're asking you for just a small number of verses, since Charles doesn't know English at all and gets exhausted trying to follow the letters."

Yes.

"Speak."

The table tapped out in English: **You know not what you ask.**

Pinson translated for the group; then he said in English: "Can't you speak some lines [of your poetry]?"

No.

"You mean you don't want to?"

Yes.

"Why don't you want to say anything?"

The table shook and turned around on itself.

"Who's there?" asked Pinson.

There was no reply. The table shook violently; then, at the end of several minutes, it tapped out: **Silence.**

"'Silence'? Does he mean we should stop?"

Scott.

"Are you Sir Walter Scott?"

Yes.

"Do you wish to speak?"

The table tapped out two lines of English verse:

Vex not the bard; his lyre is broken,
His last song sung, his last work spoken.

Pinson translated for the group. They were deeply impressed. No doubt the young lieutenant was dumbfounded. Certainly his plan to unmask the impostors of Marine-Terrace was a shambles.

The session ended. Of the many hard acts to follow that concluded the turning table sessions at Victor Hugo's home, this would have been among the hardest.

Had it really been the shade of Sir Walter Scott that had tapped out these final two lines of poetry, and about Lord Byron? Why did the participants "know not what they spoke" when they asked Byron himself to tap out a line ot two.

As a lesson in English Literature, this was surely one of the strangest in the history of the English language. How did it affect the incredulity of Lieutenant Pinson? It must surely have left him thinking. He was, after all, the only one at the seance who had any knowledge of English.

And he did not believe for a moment—or had not believed for a moment—that there was the slightest chance that the turning table could ever give access the land of the dead.

Chapter Nine

THE HAUNTING OF VICTOR HUGO

There were grisly ghosts on Jersey island: In particular, there were three murderesses and a headless man. Nothing was known about the headless man; but the White Lady was said to have murdered her infant child several millennia before, and to have been condemned to walk the barren fields of Jersey island ever after. She was said to be the familiar spirit of a nearby menhir, also called the "White Lady;" in the Jersey language, the term *La Blianche Damme* can refer to either a ghost or to a menhir.

Local legend had it that the Black Lady, also condemned to roam the island endlessly, was an ancient druidess who had sacrificed her own father on the bloodied altar stone of a dolmen. And then there was the Gray Lady, whose equally dreadful crime was mercifully without a name.

These phantasms began to haunt the imagination of the endlessly impressionable, endlessly sensitive Victor Hugo. The turning tables opened doors to other dimensions; he wondered if they might bring forth something more palpable than words, if something quasi-physical, far more terrifying than a tap, might come trailing and slouching across his bedroom floor.

Writes Jean Massin, editor of *The Complete Works of Victor Hugo*, and a leading French authority on the background and content of the seances: "It seems likely that the multiplication of seances, and certainly the growing quality of the messages, contributed to creating at Marine-Terrace an atmosphere favorable to the invasion of the most obscure forces, which had always been besieging that sad house." Hugo's unpublished *The Exile's Journal*, for April 27, 1854, describes the unpleasant atmosphere that often seemed to lay upon the poet's room. He writes that, "at night my room fills up with strange noises, there are knocks on my wall, papers stir, inexplicable noises make themselves heard." He noted that sometimes when he awoke at night, he wondered fearfully whether he was about to see some strange being strolling through his room. "Since they talk to us, they might show themselves to us," he reflected. "They are able to arouse our hearing; perhaps they will be able to arouse our sight. A black being would cause me a certain amount of fear. A white being would perhaps frighten me a little less."

His fears were not unfounded. The wandering, disenfranchised ghost of the White Lady actually did invade the turning tables.

She seems to have set the stage for her appearance very carefully, beginning with the night of February 21, 1854. We have an account in Victor Hugo's own hand, as preserved in the Jersey island transcripts:

(Note) On February 21, Charles and François-Victor, arriving back at the house at 11:30 p.m., saw the windows of the drawing room lit up. They wanted to come in by the drawing room, but the door was locked. Everybody had gone to bed. Charles, unable to explain all the light, had searched for the key. He came to ask his mother for it; she didn't know where it was; to ask Vacquerie for it, who, surly at being awakened abruptly, asked to be left alone, etc.

The next morning, when we unlocked the drawing room, the maid couldn't find the candlesticks. So it couldn't have been one of our own candles that had illuminated the room. Nor had we lit the fire the night before. What could the light have been? We chatted about it at breakfast this morning. We decided to consult the tables.

The seance was held at 1:30 that afternoon. Charles and Mme. Hugo sat at the table, with Victor Hugo transcribing.

The table did not offer much in the way of clarification. When asked by Victor Hugo if the spirits knew what it was that his sons had witnessed the night before, an anonymous entity rapped out, Yes. When Hugo asked if the phenomenon had been natural or supernatural, the entity answered only:

Night beauty.

Then the table was still. Was that all? asked Hugo. To which the table responded, **Yes.** François-Victor took Charles's place at the piece of furniture. It responded with what seemed to be a string of nonsensical words: **(Faith), goddess, doubt priest man altar temple night.**

Some months later, they would find out that the words had not been so crazy. But, for this afternoon, the seance was ended.

Three weeks later, another hair-raising incident brought the seance-goers running to the turning table, to make inquiries about the ghost called the White Lady. A Saint-Hélier baker's boy—one source suggests it was the barber—had been walking toward St. Luke's Church, which faced Marine-Terrace, when he had seen a white, motionless figure standing at the end of the street. The figure seemed to be in flames.

Philip Stevens tells the story in *Victor Hugo in Jersey*:

"Terrified, not knowing whether to go forward or back, the baker's boy [got] a grip on himself and rushed past it with his eyes closed and his hair on end. When Hugo heard all this he was rather amused, and he told Guérin, who had heard strange shrieks nearby, that he could imagine the apparition emerging from between the knobbled trunks which lined Le Dicq."

Guérin's account of hearing strange shrieks on that same night is preserved in the transcripts. He wrote: *I wrote, yesterday, March 24, 1854, arriving home at midnight, the following note: 'I heard, while passing by the Dick* [Ed.: *"Dicq"—a French version of the English word '"dyke"—is here mispelled by Guérin. This was a road leading in from the sea and following the line of an ancient dyke*], *the strange and piercing cry that I had already heard at that same place.*

I had already heard, a month before, the cry about which I speak in the note of the 24th.

Marine-Terrace, March 25, 1854

Théophile Guérin

On March 23, reporting a conversation with a friend who told him about, "a passerby having been pursued by a woman in white who was none other than a ghost," near Marine-Terrace, Hugo reputedly said, "Since we're doing the tables, it wouldn't upset me to end up not only chatting with the spirits but seeing them." Guérin declared that he would rather fight on the barricades rather than go through such an experience, to which Hugo retorted: "I'm not like you. I would experience an infinite sweetness in seeing a shade, in seeing once more those beings whom I have loved and who are dead."

It seemed important to speak to the table again.

The next day, Thursday, March 23, 1854, at 9:00 p.m., Victor Hugo, son Charles, and wife Adèle, along with Auguste Vacquerie, conducted a seance.

"Is there someone there?"

The table tapped twice.

"No? Who's replying no?"

The table tapped twice.

"But isn't there someone, since someone is replying no? Can

you say who you are?"

No.

"Is something bothering you?"

Yes.

"What?"

Domus vestra. Si vis mecum loqui, veni in viam. **[Latin for: Your house. If you want to talk to me, come out in the road.]**

Auguste Vacquerie asked: "Are you the White Lady whom the the barber saw near the house?"

Yes.

"If we went into the street, would we see you?"

Yes.

"Tonight?"

Yes.

"At what time?"

Three o'clock.

"Would we be able to see you if there were several of us?"

No.

"Must we be alone?"

Yes.

Mme. Victor Hugo inquired: "Do you love us? Are you sympathetic to our concerns?"

Yes.

Auguste Vacquerie asked, "So you don't want to speak to us here in the house?"

No.

Having more or less set up the ghostly rendez-vous for 3:00 a.m., the three participants hastened to change the subject. They summoned Molière to the table and launched into a vigorous discussion of the dead dramatist's comments in verse on his comedy, *The Learned Ladies* .

From this point on, the sequence of events is not clear. The seance seems to have ended early, with François-Victor leaving the house to spend the rest of the evening in town. No one seemed to be actively planning to go out on the street at 3:00 a.m.

But something strange did happen in the middle of the night—as a matter of fact, at 3:00 a.m. Here is the story, told in Victor Hugo's words, and preserved in the transcripts:

*I went up to bed at 11:30 p.m. I was worried and a little sad; besides, I was preoccupied, and a bit on edge on account of something I was working on at the time (**Satan: The Suns Go Out**).*

I slept badly. Toward 1:00 a.m., I heard François-Victor come in. Charles went down to open the front door for him. Victor, Charles and my wife chatted in the kitchen for a moment [where we had continued to make the table talk (Molière)]. Immediately afterward, they went to their rooms, and I heard my two sons, who sleep in the two rooms adjoining mine, come upstairs.

Everything was silent. The house fell asleep. I half-dozed off. In the midst of my drowsiness, I had a very sharp perception of surrounding objects, which meant I wasn't entirely asleep.

I had been in this state for a fairly long time when the ringing of a bell abruptly aroused me into full awakeness. In the profound calm of the night, the doorbell was ringing in the clearest and most distinct way. I raised myself up on my pillow. I listened. The world had fallen silent again, and nothing was moving in the house. I thought: "Nobody in the house is outside. It wasn't somebody from the house who rang. Might it, by any chance, be 3:00 a.m.?

I wrestled with this idea for a moment. Because of the cold, I was averse to getting up. However, I said to myself: It's odd that the bell should be ringing, and it would be strange indeed if it were now 3 o'clock. I threw myself out of bed—and I ought to say, seeing as I'm telling everything, that I moved cautiously, as if someone else were present.

The shutters of my window weren't closed, the night wasn't particularly dark, and it wasn't at all dark in my room. I took the box of matches that was on my table and struck several matches in a row against the wall; the fourth lit, and I lit my candle from it. I looked at my watch hanging from the chair back near the head of the bed. The hands said 3:05 a.m. It had been about five minutes since the ringing of the bell had awakened me.

I put out my candle. I peered outside to see if I could see anything. The sea was calm, the night pale, the terrace deserted. I went back to bed. As I was getting into bed, I saw on the wall between the two windows the phosphorescence of the matches tracing a luminous trail; I [word/s missing here], 'What if that were about to take the form of a ghost!' The trails vanished.

The next morning I told the story at breakfast. No one except me had heard the doorbell ringing. They had all been deeply asleep at the time. We resolved to ask the table this evening about this. I said that if the table invited us there [out in the street in the middle of the night] again, I would go. Auguste said, 'I'd be very scared, but I'd go, too, on the sole condition that people kept me company in the house right up until it was time [to go].' You had to go alone.

Glued to the piece of paper upon which these notes were written was an envelope containing four matches. Victor Hugo had written on the envelope:

In this envelope the four matches that I used on the night of March 23-24, 1854.

On the second night—March 24, 1854—a seance was held, beginning at 9:00 p.m. Those present were Mme. Hugo, Mlle. Adèle Hugo, Victor Hugo and Auguste Vacquerie. Seated at the table were Charles Hugo and Théophile Guérin.

The spirit in attendance turned out to be one Anacreon, a

Greek lyric poet of great distinction who lived from 570 to 478 B.C. Victor Hugo put the question to him:

"A mysterious event took place here yesterday on the subject of which we'd like some clarity. This relates to an apparition that is known in the countryside under the name of the White Lady. Will you let us talk about this event?"

No.

"Would you be able to enlighten us about it?"

No.

"After we've listened to you, would we be able to persuade you to run an errand for us with regard to the being about whom I've just spoken?"

But the table would tap no more.

Victor Hugo was as visibly shaken by his failure to wrest any information from the spirits about the White Lady as he was by the inexplicable phenomenon of her apparent coming. Soon after the inconclusive meeting with Anacreon, however—we do not know the exact date, nor do we have the transcripts of the seance—the White Lady appeared at the turning table, drew a quick portrait of herself using a smaller table one leg of which ended in a pencil, and then, after dropping a hint or two about her crime and her punishment, took her leave of the seance.

This time, she had set no rendez-vous for 3:00 in the morning.

But, one more time—though his fears were beginning to lessen—it seemed to Victor Hugo that he passed close to the presence of the White Lady, while walking along the shore late one night; and that she implored him to write a few lines of poetry to her memory. Whether this was a waking revery or not, we find the White Lady making her way with surprising composure through the turning table at Marine-Terrace on Monday, June 19, 1854. The hunchbacked French teacher Kesler was there. He—

in whom the spirits had been trying to inculcate faith in their existence for many weeks now—was fascinated by the presence of this seemingly benign female ghost. The atmosphere at this seance swiftly became one, not of ghost-inspired terror, but of philosophical inquiry, as the participants sought to interrogate the White Lady, and she sought to answer their well-meaning questions.

The White Lady seemed to bring out the gallant in the usually very shy Kesler. " The White Lady!" he had exclaimed when she first arrived. "I would very much like to see her. If she'll give me a rendez-vous, I'll go!" The Lady did not reply.

Victor Hugo had written some verses—he thought she had requested them—for the White Lady. He'd thought better of reading them, however; perhaps, he told her, he should have read them aloud before the seance had really begun. To which the White Lady answered:

I will return.

"When?" asked Hugo.

I don't know when I'll be able to come. There are times when my stone closes in upon itself. [Ed.: *The White Lady is apparently referring to the dolmen of which she is supposed to be the familiar spirit.*]

Victor Hugo asked: "Since you're free this evening, would you be able to keep a rendez-vous with our friend Kesler who wants to see you?"

Does he want to have white hair?

" I have some! Yes, I'd like some more!" exclaimed Kesler.

I will be on the beach tonight at two o'clock.

"On the Azette beach?"

Yes.

"Two o'clock is rather late," Kesler backtracked. "I would be most grateful to you if you would condescend to come earlier."

I can't come at midnight. Would he prefer tomorrow at one

o'clock, under the tree in front of his window?

"I accept most willingly, and I thank you," pronounced Kesler.

It was time for everyone to become more serious: "Will you tell us what the Rock of the Fairies is, the one where the local people claim to see apparitions?" asked Hugo.

It is my rock.

"Can we see you every night at Rocquebert?"

Yes.

"Do you live in your rock alone?"

No.

"Can you tell us who lives in it with you?"

My remorse. He is a black dwarf who beats me every time I come in.

Mme. Hugo asked: "What can we do to lessen your suffering?"

Pray.

"Can you tell us what crime you have committed?" asked Victor Hugo.

I was the first mother on this island to kill her baby.

"Has your punishment been going on for long? How long does it have to go on?"

Until the sea has invaded my rock.

"You haven't told us how long you've been subjected to such a harsh punishment."

Three thousand years.

"Three thousand years of suffering for the crime of a moment! Justice meted out by humans is less harsh!" exclaimed Auguste Vacquerie.

That is not true. The harshness of a sentence lies not in how long it lasts, but in whether it is for life. Human law that metes out forced labor for life is a thousand times more harsh than divine law that metes out three thousand years of expiation fol-

lowed by an eternity of forgiveness.

Hugo replied, rather incongruously, "You've said you had affectionate feelings for me. You've said: *basia mille.* [Italian for 'a thousand kisses'] Why do you love me?"

Because you love your children and your children love you.

Kesler joined in: "For myself, I love you because I am following my instincts and allowing you to lure me toward you who are so unhappy. You are indeed suffering. Tell me, will I have white hair before tomorrow night is over?"

If you have gotten through the entire day without committing any errors, then you will be quite fearless.

Auguste Vacquerie was still hankering after more serious stuff: "You are correct in saying that the harshness of a sentence lies not in its duration, but in whether it is for life," he declared. "But surely this is only on condition that the person being punished knows that his sentence will come to an end. Do the imprisoned souls of beings such as animals, plants, and pebbles know that their suffering will come to an end? Do they know when?"

They know that they are not condemned for life. [Ed.: *The White Lady seems to be implying: for the entire lifetime of the soul— that the soul knows that at some point on the Great Chain of Being it will be delivered from imprisonment.*] **But they do not know when their sentence will finish. The thought of certain deliverance is equivalent to the thought of deliverance in the near future. The certainty is the reality.**

Vacquerie pursued this. "We other men, who are also punished beings, we entertain the hope, but we do not have the certainty, that our sentence will end. The only thing we're sure of is life; if, in dying, we are annihilated, we will then have been condemned for life. There is no certainty of resurrection; life is a life sentence."

You know very well that you are not condemned for life.

Vacquerie declared: "I know it myself, because I personally believe in a future life. But for those who believe only in this world, it's a condemnation for life, since for them there's nothing after life."

Even they are certain of being liberated.

"By nothingness. Those whom men condemn for life are also certain to be delivered by death. There's no difference."

Yes, there is. Man metes out a life sentence, which means that human punishment would go on eternally if death did not intervene. The law decrees punishment and does not decree the end of punishment. Whereas even for those of whom you speak, the sense of being under sentence is not there without the certainty of deliverance.

Kesler had not stopped thinking about his upcoming rendezvous with the White Lady: "Tell me, dear soul," he interrupted. "You know what I'm thinking of at the moment. Do you want me to do it?"

Yes.

"But it's quite difficult. How will I do it?"

If you can't do it, don't. The White Lady seemed to be becoming impatient.

"I wanted to tell you that if it were to mean a softening of your fate, I would certainly go and see you on your rock. Would you like me to come to your rock?"

The owner of the field where my rock is would fill you full of buckshot if you did.

"Will the time come when you will find your child in the other world?" Mme. Hugo asked.

I'm certainly counting on it.

The seance ended. When the White Lady returned, almost nine months later, on Thursday, March 1, 1855, at 10:00 p.m., she was significantly more eloquent and philosophical (Kesler had failed to keep the rendez-vous, to nobody's surprise, and probably not his own). Those in attendance included the Allixes, young Adèle, and Victor Hugo. "Holding" the table were Mme. Victor Hugo and Charles Hugo.

After a few initial exchanges, the White Lady suddenly launched into a poetical description of her fate:

The mountain is my tomb; I am its soul; I am a being God speaks of under his breath; I ascend and I descend; I desire heaven and the earth desires me; stars pull me by the hair and coffin nails hold me by the feet. The darkness cries out to me: On your knees! And the sun cries out to me: Stand up! I am a martyr to the dusk: I fear the setting sun; I fear the night; the shadow is my assassin; I am she who is inconsolable standing in the obscure darkness; I weep and the stars put out my tears; I weep behind the mask of the day; I weep in the depths of God's chasm; I weep inside that immense sinister keg that the Danaides of infinity pierced full of holes. [Ed.: *The Danaides were the daughters of Danaus, who at their father's command murdered their bridegrooms on their wedding night, and were condemned in Hades to pour water eternally into a bottomless vessel.*]

Victor Hugo asked: "Are you the same person who came to me on the beach in front of my house one night and asked me for lines of verse?"

I am always she: I am she who is inconsolable and who stands on the horizon. I am the night watcher of the numberless tomb emptying its eyes into empty skulls, I am she who brings bad dreams; I am one of the bristling hairs of horror; I am the most terrible one of all, because I am the white hair and the right hair.

"Those days, when I saw you on the mountain, was it merely by chance that you appeared, or was it for me?"

For your lovely eyes—that is, for your eyes filled with good-

ness.

"It seems to me that since the winter you no longer come to the beach, and that instead you come down to the plain. Do you have a motive for this?"

I am everywhere, but I am seen only at certain hours in the north and only at certain hours in the south; I get up, and I go to sleep; souls have their laws like stars; they function like planets; there are fixed souls; there are wandering souls; there are the souls of nebulae; there are Pleiades of souls; there is the satellite soul and the sun soul; there is the asteroid soul and the world soul. The heavens have two aspects: suns and souls, night and death, radiance and resurrection. The sepulcher is a sunrise that God hides away; the day is a sunrise that God puts on display. One-half the night is given wings by eternity; the other half is given wings by immensity.

"If I were on the plain or on the beach right now, would I be able to see you?"

Don't put such questions to me.

Mme. Hugo asked: "Where have you learned to use such fine phrases? And why? Seeing as all you inspire is fright?"

The worst pain of all is the pain that elicits horror from the onlooker. To weep and to frighten: there's a punishment, because, ordinarily, sorrow attracts love and tears bring smiles. Alas! My tears are storms, and I am a hurricane driven to desperation because I am unable to caress anyone.

"You asked me to pray for you," said Victor Hugo. "Do you know that I do that every night? Do you receive these prayers directly, and do they lighten your burden?"

I am not the only one who suffers. Pray for all. If you wish to lighten my burden, forget all about me. To pray for one person alone is to cause them distress. The only good prayers are those which you sow to the winds at every tomb you pass.

"In fact, it's my rule to pray for everyone, and that's what I do. You ought to know that. But is there any disadvantage to my mixing your name and several others together in a universal prayer?"

There is a disadvantage for my name only. I am unknown to you. I am not one of your dead. I am a symbol rather than a being; I am the ghost of an entire crowd; I am the ghost of a crime rather than a criminal. I do not partake of an entity; my name is Infanticide; I am the mother of every murdered infant; I am the numberless and the invisible; I am the formidable funeral shroud fashioned in the grave from every bloodied swaddling cloth of every cradle.

"What are we to make of the apparition which at the moment has the attention of the entire island and makes some people quake in their shoes and others chuckle with merriment?"

In explanation of this, Victor Hugo had inserted the following note in the transcript: *For two weeks, the inhabitants of Bagot, George Town and Ruelle Pavee have been up all night trying to see or catch a mysterious being, dressed in a black funeral shroud, who appeared on the snow to several good women of the area.*

Nothing.

Victor Hugo continued: "What are we to make of the footprints found in Devonshire two weeks ago that the entire English press is talking about at this moment? *The Illustrated London News* published the pattern. These are foot marks in the shape of horseshoes, spaced eight inches apart, in a straight line stretching for a hundred miles and cutting across an arm of the sea, imprinted on the walls and roofs of houses as well as on the ground, and not matching the stride of any being known to man. This is indisputably a reality, and an obvious mystery. Do you know what the being is that made these footprints?"

The being you're talking about is a bird that skips on one foot with the help of its wings; a colossal polar bird that, on

account of its habit of standing on the tips of mountaintops, has lost the use of one of its feet. It's the fastest bird there is.

It must have been hard to know what to reply to this. Victor Hugo didn't seem to have; he changed the subject: "I've seen you on the mountain or on the dolmen of the White Lady; but you told us you lived at le Roquebert. Which one of those two places do you really live at?"

I have several dwelling places; I am part of a popular legend; thus have I left traces of myself in the human imagination. As for the rest: one final word. One night you wanted to go right up to a light that was shining on the sandbar, believing it was the White Lady, and you found a fisherman's lantern. Well! If you wanted to go right up to the light that was shining on the hill, you would have found a smuggler's signal. Here's the explanation, in one line: There are two souls in the two candles that cast their light upon you.

The table stopped dead.

Hugo asked anxiously: "Are you still there?"

The table shook: **No.**

"Who's there?"

Pure yes m pure.

"You who are there, do you have anything to tell us?" asked Victor Hugo. "Can you explain yourself further?" There was no reply. "Do you want us to put some questions to you?" The table did some considerable shaking, but did not reply. Since Charles was exhausted, they ended the session for the night. It was 1:00 a.m.

That night, Victor Hugo left the following note in the transcripts:

I believe it's necessary to explain the more mysterious questions asked by myself and which elicited the replies I've just recorded.

Since the beginning of the winter, I had no longer been seeing the light on the beach at night. About three months ago, across the way from Marine Terrace (it was midnight; I was just coming home), I noticed a vibrant, flickering gleaming on the hill which at first I took for the flames of the brick works. My interest was aroused. I began to observe the horizon every night at those same times when I'd come home. Whenever I settled down to observe, there was never anything to see. So I stopped thinking about it. As soon as I stopped thinking about it, the glow reappeared.

It looked like a vibrant, reddish candle flame. It was trembling visibly. It now appeared in the plain to the northeast of my house— which is quite solitary and an area where nobody lives—and on a few nights remained there, not moving for a quarter-of-an-hour and even half-an-hour.

These apparitions took place especially at the times when I got back to my house, not only toward midnight, but even between seven and eight o'clock in the evening. It's at that latter time that, arriving home for dinner one evening in the first days of February, I saw— when I'd automatically taken a look at the horizon on the summit of the hill where the dolmen of the White Lady is—a long straight flame which flared up abruptly, then subsided, then flared up again, then subsided again. It went through that strange, almost bounding motion for a third time. Then it disappeared.

In Spain I saw once on the Jaizquibel hills some smugglers' signals produced by handfuls of straw thrown in a brazier. They had the same effect from a distance. So at first I wondered if what I was seeing here was a smuggler's signal. At first, I was satisfied with this explanation. Since then, I've seen that flame again several times, at the same hour; and it has seemed to me that neither the flame near the brick oven nor the flame on the plain can be signals. I reached this conclusion by comparing these various sightings with observations I'd made the summer before on the beach; with the glow in the drawing room observed by my sons one night; with the doorbell ringing in the night; with [lacuna] drawings traced by the pencil moving of its own accord; and finally with explanations provided by the tables on various occasions, notably on the night of August 28 last. All this being said, I decided to take the preliminary precaution of not telling anyone about my intention of questioning the table on this subject.

You see that the White Lady responded.

Victor Hugo's encounter with the White Lady had come full circle. In this final seance, it had moved from the sublime—I **weep in the immense sinister keg that the Danaides of infinity pierced full of holes**—to the ridiculous—**a colossal polar bird that on account of its habit of standing on the tips of mountaintops has lost the use of one of its feet.**

Perhaps the most enlightening moment came when the White Lady said: **I am a symbol rather than a being...I do not partake of an entity; my name is Infanticide.** We begin to suspect that perhaps parts or fragments of human consciousness—the collective unconscious of mankind?—are being channeled to the friends at Marine-Terrace, energies arising from deep within the soul of man and crystallizing around certain emotionally-charged topics (this may have been what was happening when Hannibal—the warrior-consciousness of humankind?—came through the tables in the first winter of the seances).

This explanation will not assume much importance for us till we come to the roarings of ocean and comet, and begin to listen in on the large-scale global and extra-global energies which seem to be moving through the turning tables.

First, though, there is additional instruction to be had from the spirits themselves. First among their topics is God.

Chapter Ten

DOES GOD EXIST?

Time and again during the seances, Victor Hugo and Company asked the spirits why, if they were who they said they were, and therefore had all the resources of the universe at their disposal, they couldn't come up with a way of proving to the seance mavens that they existed?

It was the perennial question of humankind: Why, Oh God, if You exist, do you not reveal Your face to us? Why do You not at least explain to us why so often You seem to be absent from your Creation?

To these questions the spirits, through the months and years, had two sorts of answers in particular.

The first sort was communicated to Victor Hugo by no less than Martin Luther, at the seance of February 3, 1854, beginning at 9:00 p.m. Present were Victor Hugo and Auguste Vacquerie, with Mme. Hugo and Charles Hugo "holding" the table.

Martin Luther (1483-1546) is often called the father of Protestantism; one of its major branches, Lutheranism, is named for him. He was the German theologian who helped break the power of the Roman Catholic Church in the early part of the European Renaissance, insisting that Christ, and not the Church, was the sole mediator between God and man.

Hugo did not question Martin Luther directly about God.

What he wanted to know was whether Hugo's having access to the spirit world through the tables meant that he belonged to the noble lineage of movers and shakers of humankind who also, apparently, had had individual access to the divine. Victor Hugo framed his question in this way:

"It's a joy for us to talk to you. You are one of the great formulators of the laws of self-examination. You must be one of the spirits most disposed to opening the doors of mystery for us.

"A host of persons who have greatly influenced the destiny of the human race through their thinking are presented to us as having had mysterious beings at their ear, speaking words from unknown worlds. Socrates had a 'familiar spirit,' Joan of Arc an angel, Mohammed a pigeon, and the four Evangelists are supposed to have written the Gospels under the inspiration of four supernatural beings, a lion, an eagle, a bull and an angel. You yourself often speak in your writings of devils who get mixed up in your work. You've even intimated that you often disputed with them, since these demons seem to have been beings who importuned you rather than visiting friends. Can you tell us if the various manifestations of the mysterious that I've just enumerated have any relation to the phenomenon that's taking place right now?"

To which Martin Luther replied:

The Word of God chooses certain spirits. The sound of His voice is thunder, ocean, wind. Man is the terrified passenger in His world; life is an Ark that has lost its way. And so, to quiet man, God softens his voice. He silences the thunder-clap, the sea and the storm.

And while mariner-humanity inside the Ark is driven to despair, God extends hope to him by using animals: The dove saves Noah, the donkey saves Balaam, the lion saves Androcles, the pigeon inspires Mohammed, and the four Evangelists listen to their four beasts. The language of the divine takes on yet another form. Man is placed between beast and angel. He has one ear to the ground and one ear to the sky. When the beast becomes silent, the angel speaks, but it is always the angel. The beast is the angel in disguise, the apparition is the angel revealed. I heard the angel. Socrates spoke to him, Joan of Arc obeyed him, and Jesus rejoined him.

Now, how is it that I, hearing the divine word, could have been allowed to doubt it? How is it that Socrates, faced with drinking the hemlock, could have been allowed to doubt it? How is it that Joan of Arc, about to be burned at the stake, could have been allowed to doubt it? How could Jesus have been allowed to doubt on Calvary?

Because doubt is the instrument which forges the human spirit. If the day were to come when the human spirit no longer doubted, the human soul would fly off and leave the plough behind, for it would have acquired wings. The earth would lie fallow. Now, God is the sower and man the harvester. The celestial seed demands that the human ploughshare remain in the furrow of life.

Man, do not complain about the fact that you doubt. Doubt is the specter that holds the flaming sword of genius above the gateway of the beautiful. Shakespeare doubted, and he created Hamlet; Cervantes doubted, and he created Don Quixote; Molière doubted, and he created Don Juan. Dante doubts, and he creates Hell. Aeschylus doubts, and he creates Prometheus. Every creator doubts, and the result is that they create gods. As for me: From my doubt, I created a religion.

But Hugo was still anxious to know if his table-turning experiences were "the latest link in the vast chain of revelation that had begun in the Middle East and had ended with this very spirit,

Martin Luther."

The table's reply was bewildering.

What table are you talking about?

A startled Victor Hugo answered: "About the one that's here, that Charles is holding."

I don't see any table.

"Then you have something to learn from us, we creatures of earth and shadow. Know this: that we communicate with you by means of a three-legged table. Tell us how you for your part talk to us? Should I assume that you are not aware of how our replies come to you? Do you perceive us in some manner? Tell us what we are for you."

Spirits.

"But in what shape do we appear to you?"

The spirits of the dead see the spirits of the living through their foreheads; the spirits of the dead breathe the perfume of roses across space and hear the songs of birds through the sky. The human spirit is the great perfume and the great song of the earth. You come to us scented and melodious. [Ed.: *This passage may contain a pun in that we are 'scented and melodious' at our own funerals.*] **Perfume and song are formless; our conversation is an exchange of harmonies; the idea is the keyboard, and the musician is God.**

"From what you say, it would seem that from your point of view the human spirit is quite impersonal. Do you know who the humans are who are here? Do you know their human names? And do you come to us instead of coming to others? Have you a determining cause for coming here?"

The table shook; Martin Luther seemed anxious to leave. After another exchange or two, the spirit (now identifying himself as Shakespeare) told to Hugo—a little reluctantly, it seemed—that the spirits came to the exiles at Marine-Terrace because:

You are chosen.

"Is that all?" asked Hugo.

Yes.

And then—after just a few more words—the spirits departed and the table was still.

The second sort of explanation for why God does not reveal Himself and His mysteries to us has to do with the inadequacy of the contents of the costume boxes filled with images and concepts in our heads. Whatever He may want to say, even He is limited by the unGodlike, completely time- and space-engendered ideas and metaphors which bind down the consciousness and the awareness of humankind.

The "inability" of God—and of the spirits—to do more than broaden our understanding just a little, since they are limited to expressing themselves through us and with us and by us, is apparently the substance of what 'Idea' tells Auguste Vacquerie in the following passage (it is a subject upon which 'Galileo' and the Shadow of the Sepulcher will elaborate at tremendous and brilliant length in Chapter Twenty-One.)

The seance at which Idea held forth took place Monday, July 3, 1854, beginning at 1:00 p.m. Auguste Vacquerie was present, as were Mme. Hugo and Charles Hugo, who sat at the table.

Vacquerie had begun by taking up with Idea the problem of human suffering. If, the ever-earnest young Vacquerie wondered, we suffer on this earth because we must expiate a sin we committed in a previous existence, why did God, who created us, set things up in this way in the first place? Why did He, who could do anything He wanted, introduce suffering at all?

Vacquerie ended his question by swearing to the talking table that it would be doing a very great service to mankind if it condescended to answer this question.

The powerful entity who went by the name of Idea answered in this way:

You've just knocked at the back gate of the dark castle. You want to escape, and you tell me, 'Open up!' Which shows that you don't know who we are. Prisoners, we are your jailers. All our explanations are dungeon keys. We are the invisible turnkeys of the stars. When we unlock a sun, we unlock shadow. When we unlock infinity, we unlock one cell. When we unlock God, we release one person from solitary confinement. We are baleful lights enlightening with darkness. We assert without being able to prove, and we cast doubt even as we pour forth truth. We, like yourselves, are condemned. Under the sky of earth, Love is a galley slave, idealism is a galley slave, repentance is a galley slave, hope is a galley slave. Truth is a shadowy lantern hanging in the vault of the human skull. The savage dungeon rears up out of the fearful firmament. The wind blows all around you with an eternal groaning. Even death cannot remove your prisonhood. [Ed.: *In death—or on the reincarnational road—do we tend to retain the same thoughts and concepts that we had on earth?*] To die in that Bastille is to be imprisoned still. The gravedigger doesn't hollow out a breach there, but only battlements. Nothingness is the ghost of this castle. Doubt haunts it. Mystery rises up from all four corners of the room. The black sentinel of ignorance is always there, always ready to balk the spirit, to enclose it in infinity, to consign it to immensity, to throw it into the back of God's lowest ditch, and to garrot it with light beams.

Vacquerie responded: "Enlighten us. What do you mean when you say your explanations are dungeon keys and that you are the jailers? Are you not, rather, the liberators? Because the light you bring us, although mixed with shadow, nevertheless represents more light for us, and light and liberty are exactly the same thing."

We want to liberate you; we cannot. At the end of all our explanations, even the most profound, there is a wall. Infinity, for us, as for you, is an impasse. All we can do is give you a change of cell, give you a little more light and air. We can enlarge the skylight, but we can't tear down the wall. A window presupposes a prisn. We are your windows. We are at one and the same time light beam and bar. We cast shadows because we pour in light. Don't forget that it is the sun alone which produces shadows; that is, reflections. Shadows of whom? Of God. Reflections of whom? Of God. Here is the difference between the punitary worlds and the worlds of reward: In the punitary worlds, God sees himself in black; in the rewarded worlds, God sees himself with crystal clarity. Only Paradises mirror invisibility. [Ed.: *In chapters to come in this book, the spirits will develop "worlds of reward" and "punitary worlds" as major concepts.*]

Vacquerie replied: "Now I understand you. We are in a dungeon in a prison. You don't open the prison, but you open the dungeon."

We've brought you some light, but that very light is even more shadow. We've brought you out of the catacombs, but we haven't brought you out of the prison. You were in the cellar of the Bastille; we've put you on the roof. Before, you couldn't even see the sky; now, you can see it. But all you've done is exchange ditch for battlement, solitary confinement for the abyss. It should be quite clear to you that we remain your jailers even while we're your liberators. We remove your handcuffs, but we don't give you a nail file. We make you less unhappy, but we don't make you more free. We make you mount up to the sky, but it's by way of the prison staircase. The sky opens before you, but it's been opened by a prison-house key.

Vacquerie summed up grimly: "The upshot of all this is that it isn't possible for you to give us a decisive and irrefutable explanation for this terrible problem: 'Why an infinity of goodness and power creating so many hells?'"

I don't know what Archangel Love will say to you.

"But, you—you can't give us an explanation?"

No.

Auguste Vacquerie, despairing of finding enlightenment regarding the perennial questions of mankind, went on to quiz Idea about the secret world of animals. That amazing topic—upon which the spirits were to elaborate ideas which were more than 100 years ahead of their time—we will address in the next chapter.

Chapter Eleven

THE SECRET WORLD OF ANIMALS

As seance followed seance, the spirits had more and more to say about the unknown world of animals (from here on in, we will use the word 'animal' interchangeably with 'beast,' this latter term including birds, fish, and so on). It was true, of course, that animals were the reincarnation of criminals who had taken life on our earth to expiate a crime committed in a previous existence (the same was true for plants and stones). It was also true that animals, since they didn't understand that they were being punished, suffered more than humans.

But, as the spirits began to explain, animals had compensations. They could glimpse eternity—catch sight of ghosts, angels, and even God. Balaam's Ass had been able to see the Angel of the Lord with the flaming sword; that had given him his power to influence Balaam. The Dove of the Ark had been guided by God to the landing place for Noah's gigantic boat.

Moreover, animals (and plants and stones) knew what crime they had committed; such knowledge was not granted to man. (Did that mean that, since animals were also aware that they were suffering, they could put two and two together and conclude that they were being punished? No, since this would have required the beasts to have the faculty of reason, which they did not have.)

What all this meant was that animals were not just animals.

They had powers, and these enabled them to thrust forward, even become the Jesus Christs of their hierarchies and sub-hierarchies of the beasts, even reach far beyond their places on the Great Chain of Being—which was essential, the spirits would make increasingly clear, if all of soul-filled creation on earth were to do the things that it now had to do.

It would take the spirits a while to explain all this. The first thing to explain was this ability of beasts to glimpse their Creator.

This compensatory faculty of animals to be able to glimpse vaster dimensions of reality, Victor Hugo himself had glimpsed, as he revealed to the entity calling itself 'Drama,' during an afternoon seance on April 24, 1854:

"You've reminded me of something I wanted to ask you about. I've often wondered if animals saw things that we don't see, and if this weren't one of their compensations for being animals. That idea came back to me tonight when I heard the dogs barking on the empty terrace at a time when nobody was passing. I wondered if it were so that man thinks, but he doesn't see; and animals don't think, but they see; if that were how the incompleteness of animal nature was somehow balanced in God's eyes. Dogs can see ghosts and souls going by, and they bark. While that's happening, we're in the dark; we wonder: Why are they barking? They see what is mysterious, but they can't understand it; perhaps we would be able to understand it, but we don't see it. I've written this quickly, but that should be enough to give you the gist of my thoughts. What is your thinking on this? Would you care to enlighten me?"

There are mysterious compensations for mysterious ills. Animals are prisons of the soul. But these cells are pierced with windows which open out onto infinity, even though they are low and narrow and heavily barred. Shadows are cast by the bars and light seeps down through the air-vent. The animal sees

man and glimpses the angels. The beast's glance spans a wide spectrum, its eyelashes encompassing the material at one end and the idea at the other. The eye of the dog you're whipping is watching the angels smiling. The barking of dogs is a stammering which the Great Deaf-Mute understands; the roaring of beasts is the wailing of the new-born infant the Silent Grandfather hears. The words men speak contain only half the prayer; the voice of the animals contains the other half. The earth is filled with ears; for every mouth there are two ears; the first is the one that forgives, the second is the one that punishes. Animals, flowers and stones have their existence in-between, on the one hand, man, who does not see his soul, and on the other, God, whose countenance they glimpse; and this in such a way that, when night falls, from every part of the animal world—dens, nests, woods, waves, the dark—an immense noise rises up: the prayers of muzzles, of beaks, of fins, from maximum security prisons, from minimum security prisons, from eyelids that weep through eternity but that are never wiped. God says: I hear you; and the lion learns patience; and the bird's sleep is less disturbed; and the dog yaps but now at the robes of angels. 'Forgiveness' is the only word in the human language which the beasts can spell. All the other words would fall into the sea, but there would be no notion of drowning; forgiveness is Noah's Ark.

But human beings have certain preconceptions about beasts. Some we regard as evil, others as good. Drama launched a final sally at Hugo, exhorting him, as a poet, to have not only compassion for the beasts which we think of as "good," but also for the beasts which we regard as "bad"—in fact, to have compassion for all of God's creatures and creation, including even those parts of it which we humans make into tools with which to perform evil actions.

Drama made these statements after Hugo, responding to the

spirit's revelations about the compensations of animals, mentioned: "I placed in a rose's mouth this line addressed to a caterpillar: *Come to my place. My buds are where souls hide.* Did I write this line blindly? Or did I, like the dog in the night, glimpse something?"

Yes, you glimpsed something; but the rosebush is not the only place where souls hide. Why do you poets always talk with love about roses and butterflies, and never with love about thistles, poisonous mushrooms, toads, slugs, caterpillars, flies, mites, worms, vermin and infusoria? Certainly, these are ill-favored creatures; but...and then there are the pebbles and the seashells! Why don't you talk about bed-bugs with love? about fleas?... Why don't you pity the sufferings of vile, horrible beings? Why don't you take pity on the tortures of the infinitely tiny creatures condemned to live in the excrement of the infinitely large?

Drama went on to enumerate the sufferings of inanimate objects—iron suffers, bronze suffers, the iron collar suffers—and even of inanimate objects created by humans for offensive and defensive purposes—the cannon suffers, the guillotine knife suffers; you pity Joan of Arc, pity the stake as well. Then the spirit returned abruptly to the theme of feeling love for all beasts. This was to make its final point that, in speaking as it had, Drama was not merely mouthing sentimental rhetoric about animals:

What I say is very precise, and I wish to emphasize that I am not talking about the vague feelings that poets have had about universal life....I'm talking about the actual, vital life of beasts, of flowers, of stones, just as I would talk about your lives. I want to stress the importance of this attitude, I approve of this attitude, and I command poets to write lines of this sort, just as I would command my valets to do something... I want you to rehabilitate the toad's unhappiness and the thistle's despair. I would be most happy if in this house you spoke of tigers with pity and tiny earthworms with respect. I would be delighted if from now on you spoke of the gentleness of all non-human creatures!

And, on this note, the session ended.

Two months later, the ability of dogs to glimpse the supernatural became frighteningly apparent to the seance goers.

It happened during the period when the group was trying to, and sometimes succeeding in, talking to the White Lady. This particular evening—June 23, 1854—they had been expecting her.

What they got instead was a violent, a sustained, even an angry, shaking of the table.

Victor Hugo, Vacquerie, Guérin, Kesler, and a maid named Julie, made up the attendance at the seance. Mme. Hugo and Charles were holding the table. As the piece of furniture vibrated and trembled violently, Charles called out:

"Calm yourself! Speak. Who are you?"

The table shook even more violently. Then the trembling piece of furniture tapped out:

The Grim Gatekeeper.

"Explain to us what the Grim Gatekeeper is," demanded Victor Hugo. "Are you Death?"

No.

"Tell us who the Grim Gatekeeper is."

The ghost who opens the shadow. The one who holds the keys to suffering.

They couldn't think of who this unhappy spirit could be. The table was shaking so violently that it was constantly falling over on its side. Only with great difficulty could they right it. It was tapping so quickly that they could hardly count the taps. "Do you have something to tell us?" asked Hugo. "Speak!"

I suffer.

"What can we do for you?" pleaded Mme. Hugo.

Pray.

"We will pray for you," offered Victor Hugo. "Do you have anyhing to add to that?"

The table shook convulsively. Mme. Hugo asked Archangel Love to intercede.

The table tapped out swiftly: **They're barking.**

Victor Hugo's notes record that at that very moment they suddenly heard the dogs barking loudly all around the outside of the house. "Is this house surrounded by ghosts and spirits?" asked Guérin.

Yes.

Asked Victor Hugo: "Are the other houses haunted in the same way by invisible beings?"

No.

"Call repentance to yourself," begged Mme. Hugo. "Calm yourself."

The Grim Gatekeeper tapped out violently: **Shut up, dogs!**

To everybody's astonishment, the barking of the dogs outside subsided rapidly.

"Do you hear us, we who are here?" asked Mme. Hugo. "Don't listen to the dogs, and pray."

The barking of the dogs faded away completely.

"The dogs aren't barking anymore," declared Victor Hugo. "Are you able to talk to us now? Who are you? Were you once a soul enclosed in a human being like ourselves? Have you lived before? What crime did you commit to make you so unhappy? Speak!"

The table was once again moving violently, convulsively. It tapped out:

Oh! The horror!

"What does this mean?" asked Victor Hugo. "Explain this to us."

The Danube, the Thames, the Seine, the Neva, four sources of blood which run from the four wounds of Jesus Christ. [Ed. *This seems to be a reference to the European dictators' wars and crimes which were so oppressing the spirits of the exiles on Jersey island. It is linked up here with the sufferings of Jesus on the Cross, with which the exiles tended to identify.*]

Hugo replied: "We feel the same horror as you do about what's happening. Your thoughts are our thoughts. Do you know this?"

Yes.

"Are you suffering less?"

Yes.

"Why were you suffering so much a little while ago?"

The ghosts.

"Are they no longer there?"

No.

The group pursued this line of inquiry for a few minutes. But the Grim Gatekeeper was not at all forthcoming. The barking picked up again. The table moved convulsively.

"Do you hear the dogs?" asked Hugo. "Can you tell us why they're barking?"

They see the blackbirds.

"Do you mean, the ghosts?"

There was no response from the table.

A few brief, unenlightening exchanges followed. The dogs went on barking loudly. Abruptly, the table swiftly rapped out the words:

Shut your mouths, dogs.

The dogs immediately stopped barking.

Here are Victor Hugo's notes on this moment, preserved in the transcripts:

It wasn't only the house dogs that were barking. There were yappings from near and far. The dogs were howling all across the plain and all across the beach. And we could hear very clearly that they all stopped at the same time.

The table was silent.

The Grim Gatekeeper had vanished. The dogs would not be heard from again that evening. Instead, not the White Lady, but the Gray Lady, would come tapping through the table. She would reveal to them that she was the ghost of a Druidic priestess who had sacrificed her father on the altar of the Druids 3,000 years before.

Had the Grim Gatekeeper, with all his violence and his negativity—which had somehow provoked the barking of all the dogs in the area—cleared a path for the Gray Lady to come?

What grim gateway had the Grim Gatekeeper opened up?

They would never know. He was never to return to the table.

This was by no means the last time the seance-goers would hear the dogs barking in the night in some mysterious complicity with, or some reaction to, the spirits that seemingly milled around the turning table. And the spirits had still more to say about the strange, secret spiritual world of the beasts, particularly those, like Balaam's Ass, who had managed to reach out and touch the realm of man and thereby carve out for themselves some important and esoteric niche in their hierarchy of the beasts.

At the seance of July 7, 1854, Théophile Guérin had a long-considered and carefully-worded question to put to the spirit called Idea:

"On the subject of beasts, Balaam's Ass told us that man did not know what his mistake was and that the animal did not know what its crime was. Regent's Diamond recently informed us, to the contrary, that the beast knows why it is a beast. He insisted on this, even declaring that we should think of the crime of every beast, of every plant and of every stone as the counselor, guide and shepherd of that beast."

[Ed.: *The transcript of this seance has been lost. 'Regent's Diamond' seems to have been one of the few spirits who was a personification from the world of stones.*]

Idea's answer went as follows:

The world has made progress not only with regard to mankind, but also with regard to animals, plants and stones. In the beginning, Hell was everywhere. Mankind knew nothing of its real nature; the beast knew nothing, the plant knew nothing and the stone knew nothing. A deep shadow lay upon universal consciousness.

Saviours came. Moses taught mankind that he had a right to live. Socrates showed him that he had a right to think. Jesus revealed to him his right to love. These three men took with them to the grave, each one in his turn, some part of the shadows that lay upon the earth.

That part of the world capable of rational thought became aware of its punishment: Humanity knew that it was being punished. Then an immense light shone forth. The hand of God came out of the night; it held a lightning bolt. In the gleam imparted by that lightning bolt, humanity caught a glimpse a God who was smiling. The thunderbolt of the Bible is a twilight; the flames of the Gospels constitute a dawning.

[Ed.: *Idea seems to be suggesting that it was only after the advent of Christianity—presumably, with Paul's notion of the Fall of Man which can only be redeemed through the love of Jesus—that humanity came to understand that divine love lay behind its state of being punished.*]

The beasts, the plants and the stones: They, too, have had their Jesus Christs. Balaam's Ass was one of those. The same half-light shone on animals as shone on man, in the wake of these Passions of predestined beasts. The Lion of Androcles

118

took suffering upon himself for the tiger. The Dove of the Ark fluttered through the sky for the serpent. Saint Antoine's pig shielded the goat with its love. Balaam's Ass took thought for the thistle. The Lion of Florence—he who is the greatest of all—saved the stones of his city. So then, what came to pass? God said: 'Man knows his punishment; beast, plant and pebble will know their crime. I let man know half the mystery; I'm letting beast, plant and pebble know the other half.'

In speaking thus, God had taken a revolution into the hearts of beasts that cannot speak. The den had had its Calvary; the angel had had its Golgotha. The stable had had its cross. The bird's nest had brushed against heaven. It is only that, mystery being the garment God wears, He does not reveal to dead animals that when alive they have saved beasts, nor does He let plants and stones know that they have been their own saviours. Beasts, plants and stones still on earth will tell you that they know their crime. Balaam's Ass, the Lion of Androcles, the Dove of the Ark will tell you that they do not know theirs. Why has God decreed thusly? Perhaps because He does not want the benefactor to know what benefit he has conferred. Perhaps because He wishes to hold back some portion of happiness from the already blissful. Perhaps because he wishes to spare the newly-deceased beasts the shock of knowing what crime they have just expiated, and that, when he bestows Paradise, he always gives away only a little so that eternity may remain full.

Guérin did not fully accept this explanation. He protested: "In the midst of the splendid things you've just told us, there is one point that seems obscure to me. You say that man and beast each know half the secret: that man knows his punishment, and the beast knows its crime. I have trouble understanding that distinction. The beast has awareness of its crime; it is also aware of its suffering (since, if it were not, it wouldn't be suffering). To know that you have acted badly, and to know that you are suffering: Is that not the same thing as knowing that you are being punished?"

For it to know its crime is not for it to know its punishment. By punishment, I mean hope of deliverance. By punishment, I mean certainty of forgiveness. By punishment, I mean ascension. Man knows that he is suffering, but he also knows that he is mounting ever upward. The beast knows that it is suffering, but it does not know that it is freeing itself from suffering. It has instinct and suffering, and the knowledge of its crime. But, between that instinct and that suffering, it lacks the faculty of reason. The animal suffers and knows; man suffers and thinks. The working of the mind that reestablishes the connection between suffering and punishment, that is to say, the connection to forgiveness: Man has that, and the animal does not. Man reasons; the beast does not. Man is logical; the beast is not. Man makes calculations; the beast does not. Man draws conclusions; the beast does not. Never does a dog total up the blows it has received. A cat doesn't know how old it is. A monkey may be able to put a clock out of kilter, but it can never set the time. The beast represents the absence of mind; what is quite simple for you—drawing the conclusion from suffering that there is punishment—it finds impossible. If the beast reasoned, it would speak. Language is nothing but the beating of thought's wings.

But Guérin was still not satisfied:
"You say that by punishment you mean hope of deliverance, and that the beasts don't know their punishment...The White Lady told us quite the opposite. She told us, in her own terminology, that beasts, plants and stones knew that they were not condemned

for life, and that they held in their heads 'the thought of certain deliverance.' In what sense are you telling us that beasts have neither the certainty nor even the hope of being liberated?"

The animal knows what crime it has committed. It knows it will be forgiven for that crime. While awaiting that pardon, it knows that it is suffering. What it cannot do is reestablish the connection between that suffering and whatever else may be involved. Where reason begins, the animal leaves off. For it to attempt to draw the simplest conclusion is for it to stare into the abyss. There is no such thing as a naive animal.

And there the dialogue on animals ended, at least for a time.

But the gods that governed the turning tables—if there were any such—were not content with merely intellectual argument; all along, they had sought to provide concrete examples. In January, 1854, there had begun to appear at the turning table—slowly, with a word here, a gesture there, a line of poetry there—he who would come to be for this sub-echelon of humans the most beguiling of all the Jesus Christs of the hierarchy of beasts: The Lion of Androcles.

Chapter Twelve

THE LION OF ANDROCLES

Androcles was a Roman slave, the hero of a first-century story by Aulus Gellius. One day he saw a lion in pain and removed the thorn embedded in its paw. When Androcles was later sentenced to die in the arena, the lion recognized him and refused to harm him. The story was the subject of a play by George Bernard Shaw, **Androcles and the Lion.**

Thus *Grolier's Encyclopedia* on Androcles and the lion. This thumbnail sketch alone is enough to show us that, in the cosmology of the channeled spirits of Jersey island, the Lion of Androcles is cast in the same mould as Balaam's Ass. He is an imprisoned soul on the animal rung of the Great Chain of Being who has reached up to the next level and helped an imprisoned human soul. Is this what made him, as Idea tells it to Guérin, one of the Jesus Christs of the world of beasts?

Whatever the reasons, this lion who did not forget the person who did him a good deed is a member of the pantheon of beast-spirits of the turning tables of Jersey island. It seems as if, like Balaam's Ass, or the Dove of the Ark, or the Pigeon of Mohammed, he shuttles between the spirit world and humankind. The first glimmer of his mission to the seance-goers at Marine-Terrace peeped forth on January 6, 1854, when, at the tail-end of a long seance

filled with surprises, he shambled through to deliver the self-portrait of himself, the Lion of Androcles.

Manes are the hairpieces of sovereign brows. The lion is the
poet of the solitudes. The lion is up and about before the rising
sun. The lion forgives, the lion muses. The lion is the roaring
of the wind, the silence of the desert.

My mane is the whip of the air. My claw is might, my glance
is goodness. My muzzle tears the tiger out of the desert and
rends babies from their mothers.

The lion had dominion over the tiger. In the Roman Circus,
he bestowed the graces that Nero refused to bestow: He spared
Androcles, he saved Daniel, he grew as still as God Himself, and
he kissed the foot of Ideal Behavior. The lion is the power that
makes men great and the mercy that makes men good.

I am that lion.

I salute you.

And then he was gone.

It was to become obvious very quickly that this wasn't one of
your ordinary, garden-variety type of channeled emblematic animals. It wasn't just that he spoke beautifully, and (as we will see)
wrote beautiful poetry; so did practically everyone else who passed
through the tables at Marine-Terrace. It was also that he was
fierce, fearless, rude and unpredictable. Apart from his poetry, he
hardly spoke at all, and when he did it was mostly to hurl insults.
He didn't dialogue. He didn't show up for appointments.

But he was quite the warrior-poet! He engaged in poetry-duels
with Victor Hugo. They borrowed lines from each other; and, at
one point, they simultaneously created virtually the same poem.
Perhaps most important of all, the Lion of Androcles dictated one
of the most beautiful channeled poems ever to wend its way out of
that mysterious place where channeled poetry is created—-a poem
that seemed to testify to the truth that, in the Hugolian universe

of the turning tables, animals do not know that they are being punished, and do not have the power of reasoning, but can see God.

When the Lion of Androcles had finished reciting his self-portrait, he had saluted the group—had been saluted by them in turn—and had left abruptly, promising to return that following Tuesday, Jan. 10, at 9:00 p.m.

But it was the seance mavens themselves who missed the appointment. When, on February 17, the Lion suddenly re-appeared—interrupting a poetry-reading by Shakespeare!—he was somewhat less than majestic:

Good day, imbeciles.

"Who are you?" asked Vacquerie.

The Lion of Androcles.

Victor Hugo, Mme. Adèle and Charles were at the seance along with Vacquerie. The latter confronted the lion jovially: "Do you have a communication to impart to us, aside from this friendly greeting?"

Ask me questions in poetry, just as you did with Aeschylus and Molière.

The group had always prepared such verse questions—which Aeschylus had insisted these greats must have—carefully in advance; they didn't want to try to pass off dashed-off poetry on these illustrious dead. Mme. Hugo pointed this out to the Lion of Androcles: "If we'd known you were coming, we'd have prepared verses. Improvised ones can only be unworthy of you."

This kick in the ass makes donkeys of you all. Farewell.

And then the Lion was gone.

This disturbing interchange provoked a lively discussion among the seance-goers. What "kick in the ass" had the lion been referring to? Had he taken the excuse offered by Mme. Victor Hugo as a refusal, and been insulted? They begged the table to give them an explanation. It yielded up no tapping. They would have to wait till tomorrow and ask again; that was when the next seance was scheduled. And thus it was that, on Feb. 18, Vacquerie asked Aeschylus, now in attendence, why the Lion had acted as he had. Was it because the group had failed to show up for the rendez-vous of Jan.10? Aeschylus responded:

This lion is enormous, and full of catastrophes,
You were in the wrong, thinkers, to put him out of sorts.
It will be necessary for Hugo to toss him several stanzas,
So that he has, if he returns, some tasty bones to munch

Whether or not the Lion had taken offence, it was now Vacquerie who took offence— all the while insisting that he wasn't. It was Vacquerie in particular who had, he explained, been toiling to prepare the questions-in-poetry for Aeschylus. And now he was being told dismissively—there was not even a mention of him-self!—that it must be Hugo who composed the lines for the Lion of Androcles. This was hardly an expression of their gratitude to him for his efforts! Vacquerie protested mildly to the late, great Greek tragedian.

And so, I will unsay it. Write lines for that Lion.
You are the one I choose. Above all, make them fine.
Since before this lion consents to eat his lunch
There must be lots of marrow in those bones to munch.

But what if Hugo were more than willing to write the lines? Would Vacquerie still get to do them?
Yes.
It wasn't till March 23, with Molière in attendance, that the Lion of Androcles came pouncing back to the tables. Vacquerie,

his verse-questions ready, prepared to read them. He was left open-mouthed; just as quickly as he had come, the Lion pounced off. Disgusted, Vacquerie read his lines to Molière.

This rapid coming-and-going perhaps wasn't as arbitrary as it looked. The stage had been set for a dramatic confrontation between Victor Hugo and the Lion of Androcles. Claudius Grillet writes:

"From time to time, the tables and Hugo borrowed from each other. It was as if the tables read the poet's mind and responded to the preoccupations that besieged him at that moment, while he in turn exploited the themes they presented to him, and submitted himself to their literary influence.

"Of what I now wish to demonstrate, a lion shall be the witness. Guess who came through on March 24, 1854, in answer to the conjurers' calls? The Lion of Androcles! You should know that, a month earlier, on February 28, Victor Hugo had completed a long poem whose title was To the Lion of Androcles. Thus this animal, before haunting the drawing room, had sojourned for some time in the poet's study at Marine-Terrace."

It now emerged that Hugo, like Vacquerie, had responded to the Lion's initial request to Ask me questions in poetry, just as you did with Aeschylus and Molière. He had the very poem with him that night. And, since Vacquerie had used up his Lion poem on Molière the night before, the way was now clear for Victor Hugo to read his poem to the Lion without offending his sensitive friend.

He read the poem—it was 96 lines long—from beginning to end

"To the Lion of Androcles" would appear in *The Legend of the Centuries*, in September, 1859, in the section entitled *Decadence of Rome*. It's a brilliantly Hugolian tirade against the decadence of the modern city. On the face of it, it's a brilliant tirade against the decadence of ancient Rome. But Hugo is aiming at modern-day

Paris, that city of sin now ruled by the tyrannical Napoleon III. The soul-destroying nature of the modern metropolis was the theme that the great poet Charles Baudelaire had recently taken up, but splenetically, darkly, without hope of redemption. In Hugo, the theme would be counterbalanced by that of a world of nature which retained a certain primeval goodness, where the animals, however savage, were at least less savage than man--and able to glimpse God!.

In the last few lines of his poem, Hugo brings the Lion of Androcles into the hideous city whose shocking state of corruption Hugo has just described, for almost a hundred lines, in excruciating detail. This beast has come from the desert, where it lives in a state of serene, amoral purity as compared with the unparalleled licenciousness of the ancient Romans. The Lion beholds what is in the city; and then, with a sudden, thoughtful impulse of love and pity, it turns back toward the desert; for, writes Hugo: "Man being the monster, you, O lion, are the man."

Now the Lion of Androcles, deigning for the first time to linger awhile at the seance, recited his own poem. It began where Hugo's poem left off: with the Lion entering the desert. But the tormented, unholy city is not there. We are alone with the lion in the middle of his desert.

> The desert was somber, arid, impassable
> The sandy plains gave way to dunes.
>   At the time when day is born,
> Alone in these vast places where God
>   speaks and shows himself,
> Like a king toward a king, I go to encounter
>   The sun which comes toward me.
>
> We climb, both of us, in our superb haughtiness,

The slope, he gilding it and I trampling its grass.
    We recognize one another.
I am proud to have him for host of my lair,
He is proud to see mingling on my belly
    The hairs of my mane with his rays

Thus lived I, alone, dreaming beneath my mane,
Conducting the sun in the sky to my den,
    Majestically, mercifully,
Dreaded without anger and strong without violence,
And saying to the desert: judge if your silence
    Be worthy of my roaring.

I opened to the clear brightness my dazzled eyelid,
I listened from time to time to the prophet Isaiah
    Singing the praises of the God he served,
Because we are warriors in the selfsame army
    Therefore responded we one to the other: I
    the lion, he the angel,
From the two ends of the desert.

Gentle goodness was the breath of my mouth.
I could have brought about calm in the wild hurricane
    Tamer of surging floods.
I could have, in applying to it my marble will,
Under each one of my feet stronger than tree trunks
    Held captive one of the four winds.

The desert was vast, impassable and somber,
I reigned luminous like a lighthouse in shadow,
    There I lifted up my lofty brow,
In the endless desert that begins again and again

I was alone, I was alone on that beach as immense
As an immense page.

Did Victor Hugo write this poem himself, communicating it unconsciously to the psychics around the table? Certainly, he didn't think so. At the very end of the first edition of the poem, Hugo took great pains to dissociate the poem—and himself—from the turning tables; in a note, affixed "in the margin," he wrote as follows:

You will find in the volumes dictated by the table to my son Charles, a response of The Lion of Androcles to this poem. I note this fact here in the margin. I am simply affirming the existence of a strange phenomenon to which I was a witness several times: The phenomenon of the ancient pedestal table. A three-legged table dictates poetry by means of tappings and stanzas emerge from the obscurity. It goes without saying that never did I mix in with my lines a single line emanating from this mystery, nor with my ideas a single one of those ideas. I always religiously left them to the Unknown, which was their unique author; I do not even admit to there being a reflection of them in my work; I pushed them aside even to allowing them to influence me. The work of the human brain must remain apart from, and never borrow from, these phenomena. External manifestations of the invisible are a fact, and the internal creations of thought are another; the wall which separates these two facts must be maintained in the interests of observation and of science. We must make no breach in this wall; and to borrow something would be to make such a breach. On the side of science, which defends [making such a breach], you also feel a great and true, an obscure and certain religion which forbids it. It is then, I repeat, as much by religious conscience as by literary conscience, it is out of respect for the phenomenon itself, that I isolate myself from it, making it a rule to accept no mixtures in my inspira-

tion, and wishing to keep my work, such as it is, absolutely mine and personal.

Claudius Grillet, in *Victor Hugo, Spiritist*, cites a number of examples of how, intermittently over the next few months, the Lion of Androcles recited lines from time to time that were entirely similar to those written by Hugo ten days before, or two years before, or more.

To those disinclined to believe in the supernatural origins of messages tapped through tables, this won't come as any surprise. But even the most hardened skeptic has to wonder, with regard to a seance which took place on April 25, 1854, what strange operation of the human soul was manifesting itself here. Something happened which is likely very rare in the annals of channeling: The simultaneous creation of poetry—of a high order—by a discarnate-entity poet on the one hand, and a real-life—and great— poet on the other.

Let's look at the narrative of Claudius Grillet:

"We are no longer talking about mutual borrowings that presuppose that one work was written before the other. We are talking about simultaneous creation. [During the seances,]...the Lion is improvising. That sort of an effort can't be sustained without causing a certain fatigue. Bear in mind, too, that the dictation of his lengthy poem has not been accomplished at a single stretch [it has been spaced out over more than one seance], and betrays a certain hesitation at times.

"It so happens that, on the evening of April 25, the Lion, in the course of a superb improvisation...hesitated. The table stopped tapping. He was in the middle of railing against tame lions, who, not content with just agreeing to be slaves, also consented to being accomplices to human despicableness, and to becoming, in the Roman arena, the executioners of martyrs.

And, monsters fed on massacre and shame
Tame giants on whom oppobrium is heaped,
Heartless and mindless,
They raise against saints their sacrilegious paw
And their blood-stained claws that bury
    themselves....

"I am the one who has underlined the last two lines. Obviously, they did not satisfy the tapping spirit. He terminates his stanza, and goes off to redo them.

"During the interruption which lasted several minutes, Hugo, for his part, got down to work, and wrote the following three lines, showing them to no one else but Auguste Vacquerie.

They tore open the saints expiring in the mire
And their hideous claws enlarged the wound
    In the side of Jesus Christ.

"Almost immediately, the table began to move again, and completed the Lion of Androcles's stanza in the following way—almost in the same terms as Hugo:

Their paws tore open the martyrs in the mire,
And Jesus Christ took their claws within his wounds,
    O gibbet, for your nails.

"Bear in mind that Vacquerie, himself a poet, plays no role in this. It was Charles Hugo and Théophile Guérin who that evening placed their hands on the pedestal table.

"The moment he had heard the table's lines out, Hugo read his own aloud. There was general consternation around the table.

Mme. Hugo asked the Lion/table: 'Did you read my husband's lines before doing yours?'

"The reply was:

"No."

And that is almost the last that the seance-goers heard of the Lion of Androcles, at least explicitly. On the night of Sunday, August 6, 1854, he appeared only long enough to proclaim—in Latin, mysteriously and beautifully:

Omen, Lumen, Numen Nomen Meus. [**Portent, Light, Numinous Divinity, is My Name.**]

This numinous divinity was about to pave the way for even more numinous goings-on. These would include a visit from The Ocean, a visit from a Comet, and a voyage to the planet Mercury.

These visits would be, in some baffling manner, bound up with the ancient art of alchemy.

Chapter Thirteen

ROARINGS OF OCEAN AND COMET

We shouldn't be too surprised to find Victor Hugo participating in a seance at which The Ocean spoke. After all, the poet regarded himself as the reflection of nature itself.

However that may be, on April 22, 1854, at 4:00 p.m., no less an entity than "The Ocean"—first introducing itself as your neighbour—came tapping through the turning tables at Marine-Terrace.

Guérin and Victor Hugo were present, with Mme. Hugo and Charles holding the tables.

Hugo had been asking the spirits if they might be able to write music. For years he had dreamed of a federation of France and Germany; now—perhaps partly because he had been enchanted for many months by the sound of the ocean outside his window— he asked this entity if it could write a mega-*Marseillaise* for him, a national anthem of freedom for the future Federated Republic of France and Germany. Hugo himself, of course, would write the lyrics.

The Ocean agreed, and began to dictate a string of musical notes. Théophile Guérin, the sole person present with musical ability, took them down.

When the table had finished tapping, Hugo asked The Ocean what it would like to call its composition.

My Noise, it replied.

"What name would you like to give it?" asked Hugo.

The Thundering.

They would have to have a musician make music from these notes.

And, on that note, the session ended.

The next day, at 2:30 p.m., with Guérin, Charles and Mme. Hugo present, Guérin had bad news to report. The composition, he told The Ocean, made no sense when it was transcribed. Perhaps he had transcribed it wrongly. "Where should we make the changes?" he asked.

The Ocean seemed confused. It suggested falteringly that they **change the key to fah.** Then it tapped out a series of seemingly irrelevant syllables, beginning, **To a daff—**

Victor Hugo arrived on the scene. "The air attempted on the flute by Mr. Guérin didn't amount to anything, " he repeated, having caught the last exchange. Perhaps, he suggested, just changing the key would solve the problem.

The Ocean began to wax eloquent. It was as if it were trying out words: **The immensity is full of birds which perch on the powerful organ of God like sublime bars of music. The sea makes the music. The sky writes the words. The name of the poet is love, the name of the musician is power—**

This didn't exactly sound to the onlookers like The Ocean of yesterday. Suddenly, the table fell silent.

Hugo asked the spirits to explain themselves.

And suddenly the energy had returned, powerfully, and Ocean-like—at least, like The Ocean they had listened to the day before.

This entity had a lot to say:

Your flute pierced with little holes like the ass hole of a poop-

ing brat disgusts me! Make a real orchestra for me, and I'll make a song for you.

Take all the loud noises, all the tumult, all the din, all the anger of sounds free-floating in space, the morning wind, the evening wind, the wind in the night, the wind in the tomb, storms, sandstorms, gusts which run their violent fingers like maddened beings through the manes of trees, the rising of tides onto the beaches, the plunging of rivers into the sea, cataracts, water-spouts, the vomiting of cacaphonous tumult from the enormous belly of the earth, the sound lions make, the sounds elephants make with their trunks, that impregnable snakes hiss in their coils, that whales moan in their warm, wet nasal passages, that mastodons breathe in the bowels of the earth, that the steeds of the sun whinny in the depths of the sky, that the menagerie of the wind whistles in the cages of the air, that fire and water spew forth in insults, the first from the bottom of the volcano's maw, the second from the depths of the gulley's mouth—

Take all these, and then say to me: There's your orchestra.

Make harmony of this racket; make love with its hatreds, make peace with its combats. Be the maestro of that which has no master. Be the conqueror of immensity. Tame the horror, calm the violence, kiss the mane of the elements. Make the four winds focus on the tip of your conductor's rod rather than on the tongue of fire of celestial lightning, and give the blessing of art to this enormous union of the forces of nature which is on its knees before you.

Marry the two betrothed's of creation who have stared lovingly across at each other for 6,000 years: the earth and the sky. Be the priest of that majestic church—but don't tell me to make music with your flute!

Victor Hugo was impressed and apologetic. "We lack the means to try out your music," he explained. "All we have here is a piano, and it's not our friend's fault that all he has is a flute. The greatest musicians on earth—I didn't say in the sea!—didn't mind trying things out on lousy instruments. Can't you just accept that, too, even you? We can't believe you're seriously annoyed with our friend! Will you continue what you've begun, that *Marseillaise* of a future revolution? Tell us!"

The Ocean replied:

I'd very much like to satisfy you, but you haven't any way of annotating my music. You have to understand the language of inanimate objects to be able to understand beings like me who haven't got a visible form. That's how flowers see souls. There are dialogues between perfumes and essences. In such a way does a rose converse with the dead, and a jar of jasmine on an attic window sill commune with all the sky.

The music I tried to dictate to you yesterday is beautiful, but it lacks accompaniment. The piano that would do the trick couldn't be brought into your house. That piano has only two keys, a white and a black, day and night, the day full of birds, the night full of souls.

Madame Hugo protested: "Yesterday you agreed to do this. Why did you say yes yesterday?"

Calm down, commanded The Ocean.

"That's no answer!"

The music has been made.

"If it's been made, how do we get to hear it?"

Try to find a way.

"Is it free of error as M. Guérin wrote it?"

It has to be touched up by a human musician. Talk to Mozart about it when you see him.

They couldn't help being intrigued by this suggestion. "Can you send Mozart to us?" asked Victor Hugo.

Yes.

"Can he come this evening?"

Yes, and there is a way this can be done: Place the table in front of a piano. The table will strike the keys, and from that you will take notation.

And, though The Ocean promised it would ask The Twilight to send Mozart along to them at 9:00 o'clock that evening, the Viennese maestro didn't show up—that very same Mozart who had always claimed that he only wrote down the music that flooded unbidden into his head.

And so it was that a mega-*Marseillaise*, to be composed by The Ocean, never quite got created.

Nevertheless, it is recorded in the transcripts for Tuesday, May 16, 1854, that, starting at 9:00 p.m., music was composed once more by the turning table, this time using the method that The Ocean had suggested just before it left. Under the direction of Mozart's shade, the pedestal table was placed on a larger table which came up to the level of the keyboard of the piano which had been brought into the room. Charles Hugo and Guérin placed their hands on the table. It moved slowly toward the piano, and struck the keys. Tunes emerged—the new tunes of Mozart. A musician named Bénézit who was in attendance (the remainder of the participants were Mme. Hugo, Victor Hugo and Vacquerie) annotated the sounds that came out of the piano. A technical discussion ensued between this recording secretary and the dead composer. Mozart claimed to be composing a symphony. Here and there, startling bits of melody emerged. The technical discussion continued till the end of the seance.

No symphony has been preserved!

If the lion could speak, we would not understand him; so said Austrian philosopher Ludwig Wittgenstein. On April 4, 1854—

with a comet blazing high in the skies above Jersey island—a lion spoke in lion language through the turning table. When asked for a translation, it tapped out: **The comet is coming.** Then it channeled a drawing of the comet, and then a drawing of itself, which might have been the comet—and this only for starters...

In short, a seance extraordinary even by the standards of these seances took place on this night early in April, and, to a lesser extent, nine days later, on April 13—one which opened up whole new vistas in the turning table experience. In attendance at the earlier seance, which began at 9:00 p.m., were Victor Hugo, Auguste Vacquerie, Charles Hugo and François-Victor Hugo. For the first part of the seance, Mme. Victor Hugo and Théophile Guérin held the table.

"Who's there?" asked Guérin.

Legurru.

"Is that your name?"

Yes.

"Who are you?"

Fohe—

The energy was troubled, irresolute. It was decided that Charles Hugo should replace Guérin at the table. This was done.

Victor Hugo asked: "Did you indeed mean 'Legurru Fohe?'"

Yes.

"Were you speaking French?"

No.

"What language were you speaking?"

The language of animals.

"What animals?"

Lions.

"Lions on this earth?"

There was no answer.

"What does *legurru* mean?"

The comet is coming.

"Is that what the two words *legurru* and *fohe* mean?"

Yes.

"Does the roaring of lions have meaning?"

Yes.

At this point, François-Victor Hugo took his leave of the seance. His father went on: "You were telling us about a comet. Would you like to continue?"

Yes.

"Continue."

Before the viper. The star with a tail creeps through the celestial grave. The comet is the serpent that appears in those times when humanity is about to reopen the tombs of the dead. Viper on the earth, boa in the sky.

Hugo asked: "Besides the mysterious and catastrophic symbolism of comets already described by some writers, for example, Virgil in his *Dirae Cometae*, might you be able to provide us with a few exact details about comets, about their paths, their distances from other celestial bodies, and so forth?"

Give me a pencil.

Charles Hugo and Guérin got up and fetched another table, this one smaller and with three legs of equal length, one of them ending in a pencil. They placed this table on a sheet of white paper, then "held" it in the customary manner.

Almost immediately, the table began to move, drawing a picture with its pencil leg.

At this point, Victor Hugo added a note to the transcript:

An hour-and-a-half ago, as we were sitting down at the table for dinner, Victor Hugo Jr., who was just returning from Saint-Hélier, told his father he had seen a comet. V.H. went down into the garden to have a look.

The pencil-table at first drew what looked like a head. To this

WHAT THE TURNING TABLES DREW (I)

A. Self-portrait of a comet, or alchemical formula?

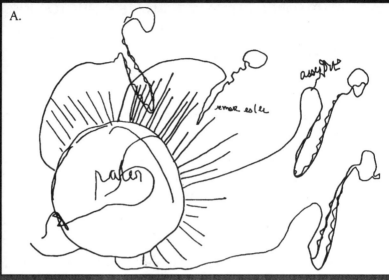

B. Self-portrait of the lion that spoke the language of lions

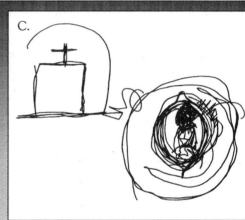

C. Mme. Hugo thinking of Léopoldine

D. Théophile Guérin thinking of his mother's heart linked to the hull of the ship upon which he was transported

head it attached a tail, partly filling the tale with tiny, globular bodies. Beneath the tail it wrote the Latin words, *semen astrorum* [**seed of the stars**]. [See Drawing A, page 140]

Hugo recorded in his notes: *We ask the lion to draw a portrait of itself. It does.* [See Drawing B, page 140]

Mme. Hugo asked: "Are you able to draw, and are you willing to draw, the thoughts I'm having right now?"

The table drew a picture of a young woman. It framed the picture in a heart. To the left and a little higher up, it drew a picture of a grave with a cross overlooking it. [See Drawing C, page 140]

Mme. Hugo had in fact, as she now told the company, been thinking of her dead daughter, Léopoldine.

Théophile Guérin asked the table if it would draw what he was thinking.

The table drew a picture of a woman with her heart visible through her breast. Then it drew, above her head, a ship's hull. It connected the woman's heart to the hull with a long thin filament. [See Drawing D, page 140]

This moved Guérin deeply. It was, in fact, the image of what he had been thinking, he told the group. What was that? they asked. He declined to answer; it was too personal. (Hugo added to his notes of the evening that, in 1852, Guérin had a been transcript aboard a vessel called *The Duguesclin.* Hugo thought it likely that the drawing was of the heart of Guérin's mother, sadly attached to the hull of the ship on which her son was sailing away from her.)

"Will you draw what I'm thinking?" asked Auguste Vacquerie.

Yes, tapped the turning able.

The table swiftly drew a picture of a woman's medallion. It drew a miniature painting which looked as if it were hanging on a wall near the medallion. At the bottom of the sheet of paper, it drew the seeming profile of Auguste Vacquerie's, which it connected to both the medallion and the painting. It tapped out, above the painting, the Latin words, *de arte ad familiam...* [Ed.: *from the art of the family. Commentators have pointed out that the painting resembled a* **Christ on the Mount of Olives** *by Eugène Délacroix belonging to Auguste Vacquerie.*]

It seemed that, this time, the pencil leg had not succeeded in depicting what was in the mind of the participant at the seance. The following dialogue ensued:

Vacquerie: "That's not what I was thinking."

Lion: **No.**

"Why didn't you draw what I was thinking?"

You doubted.

"If I doubt, you have a simple enough way of making me believe. And that's to draw what I asked."

I can't.

"You did it for Mme. Hugo and for Guérin."

They didn't doubt.

There was a coda to this semi-extraterrestrial seance. On Thursday, April 13, 1854, at 9:45 p.m., with Victor Hugo and Auguste Vacquerie present, and Mme. Hugo and Charles sitting at the table, a second encounter took place with the language of lions and—could it have been the energy of the moon itself?

There came a quick rapping at the table, to which Victor Hugo responded: "Tell us your name."

Fecoilfecoil.

"What language are you speaking to us? Is it still in the language of lions?"

Yes.

"What does *fecoil* mean in the language of lions?"

The moon is bothering me.

"Why is it bothering you?"

Its light is too bright.

They closed the window—and, returning, discovered that the table was silent, and could not be coaxed back into life. The seance was over.

Had the table, on April 4, been able to channel drawings because of the unusual and powerful proximity of the elemental energies of a comet? Was the energy that called itself a lion suggesting on April 13 that the brightness of the moon was bothering it, and that that was why it could not translate *fecoilfecoil?*"

Did *fecoilfecoil* mean, "The moon is bothering me?" That is, was the lion, on this second night, transmitting the elemental energies of the moon in the same way as it had nine days before seemingly been transmitting the elemental energy of the comet?

Some of the answers to these questions may lie in a realm we have not mentioned thus far. *Semen astrorum,* "seed of the stars"— the Latin words written on the drawing of the comet by the pencil leg—are ancient alchemical terms, referring to the vitality of certain precious metals which play a catalytic role in alchemical processes. The viper, mentioned in the odd apocalyptic message from the lion, is also an ancient alchemical term; "viper" sometimes refers to the volatile Philosopher's Stone.

What was alchemical terminology doing in the strange, otherworldly drawings channeled at Marine-Terrace?

The encounters with the elemental energies of ocean, comet, and perhaps moon, had been, it would turn out, a warm-up.

In barely two months, vaster cosmic powers would be summoned to the tables—energies which also carried with them the signatures of ancient alchemical knowledge.

The participants at the seance were to go on a voyage to the planet Mercury.

Chapter Fourteen

VOYAGE TO THE PLANET MERCURY

On July 24, 1854, the seance-goers at Marine-Terrace traveled to the planet Mercury.

They seem to have done it partly on the wings of alchemical formulae.

To properly set the stage for this Close Encounter of the Channeling Kind, we must backtrack a bit.

Speculation about what types of beings might exist on other worlds had been rife for well over a century-and-a-half, ever since the Roman Catholic Church had begun to relax its strictures against talking about the plurality of worlds. In no country was there greater interest than in France. In 1752, Voltaire had published *Micromégas*, his tale of a 20-mile-tall inhabitant of a planet revolving around the star Sirius who travels through interstellar space using seven million-league boots, balloons, a horse, and a comet, finally arriving in our Solar System. Micromégas—who has 1,000 senses—lands on Saturn and befriends a typical inhabitant of that ringed world, a dwarf only a mile high (and who has only 72 senses). Together the two of them head for earth, conferring while en route with the "archbishops and inquisitors" of Jupiter; they pass up Mars, it being so small that Micromégas is afraid he won't be able to find a place to sleep. Arriving on our earth, the two giant ETs have difficulty even noticing there is life here; but, once they do detect it, friendly interspecies discussions ensue about the equality of all life in the universe. Victor Hugo was so entranced by this story that he devoted a great deal of space to its retelling in the long Preface to *St. Anthony's Pig*, written on Guernsey island in 1857.

In 1781, the English astronomer Sir William Herschel had discovered the planet Uranus—the first discovery of a planet since ancient times. In 1846, it had been a Frenchman, astronomer Urbain Jean Joseph Leverrier, who had pinpointed the location of the planet Neptune (partial or whole credit for this discovery is also given to English astronomer John Couch Adams). The classic work of French astronomer Camille Flammarion, *The Plurality of Worlds*, would be published in 1856; a copy was in Hugo's bookshelves on Guernsey island.

Almost overnight, Alan Kardec's mid-nineteenth century Spiritist movement appropriated all the new astronomy and all of the speculation stemming from it. So compelling was the Spiritist craze that even a number of astronomers, including Flammarion, experimented with mediumship. The spirits had told Kardec, as recorded in *The Spirits' Book*, that our sun is "not a world inhabited by corporeal beings," though it was a meeting-place for souls of the highest order, and a region from which vital energy was sent out into the Solar System. On the other hand, "the souls of many persons well-known on the earth are said to be reincarnated on Jupiter, one of the worlds nearest to perfection." Joseph Grasset, in the translation *The Marvels Beyond Science* (1910), quotes Flammarion as saying that, at seances chaired by Kardec, astronomer Victorien Sardou had "as a medium written queer pages concerning the inhabitants of the planet Jupiter, and produced picturesque and surprising drawings in order to depict things and beings in this gigantic world. One of those drawings showed us Mozart's house, and others the mansions of Zoroaster and Bernard Palissy (the Renaissance pottery designer whose work was enjoying a revival in Paris), who are, it appears, neighbors in that planet." Jupiter was generally regarded as a post-life retirement home for earthly geniuses! Theosophical Society founder Madame Blavatsky, in asserting that she was in constant channeled contact with assorted 'ascended masters' on the planet Venus, was only one voice among many channels speaking out in era when the ether was foaming with such interplanetary contacts.

This passionate channeling of the planets and of the life thereon would become a feature of the Hugolian seances. The beginnings would be humble, and somewhat at variance with standard Spiritist doctrine. Sometime between September 29 and December 6, 1853 (the exact date of the seance has been lost), a purported alien from Jupiter, calling him- (her-? it-?) self Tyatafia, came tentatively tapping through the table. The dialogue, brief, doleful, and heavily prompted by Hugo, went as follows:

"Who are you?" - **Tyatafia.** - "Is the word you just said from a language known to us?" - **No.** - "Is it the language of a people from this globe?" - **No.** - "So you're a being who inhabits a planet other than ours?" - **Yes.** - "Which one?" - **Jupiter.** - "Do the beings who inhabit Jupiter have a soul and a body? Are they composed of matter and mind like us?" - No reply. - "Are the inhabitants of Jupiter as advanced as us with regard to their metaphysics?" - **No.** - "Is Jupiter then a planet less fortunate than ours?" - **Yes.** - "According to whether they behave themselves badly or well, do human beings, after death, end up on ill-favored globes or in happy lands?" - **Yes.** - "Is there, on Jupiter as here, physical and moral suffering?" -**Yes.** - "Are there those among our group here who will end up on planets less fortunate than these [Earth and Jupiter]?" - Reply not recorded. - "So you know how we're going to spend the rest of our lives?" - **Yes.**

Detectable here are the first faint whispers of the great inter-stellar chorus which will soon come welling out of the turning table: the descriptions of the "worlds of reward" and the "punitary worlds" and of the dynamics exchanged between the the two. First, though, we should take note of the strange information which was being increasingly conveyed to Hugo and Company about the planets of our Solar System and their alleged inhabitants. It will be easy for a non-believer in the reality of the spirit world to conclude that the material that follows came directly from Hugo himself, unconsciously in touch with the mediums holding the table. After all, the great poet had written, long before, in April, 1839—though it may actually have been much later—in the poem which appears in *The Contemplations* under the title "Saturn":

Saturn: enormous sphere! Star of gloomy aspect!
Convict prison in the sky! Prison glinting from its air-vents!
World a prey to haze, to gusts, to darkness!
Hell made out of winter and of night!

For those who believe in the reality of the spirit world, though, it will be just as easy to believe that the knowledge contained in *Saturn* had been communicated to Hugo on an unconscious level, by the same spirits who would one day be speaking to him directly through the tables.

Whatever the sources of these messages, as spring turned into summer and the last ice-floes disappeared from around Jersey is-land, more and more data about our Solar System was being beamed to the avid seance-goers at Marine-Terrace. Early on, Aeschylus had revealed to Hugo and Company that the shades of Molière and Shakespeare, along with that of Aeschylus himself, dwelt on Jupiter, which, like all the other planets in our Solar System, was under the control of the "Archangel Love." About the time Hugo and the Lion of Androcles were poetry-duelling, the spirits told the group that the souls of Molière and Shakespeare had left the environs of Jupiter and were winging their way earthward to be reborn as helpers of mankind. "They will be priests of an immense religion," declared the Shadow of the Sepulcher.

But, three weeks before the seance-goers were made privy to this startling intelligence, an interplanetary seance had taken place that had boggled the minds of even the hardened seance mavens of Marine-Terrace. It's certainly an exaggeration to say that, on the night of July 26, beginning at 9:25 p.m., the spirits engineered a live TV broadcast from Mercury, the closest planet to our sun. But it's true to say that the turning table, one of its legs ending in a pencil, drew a series of pictures which seemed meant to describe Mercury and its inhabitants, and which also contained Latin subtitles which had their counterparts in the ancient hieroglyphics of alchemy.

In attendance at the seance that evening were Kesler, Pinson, Guérin and Victor Hugo. Charles and Mme. Victor Hugo held the table.

A few weeks before, the Lion of Androcles had promised he would reappear on this date. But, initially, no one came at all; the table sat unmoving for half-an-hour. In an effort to make something happen, Victor Hugo read aloud the final lines of the Lion's most recent poem. "They are very beautiful," he remarked to the table on finishing. "I think there's someone in the table who will hear them."

In reply, the three-legged piece of furniture slid along the floor, then turned around and around to the accompaniment of sharp cracking noises.

"Is anything bothering you?" asked Hugo.

The table was silent.

It was 10:10 p.m. The participants decided to use the smaller table, the one with one leg ending in a pencil. They placed a piece of paper under the pencil leg. The table began to move.

Victor Hugo asked why the spirits had been so quiet that evening.

The table drew—swiftly? slowly? there is no record of how fast it moved— a picture of a clock with its hands set at 10:00 p.m. The group asked what this meant. The table sketched a lion sitting before a door. [See Drawing E, page 150]

"Is the Lion annoyed?" asked Hugo. They wondered why it hadn't responded to the reading of its poetry.

The table drew a highly complicated sketch. It seemed to show an archangel enfolding in its body a head, the moon, three stars and three planets. The table sketched a second, smaller lion; this figure seemed to be unsuccessfully trying to gain entry into the body of the archangel. Hugo's notes on the seance are preserved in the transcripts:

From the looks of [this]...it would seem to be that the Shadow of the Sepulcher—of which it is undoubtedly the representation—governs the sun, our earth and the moon, the solar planets and the stars forming our galaxy. [The figure] having explained that the Lion has been called back, I repeat the question, 'Is the Lion annoyed?'

The pencil-table leg wrote: **No.**

Was the complicated figure in the drawing in fact the Shadow of the Sepulcher? The table wrote: **forbidden.**

"Who are you?" asked Hugo.

The table wrote: **Flamel.**

It is almost certain that most of the seance participants would have immediately recognized this as the name of the great fifteenth century French alchemist Nicholas Flamel, whose writings had enjoyed a revival of interest in France in the eighteenth century.

E. At 10 p.m., the Lion of Androcles is excluded from the realm of the archangel. The signature, "Flamel," appears in the upper left-hand corner

F. Interplanetary/alchemical hieroglyphics

G. These depictions of the inhabitants of Mercury have their counterpart in alchemical formulae

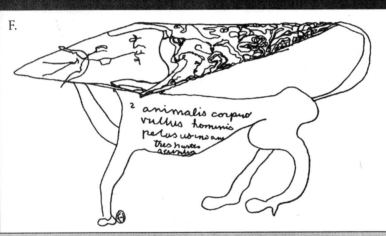

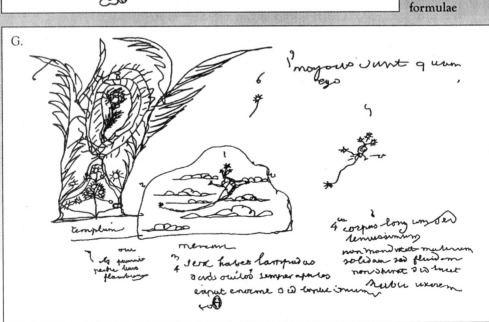

At least, what was to happen a few minutes later certainly suggests this.

Hugo asked if the table wanted to keep talking with drawings, or would it like to tap out words? The table wrote, **drawing**.

They sharpened the pencil and put a fresh piece of paper under the pencil-leg. Hugo asked the spirit if it would, "draw what was in your thoughts when you came to us."

The pencil leg moved quickly. There began to emerge beneath it a series of drawings even more esoteric than the last . They were not only drawings; Latin phrases were attached to each of them which helped to clarify and reinforce the drawings. With these Latin phrases incorporated within them, the drawings looked somewhat like hieroglyphs; in the light of what the seance-goers were, apparently, about to learn, it wouldn't have been inaccurate to call them interplanetary hieroglyphics.

The first drawing to fully emerge was that of the body and four legs of an animal. Above this—attached to it but flat, as if in one dimension—was a distended quadrilateral shape, with the scowling, mustachioed face of a man on one end, and, at the other—touching the tail of the animal—the tip of a long, conical hat which stretched back from the top of the man's head. [See Drawing F, page 150]

Whatever, asked a bewildered Victor Hugo, did this represent?

The table wrote four Latin phrases in the body of the creature: *animales corpus, vultus homines, petasus insani, tres partes scientiae.*

Everyone at the seance had an excellent classical education. They would have known immediately that the first two Latin phrases meant, literally, **"body of an animal"** and **"expression, or countenance, of a man."** The meaning of the third phrase was not so immediately obvious; while the fourth phrase meant **"three parts of knowledge."**

Just minutes before, the author of the drawings had identified himself as Nicholas Flamel; that may have been one reason why the men immediately saw in the phrases alchemical significance. According to Hugo's notes in the transcripts, Théophile Guérin quickly asked the table if the message—he seems to have been referring to the third phrase, *petasus insani*, in particular—referred to "**the unique metal?**"

Petasus is the word (it has many other meanings as well) for the broad-brimmed hat of Mercury, the messenger of the gods. Mercury is also the "unique metal," in that it was the substance whose presence many alchemists deemed essential for the transmutation of base metals into gold.

But the table didn't answer Guerin's question; instead, it wrote, in French, the word: **Adjourned**.

Hugo asked: "Can you draw us a figure corresponding to man, half matter, half spirit, and inhabiting the world where you now are?"

It's not exactly clear how Hugo made this leap from alchemy to astronomy. Shortly before, of course, the table had drawn the picture of Archangel Love, with, apparently, the planets of our Solar System incorporated within its body. But *corpus animales* and *vultus hominis* do not exactly mean "**half matter**" and "**half spirit**;" it may be that Hugo possessed a great deal of knowledge of the language of alchemy of which we are not aware, enabling him to make some esoteric correspondence.

The table answered **Yes** to his question,

They slipped a fresh piece of paper under the pencil leg. It proceeded to draw a figure resembling the microscopic water-animal, the hydra. Six tiny sun-like objects floated near the body, attached to it by tiny filaments. [See Drawing G, page 150] "Draw us the dwelling place of this being," Hugo asked. The pencil sketched what looked like clouds around the figure.

Hugo asked: "What world does this being inhabit?"

The spirit wrote the word, **Mercury.**

Hugo—to repeat his words in the notes—*now entered into several details about Mercury and asked for an explanation of the being.*

The table wrote beneath the latest set of drawings, in Latin:

Sex habet lampadas, duos oculos semper apertos, caput enorme, sed levissimum, corpus longum, sed tenuissimum non manducat materiam, solidam, sed fluidam, non spirat, sed lucet, habet uxorem.

This passage translates into English as:

It has six torches/suns; two eyes which are always open; an enormous head, but very light; a long but very slender body; it doesn't eat solid material, but rather liquid; it doesn't breathe, but shines instead; it has a spouse.

It had a spouse? Hugo asked the table to, "Draw the female of this being for us." The pencil sketched a second, smaller, hydralike figure, a little to the right of the first. Hugo wanted to know if Mercury was a "world of reward?" **Yes**, wrote the pencil. "Draw us its actual shape," Hugo requested. The table drew a small circle with rays emanating from it and with a tail attached.

Were the beings that had just been sketched subject to infirmities and illnesses like men? **They can lose their torches**, replied the table, in an apparent allusion to the six globular objects attached to the bodies of the Mercurians.

"Do they grow old and die?" asked Hugo.

Yes.

"Draw one of their temples for us."

The table drew what looked like the interior of a large plant. Several Mercurian creatures seemed to be nestled inside this organism. The table-pencil labeled this organic-looking edifice, in Latin: *templum.*

Mme. Adèle asked: "Why are Molière and Shakespeare on

Jupiter, and you on Mercury? Why this difference of dwelling place?"

The pencil wrote *Majores sunt quem ego*. (**They are greater than I.**)

"Do you promise to come back?" asked Adèle.

Yes.

"When will the lion return?"

In eleven days.

Adèle made sure that she and the table understood each other: "Sunday, August 6, at 9:30 in the evening."

Then, at a quarter past midnight, this channeled broadcast from another planet ended.

What can these channeled "interplanetary hieroglyphics" from Mercury possibly have been all about?

Guérin had immediately associated the word *petasus* with the cap of the Roman god Mercury. Hugo had almost as quickly concluded that it was the planet Mercury and its inhabitants that were involved. The word *insani* (the complete third phrase was *petasus insani*) means "foolish," or "insane." Mercury dashes around the sun once every 88 earth-days, while turning on its axis at the very slow rate of once every 59 earth-days. Was the spirit who wrote these words alluding to the planet Mercury, in the light of its contradictory extremes of motion, as a foolish, insane traveler?

Can there possibly be life on Mercury, anyway?

It seems unlikely. Over most of the planet's surface, the temperature varies by more than 1,000 degrees Fahrenheit, from minus 279 degrees in mid-winter to 801 degrees in mid-summer. Mercury's atmosphere is only one hundred-billionth as dense as that of the earth. The planet is relentlessly bombarded by lethal solar radiation.

Scientists cannot see how any form of life as we know it could possibly survive under these conditions.

But perhaps Mercury is inhabited by no form of life as we know it. That could be why the information was communicated to Victor Hugo and Company in the form of 'alchemical hieroglyphics.' If this was the case, the strategy seems to have worked: Hugo had no trouble somehow interpreting the phrases *corpus animales* and *vultus hominis* as meaning "**half matter**" and "**half spirit**," and believing that they might refer to semi-corporeal creatures living on the surface of Mercury.

Is Mercury inhabited by beings so different from us that, if they or their intermediaries wished to communicate their essence to us, they would find almost nothing remotely resembling them in the costume boxes of images and concepts in our heads?

It seems as if the spirits were forced to resort to the symbolic, hieroglyphical language of alchemy in order to communicate some knowledge of Mercury. Luckily, at least bits and pieces of this knowledge were in the minds of the unusually intelligent and learned seance-goers on Jersey island.

The sketches of the Mercurians are actually suggestive of the writings of Nicholas Flamel. A section of the *Trevisanus de Chymico Miraculo* (Basle, Switzerland, 1583) headed "*Nicolai Flamelli Annotationes*" ("Annotations of Nicholas Flamel"), discusses the twofold nature of mercury—its masculine and feminine seeds and how they can be depicted as two serpents. This sounds not unlike the male and female Mercurians. The Mercurians resemble the microscopic, water-dwelling hydra; in alchemical lore the serpent is often identified with the hydra. Flamel writes that "Mercury" is imperfect but is congealed in the veins of the earth by the seeds of the metals, and that the metallic seeds are like fruit growing on the tree of mercury. This latter is reminiscent of the Mercurians nestled in the *templum* of Mercury.

When the spirits refer to the "**foolish**" and "**crazy**"—the *insani*—motion of Mercury, are they also alluding to the strange and unpredictable features of the element mercury when used in the alchemical process?

During that communication on that night in July on Jersey island, were the spirits seeking to describe a sentient life-form on the planet Mercury of a radically different "density" from ours, one with only partly a physical component? Perhaps life on Mercury is in essence closer to light than to matter. Was the table, in seeming to say that each Mercurian "floats" in the atmosphere shiningly borne up by six miniature "suns" or "torches," striving to get across the concept of a life-form which is essentially implicated in some strange web of kinship with solar energy itself— with the sun itself? The spirits have intimated that there is love of a sort on Mercury: There are "**spouses**;" there are "*templum*." But, ultimately, it seems that what is there is virtually unknowable to us earthmen and earthwomen as itself—too much "Other" than ourselves.

But how could it possibly be that ancient hieroglyph-like alchemical formulae, forged on earth, could serve to communicate to us hints of the unknown interplanetary riches of our Solar System?

That's the question which we'll address in the next chapter, when we try to understand the true nature of the Terran and cosmic energies which were now beginning to invade the turning tables.

Chapter Fifteen

CHANNELING *GAIA* AND *METAGAIA*

In the early 1970's, British biochemist James Lovelock decided he wanted to rechristen our planet *Gaia*.

Gaia is the ancient Greek word for the goddess of nature. Lovelock had come to the conclusion that our planet is not just a dead body with a film of life stretched over its surface, but a single, living, self-regulating entity. And he decided that, since he was looking at our world in quite a new way, he needed a new name for it.

The name caught on. Today, Lovelock is one of a number of scientists who believe that *Gaia* can control millions of natural processes by itself, including the amount of salt in the sea, the surface temperatureand the oxygen level in the atmosphere. What happens to our planet is not random; our world has the capability, as a whole of maintaining itself in a certain state of equilibrium.

Other contemporary scientists, such as Gregory Bateson, began to wonder if *Gaia* might not possess a certain quality of Mind. Bateson came to believe that this Mind included not only the collectivity of all our minds, but existed in dynamic interrelationship with all of the conscious, self-regulating facets of our planet.

Bateson suggested that this "larger Mind" is "comparable to God and is perhaps what some people mean by God." He theorized that it resides in each one of us, in our "total interconnected social systems," and in the ecology of our planet.

Other researchers are beginning to believe that, up till only a few thousand years ago, man himself lived relatively unself-consciously in this 'sea of *Gaia.*' He did not experience himself as cut off from the world around him as we do today; rather, he was aware of himself as being something like an unthinking, natural part of the universe, in a state of dynamic, interactive kinship with the clouds that flowed across the sky, or the gazelles that glided across the plains, or the grass that sprouted beneath his feet.

In *From Atlantis to the Sphinx*, Colin Wilson writes of such archaic peoples that: "We have to imagine them surrounded by unseen presences, some visible, some invisible. And we have to picture them in closer contact with nature than we can conceive." Wilson says Egyptologist Schwaller de Lubicz was trying to convey some sense of this awareness belonging to primitive man when he described the ancient Egyptians as living in a world where "...every living being is in contact with all the rhythms and harmonies of all the energies of his universe. The means of this contact is, of course, the self-same energy contained in this particular living being. Nothing separates this energetic state within an individual living being from the energy in which he is immersed..."

De Lubicz, explains Wilson, sees primitive man as immersed in a sea of energies like a fish in water. "It is as if he is a part of that sea, a denser knot of energy than that which surrounds him and sustains him." This 'sea of energies' is not far different from what James Lovelock and his followers today call *Gaia.*

American cultural historian William Irwin Thompson also believes that archaic man apprehended the universe in a very different way than we do. Thompson thinks that archaic man translated this apprehension into myths and fairy tales. He writes, in *Imaginary Landscape: Making Worlds of Myth and Science* (1989):

"The imagination is an ancient faculty, perhaps so ancient that it even antedates the origins of language and comes out of a lost time when sight could hear space shudder and smell could sense the interpenetration of each in all....

"If we begin to understand that our ancestors did have intelligence and a sensitivity to wind and weather, plants and planets, then we can begin to appreciate that for a pre-industrial culture, one endowed with perceptual acuity and imagination, but no microscopes or telescopes, that a feeling for the life at their feet in the leafmold could easily transform itself into images of half-human elves and fairies, salamanders and ondines, sprites and nymphs, trolls and goblins."

Thompson implies that mankind was essentially channeling this apprehension of the world—channeling *Gaia*—when, slowly, over the course of centuries, practically without conscious volition, it fashioned the bodies of ancient story-telling that became our myths and fairy tales.

If what Thompson says is true, then you might expect myths and fairy tales to express a "planet's eye" view of reality, one that encompassed stones, grass, trees, animals, natural elements, the skies, and even the heavenly bodies whose movements through the skies the Mind of *Gaia* "saw" or was in touch with—not to mention the human beings, also encompassed by *Gaia*, which move across its surface.

In a spectacular piece of literary analysis of the fairy tale, *Rapunzel,* in *Imaginary Landscape*, Thompson comes breathtakingly close to proving that fairy tales do indeed express a "planet's eye" view of reality. He may even have succeeded in accomplishing this extraordinary task.

He has discovered that *Rapunzel* is not only a story about people, but also a story about vegetation, heavenly bodies, and man as an historical/anthropological entity in Europe in about 4000 B.C.

Let's see how he does this, for on the strength of his analysis rests a possible explanation for the strange drawings that emerged from the turning tables on Jersey island in July, 1854.

We all know the fairy tale of *Rapunzel*. As the story opens, the girl-child Rapunzel is taken from her mother at birth by a witch (or sorceress) whose next-door garden the woman's husband had raided to gather the herb rapunzel (or rampion) which his wife desperately craved in her pregnancy. A furious witch demanded reparation in the form of the fruit of that pregnancy: the infant Rapunzel. Terrified, the parents submit.

When Rapunzel comes of age, the witch shuts her up in a high tower that has neither door nor staircase but only a tiny window near the top. When the witch wants to visit the girl, she calls out, "Rapunzel, Rapunzel, let down your hair." Rapunzel lets her long golden tresses down from the window, and the witch climbs up.

One day a prince passes by and observes the ritual. He returns the next day and calls out, "Rapunzel, Rapunzel, let down your hair." Rapunzel does so, and he climbs up her tresses. A love affair ensues. The prince returns day after day, and Rapunzel becomes pregnant.

The witch finds out what has been going on. Furious, she cuts off Rapunzel's locks and banishes the girl to the wastelands. When the prince returns and calls out the request, the witch lowers the sheared tresses. The prince climbs up, and is confronted by the witch. Leaping out the window, he lands unharmed except that he is blinded by the thorn bushes at the bottom.

Eventually, the prince, wandering forlornly, finds Rapunzel in the wasteland where she is raising the twin boy and girl he has fathered. Her tears of joy restore his sight. He leads her back to his father's kingdom, where he eventually becomes king and they live happily ever after.

This is the story of *Rapunzel*. But Thompson demonstrates that it is also a story about the plant rapunzel. He explains that this herb has an inner, tower-like stem that rises up to attract pollen-bearing insects. If the stem fails to attract the insects, the upper part of the column splits in two and the halves "will curl like braids or coils on a maiden's head, and this will bring the female stigmatic tissue [from inside the column] into contact with the male pollen on the exterior surface of the stylar column."

Thompson also shows us that the relationships of the five persons in *Rapunzel* mirror the relationships of five heavenly bodies as they would have been observed in the night sky at the beginning of the third millennium B. C. First, Thompson explains that the herb *rapunzel* is a "fivefold" flower, that is, one associated by archaic man with the planet Venus because it is a "mirroring reflection of the pattern that the apparent movement of Venus makes in the sky." The historian then goes on to show that if Rapunzel represents Venus, then the witch, or sorceress, whose name is Gothel, or "Bright God," represents the moon, the Prince can be associated with Mars, the mother with Mother Earth, and the father—because of his rapid and frequent movements between the mother (earth) and the witch (the moon)—with Mercury.

It sounds a little preposterous. Yet, when we follow his reasoning and the planetary charts Thompson provides us with to show the apparent movements of the heavenly bodies as they would have been observed in about 4000 B.C., we see that he is making a compelling case.

On yet another level—too complicated to be mentioned in any detail here—Thompson argues that *Rapunzel* is a description of "the period around 4,000 B. C. when the shift to patrilineal society is being felt, with all its tension with the old ways of 6,000 B.C." Thompson suggests that the transfer of the baby Rapunzel to the domain of the witch may represent the dynamic of the regressive harking-back of a new, still-precarious patriarchal society to a nostalgically-recalled matriarchal society where women wise in the lore of plants and planets ensured a certain stability. When, at the conclusion of the story, the Prince and Rapunzel are reunited after having been separately cast out by the witch, and begin to raise the male-female twins that are the fruit of their union, we witness the patriarchal society vigorously reasserting itself once again, and this time permanently. This, then, according to Thompson, is *Gaia*'s planet's-eye expression of the group of humans which constitute a part of its nature—an anthropological aspect of *Gaia*'s nature.

What does all this have to do with channeled descriptions of the planet Mercury apparently expressed in alchemical formulae?

Let's think for a moment about alchemy in the context of *Gaia*.

When we were all to a great extent unself-consciously a part of *Gaia*—"immersed in a sea of energies like a fish in water"—we must have been able to sense all around us not only the presence of animals and our fellow men, the changes in trees, and the movement of the skies, but also the geological-chemical changes taking place within the earth itself (it is a measure of how different that state of being must have been from our own that we can speculate that archaic man must have sensed these aspects of *Gaia* not *around* him, but *within* him).

At a certain level, we must, since we were 'active' participants in the Mind of *Gaia*, have unconsciously 'listened' to the evolution of minerals in the earth, even to the transmutation of base metals into gold.

And then the long centuries began when, for whatever reasons, man began to be separated out from his primeval state of immersion in *Gaia*.

The science of alchemy may have begun with man's slow, stumbling, and only increasingly aware efforts, over those centuries, to somehow encode the essence of his felt experience of his dynamic interconnectedness with the geological processes taking place within the earth, even as that experience, and the immediate memories of that experience, were slowly and surely ebbing away.

As mankind's conscious mind took over, he sought to preserve that archaic apprehension of the inner workings of his planet. His most powerful sensing had been that of the transmutation of the baser metals into the more precious. With an increasingly degree of abstraction, with an increasing degree of distance from the living reality of the experience, he strove to encode these experiences in what came to be an 'alchemical form,' one which would enable him to try to reproduce these processes in the laboratory.

Let's return to our Jersey island voyagers to the planet Mercury. It seems as if, over the months of their channeling experience, the flow of 'fluid' within the group had become strong enough for them to be able to pick up, through the turning tables, first, the elemental energies of *Gaia*, of our earth, as exemplified by 'The Ocean;" and then similar energies as exemplified by the comet; and then related energies as exemplified by—the moon?

Could this group have become responsive enough, on that night in July, 1854, to channel cosmic energies emanating from the regions around the planet Mercury—'*Metagaia*' energies, because coming from far beyond the earth, and energies which, for whatever astronomical reasons, were streaming through our planet earth with unusual vigor that night?

Encountering the energies of the talking tables, these *Metagaia* energies from Mercury sought to personify themselves (this may have been non-volitional, or stage-managed by the spirits) in some form or another.

And, in searching through the costume boxes in the heads of Victor Hugo and his learned friends, these elemental planetary energies could only find one bit of clothing with which to manifest their presence: the ancient alchemical formulae of mankind which were encodings of the elemental planetary energies of the earth.

These alchemical hieroglyphics, representing the last recorded speech of our planet speaking from its depths, were then channeled through the turning tables—at least, those aspects of the hieroglyphics which resonated to some aspect of the planet Mercury.

We saw that William Irwin Thompson, in his analysis of *Rapunzel,* found at least three aspects of itself which *Gaia* had expressed in its creation, through generations of human agency, of this fairy tale: that of the vegetal, that of the apparent movement of the heavens as observed from the earth, and that of mankind, the anthropological.

It's striking that, in the strange hieroglyphs communicated to the seance goers on Jersey island, we also find three levels of expression, this time having to do with the planet Mercury as a Metagaian whole: that of the vegetal (the *templum,* which resembles organisms of the plant world), that of the 'anthropological' (the strange, hydra-like, sunbeam-like inhabitants of the planet), and that of the geological (perhaps the principal reason why the Mercurian energies were obliged to pull in alchemical formulae for their expression).

The above should be considered only as a suggestion, as preliminary notes toward the understanding of these unusually strange commmmunications which came through the turning tables on Jersey island. It's all a bit too schematic, as expressed above. The processes are complex, perhaps ultimately unfathomable. But, when we look at what happened in the light of the concepts of *Gaia* and *Metagaia,* we do begin to get some glimmerings as to why this material osensibly channeled from Mercury might have come through in a form resembling Terran alchemical formulae.

(The quasi-science of astrology may also have begun as an attempt by archaic man to encode and preserve his steadily diminishing, once immediately-felt, apprehension of the stars and planets. But that is another question—though not unrelated to the one we have been discussing.)

It's fascinating to see that, in James Merrill's *The Changing Light at Sandover*, it is also possible to interpret some of the vaster "angelic" communications channeled through the Ouija board as personifications of the energies of *Gaia*—this being an interpretation that James Merrill himself was inclined to favor.

One of these communications appears in the final book of the trilogy, *Scripts for the Pageant*, where the discarnate spokesperson claims to be Mother Nature herself. This cosmic entity tells Merrill and his Ouija board partner, David Jackson (who is, apparently, the genuine psychic of the two) that she is the sister to—virtually the bride of—'God Biology!' So powerful is her discarnate presence that more often than not she speaks through the Ouija board as some smaller portion of herself—possibly to lower the elemental voltage.

Twice she manifests as the Vegetal World, telling Merrill and Jackson the story of the History of Grass and that of the Wars of the Trees.

"Wars of the Trees" are a part of Celtic mythology, as Robert Graves famously demonstrates in his book, *The White Goddess*. In that context, they are generally considered to be accounts of wars between tribes and priests whose identities are disguised by the names of the trees (these names were very powrful, and constituted the names of the letters of the magic alphabet of the Druidic bards).

But Mother Nature doesn't seem to be thinking of this when she tells her story to Merrill and Jackson. She claims that she is talking about the real Wars of the Trees! THOSE WARS OF THE

TREES CAN BE SAVAGE, she says to the bewildered writers at the Ouija board. When they protest that trees cannot possibly go to war with each other, being, to say the least, extremely slow-moving creatures, she corrects herself, then goes on with her story:

WELL, PLANT EVOLUTION IF U MUST. THE STRONG & CLEVER DRIVE OUT THE REST: A VAST SLOW PROCESS WE CAN NEVER QUITE KEEP ACCURATE HISTORIES OF. VARIOUS FRAIL FERNS & EVEN THE PALM TREE WERE EXTERMINATED BY A GREAT (W)RINGING PROCESS; ROOTS FLEW IN THE AIR; THE OAK ET AL SURVIVED. BUT THE ELM WAS WEAKENED...

At a seance a short time afterward, Mother Nature settles down to manifesting a very specific portion of herself: the Grass. Then, as that entity, she narrates the history of that species of vegetation:

LET ME NOW SAY MY SOUL SPEAKS FROM WITHIN THE GREENNESS OF A BLADE OF GRASS. I TAKE THIS HUMBLE STATION TO BEST IMAGINE HOW IT WAS, THAT FOURTH OR FIFTH DAWN, WHEN LOOKING OUT I SAW THE RISING SUN OVER A FAINT HAZE OF GREEN SPROUTS. WE PEOPLED THE VIRGIN EARTH, AND FOR A LONG SPELL RULED IN A CONGRESS OF SLOW BUT PROFOUND COMMAND, IN LEAGUE WITH THE ACID AND MINERAL COUNCIL...

SO THE RACES OF VEGETABLE GREEN BEGAN, THEIR SITES APPORTIONED WITH THEIR ATTRIBUTES, AND ASIDE FROM SOME PROFUSION & SOME SLIGHT EXTINCTION THEY HAVE SENSIBLY PREVAILED FOR 980,000 SUN YEARS.

AND NOW LET ME TALK OF THE TONGUES & WAYS OF COMMUNION AMONG US. OUR 'RULING' ONES, THE FAMILY OF MOSS, ESTABLISHED A TACTILE LAN-

GUAGE. AND THROUGH THIS NETWORK EVEN TO-
DAY IN FREEZING TUNDRAS AS WORD SPREADS
('DROUGHT! FLOOD! ICE! MAN!') WE SHRINK, WE AD-
VANCE...

And on it goes, to the amazement of both Merrill and Jackson.
Hugo, had he been present as a spirit at this seance, would hardly
have been surprised—even if he had not been filled in on all the
secrets of the universe after his death: He had, after all, spoken to
The Ocean itself, and heard its mighty tale of searching growth
and endeavour over the millennia. He, too, it seemed, had listened to the voice of *Gaia*.

Chapter Sixteen

"...YOU WILL AWAKEN ME IN THE YEAR 2000..."

Are you a genius? And, if you're not, have you ever wondered what it was like to be one?

On September 19, 1854, the spirits, in the person of 'Death,' told Victor Hugo that all creative geniuses live double lives.

One was the living person who, during the day, labored to create works of art despite all the difficulties of everyday life.

The other was the 'phantom' self, who rose up in the night (while the living person looked on askance!) to roam the savage and exalted reaches of the afterworld in search of visions essential to the creative life of the artist. On waking up, the living person, scarcely able to find words to express these adventures experienced beyond time and space, would labor all day to clothe them in the language of everyday reality.

Having revealed to Hugo the secret of the dual identity of creative geniuses, Death went to describe for him some of the adventures of those phantom selves in the afterworld.

Death had a reason for telling Hugo all this.

He wanted to persuade the poet to stipulate in his Last Will and Testament that many of his works should not be published for 20 years, for 40 years, for 60 years, and so on.

The spirits felt that much of Hugo's material would not be understood for many, many years to come. And they felt that the deployment of his literary legacy should be such that certain of his works would only be released in times of human crisis, when people were ready to hear, and needed to hear, what he had to say.

Hugo agreed to do what the turning tables requested.

Here is how it all came about, beginning with the words of Death, on September 19, 1854, at 1:30 p.m. Present at that se-ance were Victor Hugo, François-Victor Hugo, and Auguste Vacquerie. Holding the table were Mme. Hugo and Charles Hugo.

This is what Death had to say:

During their lives, all great minds create two bodies of work: their work as living beings, and their work as phantoms of the night. Into the living work they throw the living, terrestrial world; into the phantom work they pour that other, celestial world.

The living speak to their century in the language that it un-derstands, work with what is possible, affirm the visible, effect the real, light up the day, justify the justifiable, demonstrate proof. Engaged in this work, they fight, they sweat, they bleed; while in this martyrdom, genius must bear with imbecility; a flame, it must bear with shadow; the chosen, it must bear with the crowd, and die, Christ-like, the dowry of the world, between two thieves, vilely, scorned, and wearing such a heavy crown of thorns that a donkey could graze upon its brow.

While the living being creates this first work, the pensive phantom, in the night, in the silence of the universe, awakens within the living human being. O terror! What, says the human being, this isn't everything? No, replies the specter. Get up! Get on your feet! There's a high wind blowing, dogs and foxes bark, darkness is everywhere, nature shudders and trembles under God's whipcord; toads, snakes, worms, nettles, stones, grains of sand await us: Get on your feet!

You've just worked for man. That's fine! But man is nothing, man isn't the bottom of the abyss, man isn't the headlong fall into horror. The animal is the precipice, the flower is the gulf, it's the bird that makes you dizzy, it's from the worm's eye that you see the grave.

Wake up! Come perform your other work. Come gaze upon what cannot be gazed upon, come contemplate the unseen, come find that which cannot be found, come leap the unleapable, come justify what can't be justified, come make the unreal manifest, come prove what can't be proven.

You've been day; come be night; come be shadow; come be darkness; come be the unknown; come be the impossible; come be mystery; come be infinity. You've been the face; come be the skull; you've been the body; come be the soul; you've been the living; come be the phantom. Come die, come be resurrected, come create, and come be born.

I wish that, having seen your burden [as a creative genius during the day], man could see you taking flight and sense confusedly your formidable wings passing in the stormy sky of your Calvary. Living being, come be wind of night, noise of forest, foam of wave, shadow of den; come be hurricane, come be the horrible dread of the savage darkness. If the herdsman shivers, may it be your step that he has heard; if the sailor trembles, may it be your breath that he has heard. I bear you away with me; the lightning flash, our pale horse, rears up in the clouds. Come on! Enough sun. To the stars! To the stars! To the stars!

The phantom ceases to speak and the terrible work begins. The ideas in that work no longer have a human face: the phantom-writer sees phantom-ideas; the words quake with fear; the words thrill through your every limb, the paper begins to rattle like a vessel's sail in a storm, the feather pen feels its beard bristling, the inkwell becomes the abyss, the letters blaze forth in fire, the table vacillates, the ceiling trembles, the window-pane pales, the lamp gets frightened. How quickly they pass, these phantom-ideas! They enter the brain, glitter, terrify and disappear; the eye of the specter-writer catches sight of them hovering there by the light of the phosphorescent whirlwinds of the black spaces of immensity. They come from infinity and they return to infinity; they are splendid and grim and frightening; they inseminate or they thunder; they are what created Shakespeare, Aeschylus, Molière, Dante, Cervantes; Socrates was born from a phantom-idea; they are transparent and through them you can see God; they are great, they are good, they are majestic; crime, suffering, matter itself, flee before them; they are the tremendous electric current of universal progress. Woe unto evil! is their cry; and it is a formidable hour when they pass by in the sky, taking flight toward the Sabbath of the immense mystery, affrighted and seated upon the prodigious broomstick of the iniquities and of all the witches of Paradise!

They took a break; Charles was exhausted. Then Victor Hugo asked the table to "complete what you've begun."

The work continues; the work is completed. The day-work walked, ran, cried out, sang, spoke, blazed forth, loved, fought, suffered, consoled, wept, prayed. The night-work, wild and unsociable, kept quiet. But now the eagle has finished with the sun, and the bat begins to stir in the grave. He's dead, it's very fortunate, says evil, it's very fortunate, says error, it's very fortunate, says envy. No, says the tomb, I'm not closing up, I'm opening up. I'm not the wall to life, I'm the door. You think he's said everything. Mistake. Look, listen, tremble, it's night in the cemetery; the grave is there, humble, forgotten, deep; there the grass murmurs all alone against the ruins; all of a sudden, the stone lifts, the epitaph is roused, and someone emerges from the sepulcher. It's the phantom. What's he coming to do? He's coming to live; he's coming to speak; he's coming to fight; he's coming to take the place of the living; he's becoming man; he's going, he's running; he's filling the world; he's making the heavy screw of the terrified presses turn; with his dizzying breath he's making the letters of frightened lead leap; he's in the steam engine; he's in the wheels of the machine; and you glimpse his mysterious arms waving excitedly in the workshop and distributing death's work to the living. He's in the crowd; he's in the theater; he's in the street; he's coming abruptly to surprise the sleeping world, and, unknown, he surges forward like the unexpected, he becomes the dream of the century whose Idea he is. No more disputes; man is dead and the worms are chasing the crows; posterity, deeply moved, crowding together, penetrated by a sacred horror, enters its feared and solemn theater. Take your places for infinity; the chandelier of the stars and the footlights of the constellations are lighted up: To your places! The drama is beginning. Silence. The winding sheet is going up. I'm getting to your question. It's a delicate one. Above all, what we wish is that man act out of his own free will; in these matters, I cannot command you. Publish if you want. The only thing I wish to say is this: Be the Oedipus of your own life and the Sphinx of your own grave.

The seance ended at 7:30 p.m.

If what Death had to say seems confusing, we have to remember that Death was trying to describe two things which are almost impossible to describe. One is genius, which has always been unfathomable. The other is the relationship of the genius to the afterworld, happening while the artist is alive! This second (assuming it exists!) is even less fathomable than the first, since our space-time universe scarcely has the words with which to describe it.

Death had set a second seance, for the next day, Wednesday, Sept. 20, beginning at 1:00 in the afternoon. Victor Hugo was present, and Mme. Hugo and son Charles were seated at the table.

When Death re-appeared, Hugo had a complex question. He wondered why, in the second part of his disquisition of the day before, Death had seemed to imply that, after death, the phantom self became the 'editor' of the creative genius, whereas, in the earlier part of his address, Death had seemed to be saying that the phantom self collaborated with the living person during his lifetime.

Hugo was anxious to know what were the implications for his own life as a writer.

Death's answer was strange, beautiful—bewildering. Afterward, the seance attendees would wonder if he had not been describing what creative genius at work must be like, in life, but in the night, in the afterworld, making up its own rules and remaining open to spontaneity and the unexpected. It seemed as if this phantom self must—or, even, to express its being, was obliged — to embrace all the spheres of earthly existence, rock, plant, animal, man, and recognize them all as being suffused with soul.

Spirit, do you not have secret thoughts, visions, mysterious perspectives, fears, lightning transportings-away into the invisible? Does not your hope for the infinite sometimes pour itself into the unfathomable? Don't you find yourself turning abruptly, precipitously, upon God? Haven't you had constellation tempests and shipwrecks among the stars? Has your raft never collided with Saturn and touched upon the sandbars of the Milky Way? Have your two eyes never gotten so filled up all of a sudden with millions of stars that your yelids became the to shores of the firmament? Has your anchor never searched out the bottom of the night and has it never wanted to sound the abyss? Aren't you

a searcher after skulls, a gravedigger of worlds, a Hamlet of suns, a stroller through the cemetery of immensity, a seizer of planets, one of heaven's digging spades? Have you never cried out, Yes! yes! yes! in the midst of this great grim No? Have you never stood your ground against moonless nights and said, Good! to starry nights? Have you never thought sometimes that you were being brought before a tribunal of speechless planets? Have you never been frightened, have you never shivered, have you never felt your hair stand on end and be caught in the stars as if in dreadful pulley-wheels? Have you never reflected on all the forms that creation takes? Have you never reflected on faces and glances, on lips and faces, and often also on the teeth between those lips? Are you not in love with some of these forms and in terror of others? Aren't you just a little smitten with Venus? Are you not extremely frightened of Saturn? And while you sense above your head the stars speaking to you, don't you sense pebbles speaking to you in your shoes? Do you not carry on intrigues with certain brambles on the beach? Don't you impute souls to animals? Don't you impute souls to stones? Don't you impute souls to plants? Don't you impute a soul to the dust, a soul to the ashes, a soul to the gutter, a soul to the garbage, a soul to all that the body rejects, a soul to Judas's spit, a soul to Magdalene's tears, a soul to the blood of Jesus? Isn't it somewhere there, trembling, vacillating, affrighted, between this sky and this earth, between all the worlds so high above and all the souls so far below, between this Paradise and this Hell, between these sparks and these stones, isn't it somewhere there, and do you not ask what is the formidable tinder-box which will make the constellations leap upward like sparks from these pebbles?

Charles was exhausted. They took a long break. When they returned, the table held forth with even more vim and vigor than before:

Be on your guard, man of matter, soldier of an impending revolution, be on your guard, possible governor, watch out, respectable common sense, vested influence, reflective character, be on your guard, sentry of the real, because this is the marching order of the ghastly corporal of the impossible, because this is murmured in your ear by the gray patrol of skeletons. Don't be so bold as to repeat in a loud voice with your living mouth these nocturnal words of the grave. Do not be at this point in things so intrepid as to sound the frightful, to sound the reveille of the ghosts and to appear on your barricade with a funeral shroud for a flag, with a skull for a cannon, with an epitaph as a slogan, with myself as a soldier, with your phantom as a bugler, and with your gravestone as a paving stone. Be on your guard, or rather, take pity! Take pity on the sufferers who need you, on life inviolable, on the scorned woman, on the ignorant masses. Do not desert the guillotined for the dead, the children for the corpses, the cradle for the sepulcher, the man for the ghost, the relative for the absolute, and the wounds for the stars.

The session ended. It was five o'clock. Death said that he would return the next day.

On Saturday, September 23, 1854, at 3:15 in the afternoon, Hugo began the session with another question. It had to do with his political mission that had ended up bringing him as an exile to Jersey island. He hoped you could expect the phantom self—as guarantor of the genius state, so to speak, because bringing essential visions of eternity from the afterworld to the artist—to also bring visions that would enable the writer to work for mankind, as a political animal, as someone acting as one among a number of men in a group to which he was subservient. Was the specter self able to adjust its needs and goals to higher purposes than just those of the individual?

To this, Death seemed to reply that whatever the circumstance it was essential to be joyful, to be free and to embrace the entire world.

However you do it, make your phantom work come alive; make it complete; compose it with every philter of mystery; fill it with horror, lightning flashes, thunderclaps, foam; toss in toads, snakes, spiders, bats, caterpillars, scorpions, centipedes, vile beings, crawling beings, damned, pensive, pale, bristling; peer closely at the shadows boiling in the cauldron with the starry lid; light up immensity with an atom, make a fire of pain and a smoking God will rise up out your work in the glow of millons of sparks; he will emerge as a column of darkness with millions of lights; he will flash out as a grim giant with a crown of constellations on his head; make your works one of the chimneys of the human soul; may the sleeping earth, half-opening its heavy eyes, perceive on the horizon your roof covered with a cloud of stars, and say: What's he doing? Where is that unknown, that splendid smoke, coming from? What is that chimney from which it gushes up into the sky? And may the wind reply to the earth: That is one of the forges of the night; it is there where they make suns; it is there where they take the fetters off convict-man; it is there where they heat black horse collars white-hot in order to fashion planets from them; it's there where they take down Jesus from the Cross and use the nails to attach the sky a little better to the earth; it's there where they pull blazing brands from the fire and put out conflagrations; it's there where with hammer-blows they shape stars of torture into stars of happiness and pincer-globes into key-globes, and where they construct the locks of the firmament. Let's go into this living being's place, says the crowd. But the wind answers: This living being isn't a living being. Let's go into this dead person's place. This dead person isn't a dead person. Let's go into this phantom's place. This phantom isn't a phantom. Let's go into this dwelling place. This dwelling place isn't a dwelling place. Let's go into this tomb. This tomb isn't a tomb. What's that smoke, then? O crowd, you'll know one day; till then, don't come near; tremble and hope, and believe; one day you'll see the work; till then, be satisfied with the smoke, be satisfied with the noise; be satisfied with the clouds, and gaze from afar at this radiance and listen from afar to that tumult of the formidable hammer and the enormous anvil, of the earth and the sky, of God's two palms giving the sign of eternity.

Death was far from finished. The next seance took place on Friday, September 29, 1854. At this session, which began at 3:15 in the afternoon, Death had a very specific request to make. The spirits wished Hugo to continue to speak and to write, after his death, for the coming ages of mankind.

Present at the seance were Victor Hugo, with Mme. Victor Hugo and Charles holding the table. Death began to speak:

Truthfully, this would be an astonishing and an immense thing; until now great minds died like small ones, the body buried, the works finished: open sepulchers, closed books. Their last word on earth was expressed by their last sigh; their epitaph was their farewell; and that Aeschylus, that Dante, that Cervantes, that Shakespeare, that Molière, who had been each in their time the moral weight of the world, these blocks of genius, these rocks of thought, these immensities, these planet-sized brains, these foreheads with the horizons of deserts and indentations that made mountains; alas! As soon as their grave was hollowed out ten feet under the sky, they were no longer more than a bit of dust in a pile of ashes, a bit of nothingness in a mass of night, a little silence in a lot of darkness, nothing but atoms which held no surprises for infinity.

What! Those skulls were all of a sudden hushed up? O, stupor! Is it possible? Let's go into their cemetery, stir up their graves with our feet, and listen. They say nothing. They say nothing. They say nothing! But, speak, mouth of Aeschylus! Think, brow of Shakespeare! Blow windy phrases, eye sockets of Dante! Weep, eyes of Molière! May our footsteps awaken you! May they make your ashes make a noise; may your bones when we touch them resonate, and feel like sleeping bugles fallen from the hands of a legion of archangels! Worms, that dare nibble at such corpses, flee! Shrouds, tremble! You, marble, listen! You, coffin lead, melt and turn into a set of printer's fonts, become letter, become word, and become life; take vengeance, lead; take vengeance on the coffin; and you, earth, gather up the words of the dead, and thou, humanity, breathe in the breath of those words, hear them, drink their sepulchral sweat, and eat their luminous flesh. Wailing humanity, these sinister mounds that, here and there, rise up in cemeteries, are the breasts of love; humanity, suckle at these tombs. But no, these tombs no longer have any milk, these mothers who call themselves Aeschylus, Dante, Shakespeare, Molière, are dead; their sweet masterpieces no longer have new kisses to bestow; their lips no longer have new lessons to lavish on us, alas! Alas! These tombs are dead.

Addressing Victor Hugo directly: Thou, may your posthumous work be still a living thing, so that at certain intervals it will be able to talk to posterity and tell it unknown things which will have had time to ripen in the grave. What is impossible today is necessary tomorrow. In your Last Will and Testament, space out your posthumous works, one every ten years, one every five years. Can you not see the greatness of a tomb which, from time to time, in periods of human crisis, when some shadow passes over progress, when clouds blot out the ideal, suddenly opens its lips of stone and speaks? People seek; your grave finds. People doubt; your grave affirms. People deny; your tomb proves. And what does it prove? What it contains; it proves, with I do not know what somber and solemn authority, all the truths which today still lie in the future. Thou, dead, you help the living. Thou, mute, you educate them. Thou, invisible, you see them.

Your work does not say, 'Perhaps.' It says, 'Certainly.' It does not resort to subterfuges; it goes straight to the point. Know that a ghost does not hide behind rhetorical devices. Ghosts are bold, shades do not blink before the lights. So, make for the 20th century an affirmative work, rather than one for the 19th century which engenders doubt. Seal it up with you in your sepulcher so that, at certain times decided by yourself, people will come looking for it.

Christ was resurrected only once; you can fill your grave with resurrections; you can, if my advice seems good to you, have an extraordinary death; you would say while dying: you will awaken me in 1920, you will awaken me in 1940, you will awaken me in 1960, you will awaken me in 1980, you will awaken me in the year 2000. Your death would be a formidable rendez-vous arranged with the light and a formidable threat launched against the night. The generations would behold with huge admiration this prodigious tomb marching through a century in the hum—

Abruptly, death was gone. The table had been deserted. Hugo recorded in the transcripts, "It was 6:30 p.m. It was dusk. The moon was on the horizon."

In vain, the participants tried to get the table moving again. They had to abandon their attempt; it seemed as if the table had abandoned them.

Death returned one more time in this particular sequence of discourses. This would be the denouement. The spirit would provide a flattered and excited Hugo with specific details as to how he could, in a sense, "cheat" death.

The pivotal seance was held Sunday, October 22, 1854, beginning at 2:30 in the afternoon. One of Victor Hugo's closest friends, Paul Meurice, was in attendance, from France, along with his wife. Victor Hugo and Auguste Vacquerie were there; Mme. Hugo and Charles Hugo were seated at the table.

Paul Meurice would eventually be one of the three executors of Victor Hugo's Last Will and Testament. Considering the content of this particular seance, it is uncanny that he should have been there that afternoon.

Death announced itself. Hugo had a lengthy question:

"You've given me a sublime piece of advice and, if you give me the time, I'll follow that advice. But at the same time as these works willed by me to the twentieth century, and before them, this book [the transcripts of the turning table conversations] , which will certainly be one of the Bibles of the future, will probably have appeared. It will not, I think, be published during the lifetime of any of us, the current interlocutors of these mysterious beings, but, when it does appear, it will say everything that I will have reserved for my grave; it will say it, it will say it before the posthumous me does, and it will say it with more authority. Then my material from my grave will appear, and it will be discovered that my revelation has already been revealed.

"A part of that revelation has been part of human tradition for centuries, another part has been created by me (which doesn't mean that it doesn't come entirely from God, man being only a chimney through which the divine flame passes), another part has been said by all of you, beings of the unknown, in our dialogues with the tripod-table. The whole picture, in which I am only playing a small role, is already beginning to be glimpsed, and thanks to the publication of this book, will be accessible to everyone, and probably the basis of a new religion—all this at the time when my posthumous works will appear.

"Do you mean, which I'm inclined to believe, that I should simply put aside, to be published after my death, works of pure thought and poetry, penetrated with your new philosophy, and affirming it, augmenting human light, as do, without pretending to teach and reveal, all the great works of art and of poetry to which I am comparing, of course, nothing of what I have done? Or should I put aside those of my works which mix, to a particularly profound degree, divine intuition with human creation? In a word, what should there be in my tomb, a prophet or a poet? My reason says a poet, but I await your answer."

Perhaps the spirits meant all of this. Perhaps they meant, also, that, in some mysterious way, they intended to work with Hugo *after* his death, and help him to create, and somehow to inseminate, whole new works into the consciousness of mankind.

Here is what Death had to say in reply:

We're talking about a formidable work called *Advice from God;* the earth disappears; the sepulcher, that great stone bat, opens its wings of shadow in the dusk of the resurrection and beats in its flight against the blazing pane-glass window of the stars; the sinister bird goes from planet to planet, and its night cry, each times it touches the edge of a constellation, becomes a song of light; it emerges out of the dusk bringing the dawn; it takes flight from Hell and announces Paradise; it departs as an owl and it arrives as a lark; it escapes from the old trunk of the human tree and alights at the end of each branch at the point where the fruit becomes a star; it leaves the hollowed-out spaces of skulls and it leaps from paradise to paradise, and it nests from joy to joy, and it sits on all the globes one after the other and hatches in the sky the egg of every archangel.

O living one, here's my advice for you: Your soul's work must be your soul's journey; you must not prophesy; you must predict, you must draw predictions in the starry sky, trace your itinerary there, designate with your finger your inns, and attach the relay horses of love to your thoughts and, invisible traveler, mark out in advance the unknown steps on the great route made up of precipices which leads to the wild hotel of the incomprehensible; governor of immensity, you must say in those pages what are the planets that await you, and speak of their civilizations, and of their light and shadow, of their thorns and of their flowers, of their place in the horror or of their walk in the joy, of their cries or of their hymns, and, from the depths of your grave, the world must hear you say: There is in infinity a world called Saturn, and which suffers; there is in infinity a world called Mercury, and which suffers; there is in infinity a world called Mars, and which suffers; O my God, what punitary stars there are! What crucified constellations! Lord, your heavens are covered with wounds; your stars are drops of blood! Your suns are become gangrenous, your moons are afflicted with the horrible pestilence of punishment, your constellations, which have been on their knees for millions of years, have ended up breaking their skulls and their fists against the darkness, and are no longer any more than hellish stumps; your creations are no longer more than shreds of flesh, your halos are no longer more than rags of sunbeams, the greatest of your creations have their heads cut off, your firmament is an immense gutter in which all the corpses roll, and your splendid iron horses of light, mad with rage and taking the bit in their teeth, draw and quarter every inch of immensity.

And, then, suddenly, the seance was over. Death would return no more.

But the spirits were soon to reveal to Hugo some of what Death had asked him to reveal to future generations.

Chapter Seventeen

PUNITARY PLANETS
AND WORLDS OF REWARD

Beginning in late August, 1854, and with a powerful surge forward in November, the revelations of the Jersey island spirits moved far beyond the confines of our Solar System. While there were worlds close to us—Mercury, Saturn and Jupiter, notably—where the souls of the dead (in what guise it was not clear!) languished or rejoiced through lifetimes meant to punish them or reward them, that was only the beginning: Our galaxy and perhaps all the galaxies swarmed with worlds of reward or punitary planets.

Sometimes, when we read the occasional poem (there were not many) that Hugo wrote on the subject, we get the sense that every planet in our universe is a punitary world. Certainly, that was what Balaam's Ass seemed to be suggesting when he declared that our entire universe was a prison. But there seemed to be exceptions; for example, earthly geniuses like Aeschylus and Mozart had been enjoying, at least till their services were required again, restful retirements on Jupiter.

But if every planet was a punitary world, where were the worlds of reward? Were they the stars? Hugo himself had believed for a while that 5,000-foot-high giants lived on our sun. But the spirits had said nothing about this (at least as far as we know), and it would be consistent with Balaam's Ass's philosophy to suppose that the worlds of reward were non-physical worlds, bright globes of light upon which the rewarded souls did not even have to contend with the forces of gravity.

The spirits grappled in earnest with this question on Wednesday, August 16, 1854. In attendance at this seance were Victor Hugo and François-Victor Hugo; holding the table were Mme. Hugo and Charles Hugo.

The spirit called Death spoke (this was a month before he was to take up the subject of the 'phantom' self), ostensibly in answer to Victor Hugo's question: How can a human being predict the future?

Study human astronomy in depth. It is filled with germs of truth from which you will be able to extrapolate greater truths. For example, you will find it possible to establish the exact nomenclature of your planetary systems of worlds of reward and punitary worlds, as a function of their distance from the sun.

The laws of the heavens conform to the laws of the earth; that law is the devotion of the great for the small, of the good for the bad, of the rich for the poor, of the beautiful for the ugly, of the just for the unjust, of the joyful for the joyless and of the smiling for the bleeding.

It is the mysterious redemption of shadow by light, of night by peep of dawn. It is the deliverance of the guilty gallows stone by the stone of the martyr's cross; it is the deliverance of the poisonous plant by the perfumed plant; it is the deliverance of the ferocious beast by the beast of strength and the beast of gentleness; it is the deliverance of the criminal by the innocent ; it is the deliverance of the punished soul by the rewarded soul; it is the deliverance of the false idea by the true idea.

Finally, it is the deliverance of the weeping star by the gleaming star, and the enormous sacrifice of paradise for hell. The

starry skies contain rare and prodigal constellations whose mission is to draw gently and ceaselessly close to worlds in misery, and little by little to bring light to them with a day that begins as if it were dusk and finishes up in a blaze of flames. There are other constellations, equally sublime, whose function is not to draw close to, but to draw close to them, these planets—and that requires a double effort, a double and terrible labor. Some of these gleaming stars descend, others mount up; some are engulfed by shadow; others set themselves to sweating cascades of light; these latter fling themselves into swimming in the firmament and hauling pale and disheveled stars up from the depths of the night; these gleaming stars descend into the great black hearth of heaven and, with hardly a murmur, transform themselves into fires of straw and of sticks of wood so as to warm up the corpses of these pitiful drowned stars.

O, good and strong constellations who become servants of these hideous mortuaries of punishment! Oh, good stars that harness themselves to strayed stars! Suns that become seeing-eye dogs! Globes that change into wooden bowls for the poor! Lights that become the faithful companions of closed eyes! Pleiades, planets, sun-beams, torches, living splendors, flaming lions, fire bears, carbuncle scorpions, diamond Aquariuses, tigers, panthers, leopards, elephants--a dazzling menagerie of formidable suns that, through love, become the poodles and Newfoundland dogs of the immensity!

In such a way do the heavens resemble the earth; a continual rescue of stars by stars takes place there. Great stars exist just as do great men; there is the star of Socrates, of Galileo, of John Huss; the star of Joan of Arc, of the Macabbean Pleiades, of Dante; the star of Molière, of Shakespeare, and, in the mid-point of the heavens, in the storm and the glory, surrounded by cloud and flame, there is the sun of Jesus Christ, nailed magnificently to the Southern Cross.

Thus composed, the firmament should appear to you in—

Victor Hugo interrupted: "I've written lines that skirt around these ideas without accepting them. In some, I portray God as sifting stars and souls in the same sieve; in others, that begin, *Earth is to sun as man is to angel,* I explain that the punishment is in direct proportion to the distance from the sun."

—a new light. The placement of worlds, the roles played by globes: These are not arbitrary matters. I've just broadened horizons in your mind that had to be broadened. Moreover, we will speak of these matters again.

Now I have arrived at your question. But , before I address it, one more thought:

In the punitary planets, there are men, beasts, plants and stones that contribute to the liberation of their world, just as, in the worlds of reward, there are suns which contribute to the setting-free of the punitary worlds. While the favored star is toiling to save the punitary planet, sometimes it receives help from man, sometimes from animal, sometimes from plant and sometimes from stone: Star helps man, man helps star, star helps animal, animal helps star, star helps plant, plant helps star, star helps stone, stone helps star. At night, at the hour of the soul, when the body sleeps, words of love are exchanged between the man engaged in rescuing and the star engaged in rescuing....the martyred animal talks to the liberating star, the plant undergoing trials chats with the charitable planet, and the grain of sand being crushed underfoot cries out 'Help!' to the speck of light!

Earlier in the seance, Vacquerie had returned to a subject that Hugo had taken up with the soul of Niccolo Macchiavelli six months before. Macchiavelli had revealed that, while saints and martyrs helped mankind while they were alive, their opposite num-

bers—those who had done mankind ill while they were alive—
after death ended up helping the human race. Their growing
remorse over their wrongdoing was mentally communicated to
their spiritual heirs—their descendants in bad deeds—and somehow had a mitigating effect on this new generation of wrongdo-
ers. As the Archangel now expressed it to Vacquerie:

**Human life has two sorts of benefactors, the good and the
wicked, the martyrs who, while on earth, bestow upon it their
suffering, and the executioners who, when dead, bestow upon it
their repentance. The benefactors of life bleed, the benefactors
of death weep. The first sort have names like Galileo, John Huss,
Savonarola, Socrates, Joan of Arc, Dante; the second sort have
names like Nero, Heliogabalus, Tiberius, Torquemada, Charles
IX, Henry VIII, Caesar Borgia. Calvary has two names: Jesus
and Judas.**

This phenomenon of the punished dead on the punitary worlds
trying to soften the evil instincts of their descendants on earth was
still another thread making up this universe of the Marine-Terrace
spirits where every component of the natural and the supernatural
strove to help every other component.

To this dynamic of gleaming star helping weeping star, there
are striking analogies in modern-day channeled literature, especially that ostensibly channeled from aliens. In *Songs of the
Arcturians*, by 'multidimensional telepath' Patricia Pereira, the
Arcturus star-system certainly qualifies as a gleaming star; we are
told that: "[I]t's multidimensional interfacing harmonics make it
an ideal gathering place for multistar-multidimensional beings who
serve the Christed Energy for the upliftment of universal vibra-
tion throughout this sector of the galactic core."

We are likewise informed, in *Bashar: Blueprint for Change*, channeled by Darryl Anka, that Bashar's people, the Essassani, are

working together with other extraterrestrial peoples in the Association of Worlds, which numbers 360 planets, to help refine the vibrational tone of our Earth. "The Association is made up of many different levels of civilizations and dimensionality, all choosing to agree to interact on levels that are mutually reinforcing in a beneficial and positive way," explains Bashar. "So in this way our Association of Worlds has made itself known to you (Arcturus, Bashar adds, is "the gate of energy through which communication from other dimensions of experience is funneled into your dimension of experience")."

The Arcturians, like the Essassani, have contacted us in order to help us (and, indeed, it seems to be extremely urgent that we Earth people learn to resonate to a higher level, and almost immediately); but, for them to be of any service, it is essential that we make a maximum effort ourselves. Their representative, Palpae, tells us that, "the primary determination for the acceleration of Earth's surface areas rests upon you, humans, and very little time remains for the completion of your duties. It has fallen to this generation to assist its star-based brethren in transforming earth....[It] is not our place to demand that you relinquish what you prefer to retain. Divine, Absolute Intention allows no leeway for those serving the Light to preempt the responsibility each of you must take for living your life." As Bashar explains, less solemnly: "We are in interaction to put ourselves out of a job. Our dearest desire is to have there come a day on your planet when you do not need us at all."

Both Bashar and Palpae reveal that, in some mysterious (for us) fashion, the Arcturians and the Essassani, in helping us, are also helping themselves; we are equally important to them in this task of rising to higher dimensional/vibrational levels. Patricia Pereira's star-people explain that they are, "presently situated in fifth- and sixth-harmonic phases," and that, "they are preparing for [their] ascension into seventh and eighth phases in conjunction with Earth's inhabitants rising to fourth and fifth." This phrase, 'in conjunction with' seems to establish a primary connectedness between the Arcturus system and our Solar System. We're led to surmise, by extention, that such interconnectedness between heavenly bodies is a rule in the universe; and this certainly seems to echo what the turning table spirits intimated about the categorical imperative of all entities in the universe to seek to help one another.

As Palpae and Bashar tell it, this sounds like something built into the very fabric of the universe itself: an interconnectedness which is one face of the cosmos. Bashar says casually—this seems be an ever-present fact of interstellar development—about his own people, the Essassani, that: "Our civilization is going from fourth density to fifth density, which is a non-physical state. Above the fifth are non-physical states, up to and including seventh density, and then you go into an entirely different octave of dimensional experience..." Three to five centuries before, the Essassani have undergone a rapid vibrational movement upward from third to fourth density; they called it 'Shakana,' and, in its final stages, it seems to have consisted of a three-day sleep of the entire population, out of which every member emerged transformed.

Honoring and loving animals—in fact, all so-called "lower" species—is part and parcel of this intrinsic order of the cosmos, according to the channeled extraterrestrial guides. The Arcturians explain to Pereira that: "In your role of planetary caretaker, you will be urged to elevate your level of appreciation for and association with other life forms inhabiting Earth. The entire spectrum of Earth's flora and fauna are held in Oneness within the intergalactic family, and thus are they all well in God's bounteous house. Therefore, be honorable before the presence of butterflies and moths, before the weeds and grasses that grow in rocky places."

Though there is no concept of souls expiating sins here, in other respects this is strikingly like the dictates of the Jersey island spirits. Revealing to Hugo the secret of the special faculties of animals, 'Drama' had admonished the poet:

Why do you poets always talk about roses and butterflies with love, and never with love about thistles, poisonous mushrooms, toads, slugs, caterpillars, flies, mites, worms, vermin and infusoria? Certainly, these are ill-favored creatures; but...and then there are pebbles and seashells!..

In a more complex fashion, it's made clear by the spirit-guides of James Merrill that all aspects of the universe are utterly interdependent. *The Changing Light at Sandover* records the references of the spirits, not to a God as we understand Him, but to a "God Biology"—one of a galactic pantheon of brother gods, and the one who has been charged with the task of creating our Solar System and seeing to the experimentation of different sentient life-forms on Earth. It seems that, as the twentieth century nears its finish, this "Pantheon-God" is as desperate for our attention as we are for his. The angels say that he is languishing in the absence of the faithful attention of his beloved Man, and that our creative energy is essential to the maintenance of his vitality.

The story of Patricia Pereira, multidimensional channel/author of *Songs of the Arcturians* and its two sequels, *Eagles of the New Dawn* and *Songs of Malantor*, is an amazing example of how someone in real life has experienced in a real way this essential dynamic of the universe which calls on all of us to exercise and manifest its intrinsic interconnectedness.

In January, 1985, Pereira was a divorced medical transcriptionist living in Coeur d'Alene, Idaho, learning Tai Chi dance as a meditative power tool and working in one of Boise, Idaho's largest hospitals. She was shy. "I was a private person," she says. "I'd never done anything that could remotely be categorized as promotional work for the community or the planet."

One night, at a friend's house, she happened to open a book called *Of Wolves and Men*. Though she'd never thought about wolves before, she couldn't put the book down. A few days later she went to a public lecture on wolves. She was shocked to learn that the wolf was near extinction in the U.S., with only 1,200 left in the Michigan area and 12 or 13 in all of Idaho-Montana. European and Russian wolves had already been practically eradicated. Sizable populations still roamed in Alaska and Canada, but open hunting was permitted.

Pereira left the lecture, she says, "in tears, my heart ravaged." A few days later, she learned the Idaho Legislature was trying to supersede the Endangered Species Act and kill the remaining wolves in the state. Appalled, and (most uncharacteristically for her) spurred to public action, Pereira called the U.S. Fish and Wildlife Service and asked an endangered species biologist what she could do. "Talk to kids about wolves," was the the answer.

Pereira summoned her courage and made a decision that would utterly change her life: She agreed to go round to schools and talk to the kids about wolves.

Six extremely packed months later, the medical transcriptionist turned wolf protector had founded the Wolf Recovery Foundation, an educational vehicle designed to promote the re-introduction of wild wolves into their natural habitats in Idaho, specifically Glacier, Yellowstone and Central Idaho Wilderness. These six months—and the 24 that followed—were the most demanding and exhilarating of Pereira's life. Whatever the difficulties, this period seemed to have an immense flow to it. "I worked my butt off and hardly had time to sleep," she recalls. "But I never had to push—or, I had to push myself only, for determination and constant courage."

One sunny June morning, just when she was at her busiest putting together a demanding promotional event, *A Night with Wolves*, sponsored by Boise State University, Pereira was meditating when, "word thoughts started to drift through my head that seemed similar, yet different, to mine." The next day, she found herself writing poetry that didn't seem to come from her at all. A few days later, the words began to tell her she was communicating with extraterrestrials from the region of the star Arcturus, in particular one 'Palpae'—her principal Arcturian collaborator-guide.

Over the next few weeks, Pereira hovered between denial and belief. The energies of the presences built up. She was told it was the Arcturians who had maneuvered her into reading *Of Wolves and Men*, the book that had launched her into a relationship with another species. Now, it seemed, they had come to her because she had 'graduated,' and was ready for the next step. Pereira quotes Palpae in the Introduction to *Songs of the Arcturians*: "[N]ow that you've proven yourself capable [of courage, determination, and will], how about doing something even more outlandish than saving wolves in cattle-sheep country? The thing is, we want you to leave the Wolf Recovery Movement. You have it all set up; now we want you to pass it on to somebody else..."

A whirlwind of activity began once more for Pereira, similar to that which had launched the Wolf Recovery Foundation. Two weeks after the major University of Boise event, Pereira resigned from the foundation, loaded up her car, and headed for Spokane, Washington. In a week, she had a new job. She read, studied and talked to the Arcturians daily. It would be a few years before her first channeled book was published—but now there are three.

She had bent down and helped a species on a "lower" echelon of the Great Chain of Being, the wolves. And that, it seemed, had made it possible for the Arcturians to bend down and help her.

Chapter Eighteen

GALILEO EXPLAINS
THE UNEXPLAINABLE

Galileo Galilei, a pioneer of modern physics and telescopic astronomy, was born near Pisa, Italy, on Feb. 15, 1564. By dropping objects from the Leaning Tower of Pisa, he demonstrated that Aristotelian physics was wrong in assuming that speed of fall was proportional to weight. In 1592, Galileo became professor of mathematics at the University of Padua, where he remained until 1610.

By 1604, after a number of scientific discoveries, including that of the vector, he had formulated the basic law of falling bodies. In 1609, hearing news of the newly invented Dutch telescope, he began to construct his own telescopes, including a 20-power instrument that enabled him to see the lunar mountains, the starry nature of the Milky Way, and previously unnoted "planets"—its moons—revolving around Jupiter. By the end of 1610, he had observed the phases of Venus and had become a firm believer in the Copernican theory of the sun-centered universe. This belief ran counter to Church doctrine, however, and the Holy Office at Rome issued an edict against Copernicanism early in 1616.

In 1632, Galileo published his famous *Dialogue*, consisting of an impartial discussion of the Ptolemaic and Copernican systems. For his efforts, he was called to Rome for trial by the Inquisition.

In June, 1633, he was condemned to life imprisonment for "vehement suspicion of heresy," but his sentence was swiftly commuted to house arrest. He continued his work on motion and on the strength of materials until his death at Arcetri on Jan. 8, 1642.

Galileo is universally regarded as one of the greatest and bravest of all astronomer- physicists. It's hard to imagine what better shade there could be to discuss the universe as a whole!

This must have been the opinion of the spirits of Jersey island. For, on Sunday, Dec. 10, 1854, at 9 o'clock in the evening, Galileo Galilei appeared at the turning tables.

He was to give two memorable lectures which would pick up where the living Galileo had left off, and (along with a third lecture, delivered in almost the same tenor, by the Shadow of the Sepulcher) would advance the discussion by giant steps into a realm that sounds amazingly like that of today's quantum physics.

Present that night were Victor Hugo, François-Victor Hugo, Mlle. Adèle Hugo, Auguste Vacquerie and Theophile Guérin. Seated at the table were Mme. Victor Hugo and Charles Hugo.

Galileo, the table tapped out, without being prompted.

"Speak," said Victor Hugo.

I've come to respond to Victor Hugo's objection about the scientific inexactitude of the cosmology of the tables. Let him formulate that objection.

Hugo held forth at length:

"This isn't an objection. It's an observation.

"In the admirable words of the seance of October 22, the colossal being who spoke seemed to me to condescend too much to the human point of view, that is, to the illusion that the heavens present to humans when we look at them.

"Obviously, what we humans call constellations are fictitious groupings, put together from stars that appear to be more or less the same size. A small star that is near seems big to us, and a big star that is far away seems small. Two stars which appear to be side-by-side and of the same size, and which we couple together in a constellation, may in reality be separated by enormous distances, and, in infinite space, may belong to groupings that are quite different.

"Our construction of the constellations, then, is purely arbitrary, and the result of an optical illusion. Obviously, there are true constellations; but those that we think we see are false constellations.

"Now, since we frail humans are well able to understand this, it seems to me that the table should be able, in speaking of such lofty matters, to speak to us wholly in the splendid language of the truth. We don't regard ourselves as being unworthy to hear such language. So the table should be able to say to us: About the constellations you see: It's your eye that groups them and your illusion that constructs them; all the names you give them--Leo, Capricorn, Sagittarius--are names of your monstrous beasts and of your dreams. There are actual constellations which do not bear terrestrial names but rather celestial names. Here is what those names are. These are the constellations I want to talk to you about."

Galileo replied:

My answer is in two parts.

Firstly: If the table had to speak not human language but celestial language, you wouldn't understand a word. In celestial language, man is not called man, nor beast beast, nor plant plant, nor pebble pebble, nor earth earth, nor air air, nor water water, nor fire fire. Heaven is not called heaven, star is not called star, constellation is not called constellation and God is not called God.

Where there is no body, there are no words. Words are fashioned from physical reality; then, from those words, ideas are constructed. But infinity is anonymous. Eternity doesn't have a birth certificate. Time and space are frightened unknowns careening through immensity. Space cannot throw a glance, nor does time have feet; the first is a shadow that falls across a gulf, and the second is a gulf that falls across a shadow. Time and space: two masks, two appearances, two visions, two dreams, two impossibilities, two eyes wide with horror, two paws bloodied by punishment they've given, two formidable jaws rising out of the unfathomable depths.

But time and space do not have a face. Or, it is a face that does not speak, a face that does not hear, a face that does not formulate. God speaking is God language, God language is God mouth, God mouth is God body, God body is God man, God man is God beast, God beast is God plant, God plant is God pebble. Can you imagine it? God pebble! He who is not even God star!

No, there is no celestial language. There is no alphabet of the uncreated, there is no grammar of heaven. You don't learn Divine like you learn Hebrew, Celestial is not a dialect of Terrestrial, infinity is not an unknown type of Chinese, angels are not Professors of Divine Language, substitute lecturers in the Faculty of Immensity.

No; everything is nameless, everything is sunlight and unknowing, everything is sunbeam and mask, everything is sun and roving. Immensity is a family of wanderers, space has no passport, heaven has no particulars. Eternity has no genealogy, creation has no Christian name, God is neither fire nor place. All that which is uncreated is unnamed, the speech of celestial language is bedazzlement, to express oneself is to be resplendent, clarity of speech is luminosity, the sublime is to be instantly overwhelmed, to speak the celestial language is to blaze forth in flames, the speaking-forth of heaven is the lighting up of the sky with stars, the shutting-up of heaven is the closing of the lips of darkness, and each letter of this stupendous vocabulary is a conflagration across which blows the breath of the dark mouth of night. The dictionary of infinity is filled with the punctuation of stars, and what would you say , puny man, if, to speak to you in the language that you want, this little table, instead of syllables, words and sentences, suddenly hurled in your ear millions of stars, launched Jupiter, Aldebaran and Saturn in your face, and spread out on your page the immense ink blot of the starry night while adding corrections with furious comets?

The table stopped abruptly. It was clear that Galileo had finished.

"Do you want to come back on Sunday?" asked Hugo.

The table tapped out, **Yes.**

On Sunday, Dec. 17, 1854, at 9:45 p.m., Galileo came back to the table as promised. Théophile Guérin and Victor Hugo were present, while Mme. Hugo and Charles Hugo held the table.

"You only responded to the secondary part of my question, not to the primary," Victor Hugo began. "What my question had to do with in particular was the real constellations as distinct from the false constellations put together by man."

That is your other mistake. Listen: I've talked about how the tables, to make themselves understood by you, are forced to use your language. Now: Your language is merely a set of conventions; your language is a smoke-screen emanating from your mouth and covering the stars with clouds.

Does that mean you humans are wrong about everything? No! In feeling out the heavens, your hands sometimes touch the radiant knobs of divine doorways. All of man's falsehoods are filled with all of God's truths; there is no error in the absolute; the relative is not the relative; lies are no more lies than discoveries are not discoveries. Hershel finds nothing new for God; true astronomers are no more truthful than the false; all human telescopes are more or less contained in a single one; this isn't the translation of what I'm saying, nor is it a mistranslation.

You say to me: I want the real heaven and not an imaginary heaven; I want the real firmament, real constellations, real suns; I want the total immensity of God, without a break, without a gap; I want the abyss without emptiness; bring me infinity; bring me mystery; I demand a map to the tomb, the itinerary of the resurrection; may they show me the incommensurable, sound out for me the unsoundable, open the seals of heaven for me. I want to search the premises of the stars. Human constellations, your papers. Big Dipper, identify yourself. Capricorn, you're lying. Aquarius, you're lying; you're a suspicious character. Firmament, you're a suspect; I want to search your pockets; no more subterfuges. Lock all the doors; let no star escape! Handcuff God; I've got to question Him! And now, dark night, come before the court. And now, radiant day, answer. And now, accused suns, rise in your seats. I am president of the night-time court of the assizes; I have a jury of ghosts; the court is declared in session. Silence in the gallery of the stars!

Let the witness Galileo enter!

I enter, and I say: O you who live, do I know heaven? Have I traveled over its immensity, not having traveled over eternity? How can you expect me to tell you about the tenants and the borders of infinity when it is not tenantable and when it has no borders? No one has ever been privy to the confidences of that immense being who is the accused, namely, mystery itself. It has no intimate friends who can confide its nature to you; it alone knows its secret. Not a single star will speak up. The conspirators of shadows will all shut up, and the secret society of the stars will cover for God. Truth will swear no oaths, the absolute will not allow itself to be intimidated, and no examining magistrate will put paradise on the stand. No clerk of this court will draw up a list of constellations, no attorney will leaf through God's file, and no sentences will be pronounced before the crowd in this courtroom, such as: The suns are acquitted, the constellations are convicted, the Big Dipper is declared liquidated, the complaint against Jupiter is dropped, and Aldebaran will be released and allowed to recirculate in the skies. As for creation, we'll keep our eye on it, and immensity is sentenced to monitoring the elevated thoughts of mankind for a hundred million years.

I, Galileo, declare that I do not know the contents of infinity; I don't know where it begins and where it ends; I don't know what comes before, after, in the middle, to the right, to the left, east, west, south or north; I don't know its inside or its outside; I see heavenly bodies, heavenly bodies, heavenly bodies; I see stars, stars, stars; I see constellations, constellations, constellations; I see sunbeams mixed with cloud-bedecked splendors with great blazings-forth of flame, bedazzlement lost in contemplation, contemplation plunged in bedazzlement; I'm caught up in the prodigious turning of the golden-hubbed wheel of heaven. Where is it going? I have no idea.

Night is the beaten track of the stars. I look up at the night and all I see are millions of wheels of all the wagons of the conquering forces of the eternal, launched at top speed toward a goal that is invisible. I am an ignoramus of the unknown. I don't know the first heavenly body any better than I know the last. I defy you to find anybody who can say any more about the night than I can: It's a mine full of shadows with veins filled with stars; you can only hollow out a shadow with a shadow, just as you can only polish a diamond with a diamond; from time to time the quarry of black marble gives the sculptor a vision of what the completed statue will look like; and God, what heaven is like. That's it. The firmament is a colossal riddle to which there are million of keys; one star negates another, the heavenly bodies all deny and affirm each other, and no one knows if these millions of gold duckets that radiate out their light belong to the realms of negativity or to the realms of positivity.

Galileo stopped. The seance had ended, at 1:20 a.m.

What did Victor Hugo think of this session? He has left his reactions in a note among the transcripts. Here they are, slightly abridged:

I'm not going to insist anymore. It's becoming obvious to me, from what the table said this evening--and on several other occasions as well--that this world of the sublime, which has consented to communicate with our world of shadows, will not allow itself to be forced by us to reveal its secrets...

The world of the sublime wants to remain sublime. It doesn't want to reveal the exact details of its nature; or, at least, it wants that exactitude to consist only of a confused vision of enormousness shot through with prodigious bursts of light and shadow. The world of the sublime wants to be our vision, not our science....It does not want human reason, or the established facts of human science, to have anything to do with its definition. ....In a word, it wants man to remain in a state of doubt. Visibly, that is the law, and I am resigned to it.

But Hugo is greatly distressed that this towering earth genius, Galileo, *who fought bravely all his life to destroy illusion on earth, now takes the side of illusion! Galileo, who could have called himself Reality, takes the side of Appearances!...He practically ended up saying Yes and No, he who was brought to his knees by No, and who got up saying Yes!*

Obviously, he can't be wrong, and he knows what he's doing; and if he refuses to explain this position of his regarding appearance and reality, it must be because appearance and reality are a part of what the human eye sees, and man must continue to live in a state of Doubt.

Hugo is concerned at the extent to which the tables mix together clarity and unintelligibility. The more secrets they reveal, the more they seem to leave the seance-goers groping in the dark. He is frustrated because, *they reveal nothing except in their own time, and never in ours. There are moments when they thicken the clouds even while they suffuse them with splendors—but with the splendors of the lightning bolt rather than the [edifying] splendors of the sunbeam. Every time we begin to see a little more distinctly, this mysterious world closes up. It seems that we must be certain of nothing; it is in that that consists the expiation of our sins on the human plane.* Hugo ends up by declaring that, despite what appears to him to be the deliberate obscurantism of the tables, he still believes that the world of the sublime actually exists, and that the spirits of the Jersey island tables are its representatives.

This immense genius, Victor Hugo, may be, whatever his good will and towering intelligence, mistaken when he writes: *The world of the sublime wants to remain sublime. It doesn't want to reveal the exact details of its nature.* Hugo lived well before relativity theory; he came from a time when men and women still believed that, behind the transitory illusions of sensory perception, behind the confused and jumbled notions we all have of what really is—there really is a 'really is'! Hugo and his contemporaries still believed that, behind the everyday world of appearances, there was an objectively real and unchanging superstructure.

That is why there are certain places that the mind of Victor Hugo cannot go to (and the minds of his extremely bright companions at the turning table). It cannot go to the place that posits

a costume box in our minds from which other-dimensional entities must pluck earthly identity if they wish to speak to us. When
Galileo tells Hugo, **You can only hollow out a shadow with a
shadow, just as you can only polish a diamond with a diamond,**
the poet cannot connect that sentence with the 'simple' statement
with which Galileo had begun—namely, to paraphrase, that, **"you
can only talk about the world of the sublime in the language of
the world of the sublime--and the world of the sublime has no
language."**

It must have been that the spirits read Hugo's worried note.
At any rate, on Monday, Dec. 18, 1854, there appeared at the
seance the formidable if benign figure of the Shadow of the Sepulcher, whom the seance-goers were increasingly coming to regard
as a sort of "district manager"—the spirit who directed (and in
some mysterious way encompassed within himself) the comings
and goings of the other spirits.

Perhaps the Shadow of the Sepulcher had come to try to succeed where his lieutenant, Galileo, had failed.

Did he succeed?

Let's listen to his words:

**I've come to bring you, not one of the keys to heaven which
must remain closed to human science, but one of the keys to
God the whole power of whom is to fling open the gates to the
loftiest progress of which the human spirit is capable. The firmament is full of abrupt and somber doors; it's an eternal din of
brass hinges and splendid nails and flaming bars and luminous
pincers. But God has no door-bolts; his way of shutting himself
up is to exist without limits; his wall is the unlimited; his horizon is the impenetrable; you don't enter into him, because in
him everything is majestically free to move to the striding of its
own soul. You could take endless trips in his bottomless being;**

you could lose themselves in this God, in this Word, in that inextricable network of flashing roads, in that virgin forest of effulgence. God is the great wall and he who is above all accessible; he escapes into the inaccessible, and he gives himself to the accessible. He does not steal away, he does not isolate himself, he does not flee. He is all alone everywhere; millions of worlds compose this enormous, solitary being; crowds of creations make up this immense anchorite; the multitudes of the heavens constitute this prodigious cavern which he is; the throngs of heavenly bodies and the populations of suns are the soul and the unity of this tranquil monk who tosses over our world his rough homespun hair shirt of clouds. Universal liberty creates this incommensurable prisoner. God is in on this mystery in secret. God is the prison master moved to pity by every slave, but a slave himself. He is nothing but misery; he is nothing but pain; he is nothing but pity. God is the mighty tear of infinity. I come then to tell you God's thoughts regarding this firmament about which you want to know more. And so, first, I ask you: Why more, and not everything? Since you're asking anyway, why ask for so little? You're not very demanding! What difference does a crumb of the sky more or less make to you? What a mediocre appetite for infinity is that which asks for an additional portion of stars and which complains to its jailer about its ration of heavenly bodies! That's some mighty will you've got ! That' s a really awe-inspiring revolt! Some fear-inspiring riot!

Several golden apples more or less for dessert! Poor mankind. My, you really would have been proud of yourself if Galileo had revealed to you, instead of the miserable point of view of the earth, the miserable point of view of Jupiter, or the miserable point of view of Venus, or the miserable point of view of Saturn, or the miserable point of view of Mars! Is the mistake of Mercury the fruit that seduces you? O, Tantalus of the heavens! Is it

Helen's illusion you want? [Ed.: *Wishing to be awarded the golden apple (obtained by Mercury) as the most beautiful goddess of all, Aphrodite bribed Paris, the mortal judge, to choose her; in return, she helped him abduct Helen, thus causing the Trojan War. Helen's illusion was that of the existence on earth of ideal beauty. Tantalus was condemned to an eternity of being plagued with hunger and thirst while food and drink were kept just out of his reach.*] Do you want the optical point of view of Herschel? Do you want the mirage of the planet to your left instead of the will-o-the-wisp of the planet to your right? Do you desire, not the absolute, but a different relativity from your own, not the truth, but a different falsehood from your own, not the true meaning, but a different counter-meaning?

Are you fond of smoke, are you a fog gourmand, are you starved for shadow? You think you're asking for a bigger piece of reality, but you're asking for a bigger pile of lies; you want a greater variety of cloud, but not the full light of day. You want to be able to make a bundle of light out of a heap of shadows; and, finding that your world doesn't see into heaven clearly enough, you complain at not having been notified of three or four more planets, and you write self-pityingly: If only I were blind enough not to know how much more there is to know! Whereupon, like petulant street urchins, you throw rocks at the streetlights of God.

You know what I would do if I were in your place? I'd ask for all or nothing; I'd insist on immensity; I'd read the riot act to infinity, I'd raise my barricade to the top floor of the sky, I'd finish the revolution, I'd want to know everything, hold everything, take everything; I wouldn't let the sky off the hook about Paradise; I wouldn't let it hide Hell from me; I'd even put myself in the abyss; I'd make my brain the engulfer of God; I'd give myself a formidable mouthful of infinity: I'd be an immense and terrible Gargantua [giant in book by Rabelais] of stars, a colossal Polyphemus [one-eyed giant in the *Odyssey*] of constellations, of whirlwinds, of thunders; I'd drink the milk-basin of the Milky Way; I'd swallow comets; I'd lunch on dawn; I'd dine on day, and I'd sup on night; I'd invite myself, splendid table-companion that I am, to the banquet of all the glories, and I'd salute God as: My host! I'd work up a magnificent hunger, an enormous thirst, and I'd race through the drunken spaces between the spheres singing the fearsome drinking song of eternity, joyous, radiant, sublime, hands full of bunches of grapes made of stars and my face purple with suns! I wouldn't leave a star unturned, and at the end of the banquet, I'd pass out beneath the table of the heavens radiant with light!

But you, you're more modest: You ask the world for alms, you merely beg from God, you stretch out your hand as you say to him: a little star, please! I'm getting to the question that preoccupies you. Your scientists are going to laugh, you tell me, at our astronomy; they'll holler: What is the meaning of these constellations which have no meaning? They're taking our optical illusions seriously! There doesn't have to be any connection between the stars we've used to make up the grouping of the Big Dipper, the grouping of Capricorn, and so, and so. There are incalculable distances between these worlds whose roles you mix together in the sky! You impute common actions to stars that the stars are not aware of! You joke about grouping together stars that are millions of leagues apart and which have never spoken together. Some gag, that! Is the sky the hand of a juggler upon which heavenly bodies leap about and perform tour de forces? Is your astronomy a conjurers' table on which gifted enough magicians can make distances do away? No constellations, no sky, no God....

O, scientists, beyond your calculations there is unity. Unity is the total of God. There is no figure one thousand, there is no figure one hundred, there is no figure ten, there is no figure two; God only counts to one. The sky is one immense constellation. There are not even two groupings of heavenly bodies; there is only one. There are not millions of leagues; there are not millions of feet, there are no distances under the sky; there is only nearness, there is only one family, there is only one people, and there is only one world.

All these little constellations are false groupings relatively speaking and true groupings absolutely speaking; the Big Dipper and Aquarius and Orion are couplings tailor-made for seeing and which don't disturb the celestial harmony; all these heavenly bodies see each other, and know each other, and attract each other, and love each other; they seek out each another and they find each other; they understand each other and they enliven each other; among them there are those who communicate between themselves; there are those who marry, who beget children, and who are entombed; there are no solitary heavenly bodies, there are no orphaned heavenly bodies, there are no widowed stars, there are no lost suns; there is not a single corner of the night that is in mourning; there is not a single day that is abandoned; there is not a single sphere that is not all by itself the hub of the heavens! the entire vault of the sky is filled with a single heavenly body that is always in the process of expanding; all the other heavenly bodies are merely the seeds of this heavenly body-flower. An immense need for devotion, that is the law of the worlds; night is a democracy of stars; the firmament is a symbolic republic that mixes together heavenly bodies of every rank and makes manifest brotherhood and sisterhood by ...

Victor Hugo interrupted: "I said: *The future is the hymen of men on earth/ And of the stars in the heavens.*"

...by divine effulgence. The heavenly-body palace helps the

heavenly-body workshop, the heavenly-body workshop helps the heavenly-body garret, the heavenly-body garret helps the heavenly-body cellar, the heavenly-body cellar helps the heavenly-body prison; the infinitely small is the younger brother of the infinitely great; a genius star an idiot star; Hercules-suns are always close to cradle-suns; the faces of happy worlds are forever peering about at the side of unhappy worlds; punitary stars are always weeping at the side of stars of reward; stars of reward are always smiling at the side of punitary stars. Consolation is the form reward takes. There is always a heavenly-body dove close to a heavenly-body tomb. There is always a sun that is dressing wounds close to a sun that is bleeding. Immensity is the love song of eternity. Love, love: You are the supreme solution, you are the final figure, you are God's billion and the prodigious sum formed by every dazzling zero in the starry firmament. You are the supreme calculation, the treasure of the sepulcher, the heritage of the dead. You are packed full with resurrection, and you turn the celestial wine-vaults into places of splendid celebration.

The table stopped tapping. The seance, which had begun at 1:30 p.m., had gone on till 7:00 p.m.

Was Victor Hugo mollified?

On Dec. 19, 1854, he wrote the following note, which was preserved in the transcripts:

I persist in making no objection. All this is enormous. Still, I don't confuse enormousness with immensity. God alone is immense. It seems to me that what was personally addressed to me confirms my earlier note. The great Biblical reproaches are there, but under a different form: According to the lights of my conscience, I do not believe that I have merited them.

As far as all the rest of it is concerned: I do not believe that I am mistaken in my thinking; but I do not believe the world of the sublime, which speaks such magnificent language to us, is mistaken either. It does as it must with respect to us: It leaves us doubting. The table ended up practically jeering at me: It asked me, What difference does a crumb of infinity more or less matter to you? I will insist no further. I believe in my heart that I am right; but I bow my head silently before the sublime being who spoke to me yesterday, and who ended with such lofty, and such gentle, words.

Victor Hugo

Chapter Nineteen

JOSHUA ON
QUANTUM HOLOGRAPHY

To know in our hearts, to understand beyond understanding, that all of the parts of the universe are dynamically and lovingly interconnected, that they are all in the same place and are all the same thing, is to have powers that are Godlike. This is the message that Joshua, the Israelite warrior who leveled the walls of Jericho with trumpet blasts and forced the sun to stop in its tracks, brought to Victor Hugo and his friends in two turning table sessions on December 28 and 29, 1854.

It is startling to realize just how appropriate it was that Joshua should have been the one to deliver these power-bestowing words. He is one of the few humans we know of in all of history who has connected with a gleaming star (our sun) and made it stop in its tracks, this being necessarily in accordance with God's purposes, and which significantly improved the fortunes of these ancient Israelite representatives of our punitary world.

Moreover, Joshua must have connected with the souls of the stones that made up the walls of Jericho. That must have been how, using sound in a way we cannot yet comprehend, he persuaded these sentient creatures of the world of stone to give way, and we can only suppose that they, too, rejoiced at the outcome, since they—like the sun—were carrying out God's will.

How was it that Joshua was able to accomplish these colossal tasks? He had an intimate knowledge of the (we had supposed) late twentieth concepts of nonlocality and quantum holography, and was able to use this knowledge to manipulate the physical world.

Such were the amazing truths which seemed to emerge from this watershed turning table session, which began at 9:30 p.m., and at which Victor Hugo was present with Mme. Hugo and Charles holding the table.

The table was a brand-new one, borrowed from the Allixes; the regular table had become permanently twisted out of shape by the movements of the spirits.

Joshua announced himself, and began:

Man is not a simple I. He is a complex I.

In his epidermis, there are millions of beings who are millions of souls. In his flesh, there are millions of beings who are millions of souls. In his bones, there are millions of beings who are millions of souls. In his blood, there are millions of beings who are millions of souls. In his hair, there are millions of beings who are millions of souls. In his nails, there are millions of beings who are millions of souls. Each breath exhaled from his mouth is a whiff of souls; each glance from his eyes is a radiating outward of souls.

The biggest nest of all is in the brain. There, every fiber is a soul that thinks; an idea takes shape only on account of the slow and painful work of every prisoner soul laboring beneath the vault of the human skull. A brain is a solitary confinement cell; an idea is an escape from that cell. All the limbs of a man's body are prison corridors. His head is a solitary confinement cell. Man is a prisoner who also serves as a prison. Man is an immense I filled with imperceptible I's; he is a world unto himself.

He is a hell to the tips of his nails and a hell to the roots of his hairs; his veins are rivers filled with drowned bodies; his bones are hitching posts hung with horses' collars; his hairs are the cords of an invisible whip with whose grim throngs the wind lashes the convicts imprisoned in his skull.

Man is filled with criminals about to be executed; he is the instrument of those executions even as he is the one about to be excuted. He is both hanged man and noose, both crucified and the cross.

He is a man who is drawn and quartered, whose four limbs draw and quarter the world, and whose arms and legs are as many furious horses bearing bleeding souls away into the unknown. Man arises in the evening, in the world of shadows, and all nature looks upon him with great dread; heaven says, it is Christ; earth says, it is Calvary. Man carries on his head a gigantic crow which is eternally in flight and whose huge wing he only glimpses at night. Muse on this abyss:

Man is an I peopled with I's who do not know him and whom he does not know. Each I in its turn is full of other I's, and so on to infinity. The I of the man lives in complete wholeness, and each I interior to the man is equally completely whole. Man knows nothing of his being. He cannot know what lives, dies and is born within him. Man is but the principal soul of the human body; there are within him the souls of other men, animal souls, plant souls, souls of stones. There is more: There are the souls of stars. Man is the world; man is the sky; man is the infinite; man is eternal; man is the seed of creation tossed to the four winds and scudding through the great gulfs of God.

An immense atom, the slightest I contains a complete pattern of all the I's. The beast contains all the I's of man. The plant contains all the I's of the beast. The pebble contains all the I's of the plant. The globe contains all the I's of man, of beast and of plant. The globe contains all the I's of man, of beast, of plant and of pebble. The sky contains all the I's of all the globes. God contains all the I's of all the heavens; but this is only the very beginning of the horizons.

You'll see; you'll see; you'll see. O, all-powerfulness of God! He has made of the world something which cannot be lost; he has placed the seed of every being in each being; he has made every fruit the pit, and every pit the fruit; he has enclosed man in the beast and the beast in man, plant in pebble and pebble in plant; he has put the star in the sky and the sky in the star, and he has placed himself in everything and everything in himself, in such a way that if one day it were to happen that a whirlwind, a flood, or a hurricane destroyed men, beasts, plants and stones; if it were to happen that a comet devoured the stars and, annihilating itself, left nothing more of creation than a single grain of sand, God would smile and, taking that grain of sand in his hands, toss it up into space while crying out: 'Emerge, millions of worlds!'

Joshua had brought the first part of his discourse to a close. To us, what he said sounds astonishingly close to a description of the new, emerging modern-day concept of a holographic universe. Here is a little of what Michael Talbot has to say on the subject in *The Holographic Universe*.

"Unlike normal photographs, every small fragment of a piece of holographic film contains all the information recorded in the whole....This was precisely the feature that got [neurophysiologist Karl] Pribram so excited...it seemed equally possible for every part of the brain to contain all the information necessary to recall a whole memory..."

"As soon as physicist [David] Bohm began to reflect on the hologram he saw that it...provided a new way of undrstanding order. Like the ink drop in its dispersed state, the interference patterns recorded on a piece of holographic film also appear disordered to the naked eye. Both possess orders that are hidden or enfolded....The more Bohm thought about it, the more he became convinced that the universe actually employed holographic principles in its operations, was itself a kind of giant, flowing hologram..."

Every part of the universe was contained in every other part! And the whole was contained in each of those parts! ...Could Joshua really have been talking about something like quantum holography? The next night, this entity returned to the turning table. It was Friday, Dec. 29, 10:15 p.m. In attendance were Mlle. Augustine Allix, Jules Allix, Auguste Vacquerie and Victor Hugo, with Mme. Victor Hugo and Charles Hugo seated at the table.

After two minutes or so, the table began to shake. Joshua made his presence known. "Do you want to continue from yesterday, or should be ask you questions?" asked Victor Hugo.

Some questions.

"People attribute to you the impossible miracle of making the sun stand still in the sky," said Hugo. "How should we take this? What do you yourself have to say on the subject?"

We come here not so much to verify facts as to illuminate ideas; however, since you, a man of ideas, are asking me about this fact, I'm going to answer you. The sun is the life of nature; night is its death. The day is a being who lives for twelve hours and who drags behind himself a corpse who is dead for twelve hours. Eliminate night, and you will have a being who is alive for twenty-four hours. I have been prophet, I have been light, and I have eliminated night. I've been the idea of sun who stops its beams from shining upon suffering. I said to my soul, you shall not go farther; I stopped the star upon worm, upon caterpillar, upon rags, upon wounds; I made the clock cease ticking,

light's hour upon the middle of night's clock-face; I stopped noon upon midnight.

How had Joshua stopped the sun? He seems to be saying that he understood that God has put the sun within himself, Joshua, and himself, Joshua, within the sun; the Israelite seems to have made contact with the sun in himself and ordered it to stop: **I said to my soul, you shall not go farther.** He seems also to have "told"--as if telling a rosary, or a mantra-- all the other aspects of the universe which he knows are in himself (and which he knows that he is in)--**the worm, the caterpillar, the rag, the wound**--and made it clear that it is also on their account that the sun must stop.

These bewildering statements were to become clearer when Joshua continued his disquisition. He would introduce the concept of "eliminating" things.

But they seemed now not to be clear--or even interesting--to Victor Hugo. He suddenly changed the subject, asking Joshua if he were the same spirit who had come to them one year earlier and predicted the downfall of Napoleon III for 1855.

You're wasting time asking me if I know Bonaparte. From the way you speak of him, Bonaparte is a bad fellow. Bad people do not come within my vision. I read words, not erasures.

Let's talk about the stars. Man will find everything, he will eliminate everything and the distances of God from himself. There is nothing but distance. Night is only distance from day, evil distance from good, pain distance from happiness, earth distance from sky. Man has already eliminated the distance of man from man with democracy, the distance of country from country with the railway, the distance of pain from well-being with chloroform, the distance of shadow from daylight with electricity, the distance of life from death with science, the distance of air from earth with the balloon, the distance of sea from earth

with the steamboat, the distance of fire from coal with the Volta pile [the battery], the distance of pearl from woman with the diving-bell, the distance of stone from house with the miner, the distance of iron from tool with the blacksmith, the distance of lead [used to create type] from idea with the printing house, the distance of gold from falsehood with paper money, the distance of cradle from grave with the mother, the distance of grave from cradle with the father, the distance of man from beast with the dog, the distance of beast from plant with the garden, the distance of plant from stone with the swallow's nest and the scarlet pimpernel tossed in the cage hanging on the old wall, and the orchard's wall, the distance of seed from wheat field by the sower, the distance of winter from spring by the ploughman, the distance of spring from summer by the farmer, the distance of summer from autumn by the harvester, the distance of autumn from winter by the grape-gatherer, the distance of snow from heat by the radiator, the distance of matter from idea by art, the distance of plastic beauty from moral splendor by the Parthenon, the distance of pain from the crown of thorns by the Calvary... [Ed.: *There follows a series of nine examples which are fairly obscure to anyone but a lover of Classical literature and history*], the distance of yes from no by perhaps, the distance of strength from love by the promise kept, the distance of two arms from the cross by the two arms of Jesus Christ, the distance of two arms from Jesus Christ by the knees of Mary Magdalene, the distance of immensity from eternity by prayer, the distance of the thunderbolt from the abyss by the lightning bolt captured by the lightning rod, the distance of Nero from the gladiator by the martyr, the distance of mystery from doubt by faith, the distance of faith from mystery by doubt, the distance of the infinitely small from the infinitely large by the eternally fallen on his knees.

He has eliminated every distance at hand's length, at feet's length, and at eyes' length; and he wants to stop there! and he doesn't want to be able to leap the distance from one star to another! And he wants to be attached to his globe forever—like an animal attached to its collar! and he does not want to be able to look at the sky in any other way than attached to his leash and he wants to be restricted solely to that nightly glance! And he wants to be the center of the universe! and he wants to put his stamp on the darkness! And he wants to bark at the stars! And he doesn't want to take a bite out of the starry worlds! Where are you, the one million leagues that can stop mankind? Let's see your empty zeros, absurd number; insane fetters, let's see your links. You are only darkness, you millions of leagues, and man is a torch with all the boldness of a torch. Watch out, heavenly distances: Man hungers for the stars, man is the great voyager, man is the great eater of impossibilities, man is the mighty igniter of realities; if you don't want him to do these things, he will force you to accept him; he will take you, abysses, in the hollow of his hand; he will boot you out, night-mastiff; he will pile you up, cloud-firewood, fog-wine shoots, obscurity-coals, and he will set fire to this darkness with the colossal spark of his spirit, and the stars themselves will cry out: Let's go watch the fire!

This discussion may seem repetitive, even tedious. To this commentator it seems to be no less than a description of nonlocality. Nonlocality posits that everything in the universe can be equipresent at every point in the universe. Thus it is possible, not to go faster than light, but to act as if the speed of light did not exist.

Once you enter the realm of nonlocality, you effectively eliminate all distances. In actual fact, it would seem that effectively there are no distances; there is only nonlocality.

Here is what Michael Talbot, in *The Holographic Universe*, says on the subject of nonlocality:

"An even more surprising feature of the quantum potential was its implications for the nature of location. At the level of our everyday lives things have very specific locations, but [physicist David] Bohm's interpretation of quantum physics indicated that at the subatomic level, the level in which the quantum potential operated, location ceased to exist. All points in space became equal to all other points in space, and it was meaningless to speak of anything as being separate from anything else. Physicists call this property 'locality.'"

Former moonwalking astronaut Dr. Edgar Mitchell, who is currently researching the concept of nonlocality, echoed Talbot's words in an interview in *Kindred Spirit* Quarterly, for June-August, 1997:

*KS: In your book **The Way of the Explorer**, you allude to an experiment carried out by Alain Aspect in Paris in 1982 as the 'missing link' between the older, dualist view of mind and body as separate and distinct—the view that has God separate from physical reality and making all our decisions for us—and the newer view, espoused by yourself, of the mental and the physical as two aspects of a single reality. Would you explain?*

EM: To my mind, Aspect proved the existence of nonlocality. He and his colleagues produced a series of twin photons. They enabled the photons to travel in opposite directions through a conduit that aimed them at one of two polarization analyzers. They saw that each photon was still able to correlate its angle of polarization with that of its twin. Since nothing can travel faster than light, then it wasn't a case of information being transferred from one particle to the other; rather, the wave aspects of the particles were in some way interconnected nonlocally and 'resonated' so as to maintain the correlation of their characteristics. They didn't behave as particles at all but like fields, filling all space, orchestrated and mediated in their properties by a mechanism not yet understood.

KS: Is nonlocality the explanation for the ability of psychics occasionally to 'apport,' or transfer objects psychokinetically, over sometimes very great distances?

EM: There are a number of sharply conflicting explanations of what nonlocality means, and so it is very difficult to answer that question; but I do believe that the notion of nonlocality was involved. We must look at the concept of quantum holography as well as nonlocality to have a good explanation of how these psychic events work. Holography, of course, refers to the indications we have from the structure of nature—for example, the brain's memory-storing capabilities—that every part contains the whole. In the past year-and-a-half, research I've been conducting with European scientists in quantum holography has succeeded in taking the idea of nonlocality out of the subatomic realm and showing that it pertains across the whole spectrum, scale-size, from the subatomic to the cosmic. The universe is a hologram, with each part containing the whole; the mathematics we've done suggests that nonlocality pertains across all scale sizes.

Not only is the whole contained in the parts throughout the universe, but everything is everywhere at once. The concept of locality suggests that we could immediately be anywhere in the universe we wanted, if could just manage to make "distance" disappear.

This seems to be what Joshua is saying. It can hardly have been easy for him to say this. If even today we find it difficult to scrape together the concepts and images needed to express the idea of nonlocality, imagine how difficult it would have been 150 years ago! Able to draw on arguably some of the best minds of the time, gathered in exile around the tiny table on Jersey island, the spirit of Joshua—if we may presume for the sake of argument that that was who this was—is forced to resort to a seemingly interminable litany of examples of eliminating distance to bring two terms infinitely closer together. Presumably, he could have gone on forever. In fact, that was probably the only way he could have made his point. He needed to somehow suggest to the seance-goers that every instance of separation by distance in the universe can somehow be eliminated—that, in fact, everything is potentially in the same place.

Seen in this context, the final portion of Joshua's second and last discourse seems to be a mad, glorious, incredible rallying-cry to humanity. Joshua is striving to make us understand that there is no distance in the universe that cannot be bridged—that is, eliminated—and that the stars themselves await mankind if only we want badly enough to attain to them. And this want, he says, is profoundly a part of the fiery spirit of humankind.

Chapter Twenty

FOUR RELIGIONS OF MANKIND: MOHAMMED ON ISLAM; CHRIST ON DRUIDISM, CHRISTIANITY AND REVOLUTION

A series of seminars on religion, given by the spirits to the Jersey island seance-goers—and with the best teachers imaginable!—began in earnest on (probably) Dec. 26, 1853, at 5:00 p.m., when no less than Mohammed coming to the turning tables to hold forth on the nature of Islam.

This was one day before Balaam's Ass was to reveal to Hugo and Company that our universe is merely a prison for mankind. We shouldn't be surprised to learn, then, that Mohammed—or this spirit representing Mohammed, or this confluence of energies somehow resonating the religious consciousness of mankind—also represented his religion, and indeed all religions, as prisons of the souls, and as excuses for acts of cruelty.

Present at the seance were Victor Hugo, Mlle. Adèle Hugo and Auguste Vacquerie. Mme. Hugo and Charles held the table.

"Who's there?" Vacquerie had asked.

Mohammed.

"Speak," requested Vacquerie.

Shadows still cover the earth. Martyred truth bleeds error from the nails that fix it to the cross. It is profoundest night. Despots say: We are the right. Priests say: We are the law. The

gibbet replies: Yes. The scaffold replies: Yes. The grave replies: No. The lugubrious hosanna of evil resounds in the song of owls beneath the starry heavens. Crows come to peck out the last glance of love from the dying eyes of Jesus. The double silhouette of gallows and scaffold rises up on the dark horizon, and we glimpse, standing off in the shadows, religion officiating at these executions in the name of the cross. Day approaches; morning is nigh. The clouds riding high in the sky, roused to indignation by what they see, are going to open their mouths and launch a flaming star, a light formidable as grape-shot, at this world of shadows. The priest-gibbet and the priest-scaffold will be overthrown. The bastions of shadow will fall, the earth will tremble beneath those who now stand on it, and heaven will open to those who are on their knees.

Auguste Vacquerie commented: "Even as we speak, three religions are fighting for supremacy in the East; talk to us about these religions and their future."

Catholicism is the rampart against the night. Ancient Greek religion is now a fortress covered with snow. The religion of Mohammed is the wall of the flesh. None of them ought to last. The Pope says to man: you are not to see; the czar: you are to suffer; the sultan: you are to enjoy. All three are mistaken. I tell you that the collapse of all the priesthoods has begun. The priest of the knout, the priest of the cross, and the priest of the crescent are three corpses which will be carried off the battlefield. The saint is no more right before God than the houri, and God no more wants a religion that brutalizes man with asceticism than he wants a religion that lulls him to sleep with voluptuousness. Let's go, my son. We must die. I gave you my standard so that you could conquer. I leave it to you to bury yourself in.

The student of comparative channeling might want to compare what the channeled Mohammed of Victor Hugo's group had to say in 1853 with some of what the channeled Mohammed of James Merrill had to say in the late 1970's and early 1980's.

Moh.:
O GOD, O ALLAH BEN ALLAH! LORDS, MEN, WOMEN!
HERE I AM, JUST AS YOU SEE ME, A SIMPLE MAN...
NEITHER ALL MEEK LIKE MY PROPHET BROTHER JESU
WHO HAD NO USE FOR WOMEN, NOR BRAINFILLED
    LIKE MY
PRINCELY BROTHER--WHAT MAN COMPLAINS OF A
    WHORE? BAH!
NO, JUST AS YOU SEE ME. AND BELIEVE ME, MASTER
    GOD,
JUST AS SURPRISED AS ANY MAN WHEN MY VISION
    CAME.
ME? ME TO SAY ALL THAT! WHY, I COULD NOT READ,
HONORABLE SCRIBES, IMAGINE! WELL, I WENT OUT,
SPOKE! IT WAS EASY! JESUS, YOU SEE, HAD A
    DIFFERENT
WORLD TO TRY TO WIN OVER TO LOVE AND MERCY...

It was not till over a year later, on Sunday, Feb. 11, 1855, at 9:30 p.m., that Jesus Christ appeared through the turning table to speak at length about the similarities and differences between Druidism, Christianity and Revolution—in this case, the French Revolution. Christ had dropped by twice before, but only to deliver one sentence on September 15, 1853, **Christ announces the resurrection**, and two on February 27, 1854, **I have the key [to freedom from imprisonment]**, and then, in response to the request of

Judas (also present at the table) to give Judas that key: **There it is, Judas.**

Attending the seance the night of Feb. 11, 1855, were Mme. Augustine Allix, Jules Allix, François-Victor Hugo and Auguste Vacquerie. Mme. Victor Hugo and Charles Hugo sat at the table.

After a brief exchange of civilities, followed by some speculation by Vacquerie about whether all religions complimented and extended one another, 'Christ'—or whatever confluence of energies was now here represented—launched into a disquisition on comparative religion that unfailingly emphasized the cruelty and prison-house nature of every religion. Here is what 'Christ' said:

Druidism is the first of mankind's religions and the first explosion of the soul into the body. The Druids radiate the soul out across the debris of bloody matter. They break the body with blows from heaven. They assassinate mankind with blows from God. They kill the child with blows of prayer. They crush old men with blows of the grave. They turn the splendor of the soul into the liberator of everything and the murderer of everything. The soul of druidism is an angel with hatchet-shaped wings. Druidism fills forest, stream, beast, stone, with flecks of blood that reflect the stars. It spreads eternity with wounds and immortality with packed sepulchers. It tears suns from the body of mankind by using torture. It submits the body to the rack of infinity, it tears its flesh with pincers made of the two sides of the firmament, it pours melted sunbeams into its veins, it draws and quarters it with the four winds, it beheads it with the golden cutting-edge of the moon, and its throws its head into the charnel-house of enormous darkness. Druidism is the soul's crime against mankind. It is eternity, immensity, heaven, stars, lightning, thunder, bandits.

Each time Christianity goes up one degree on earth its goes

down one in heaven. It teaches love in the name of charity and hatred in the name of hell. Man is everything; animal, plant, stone, nothing. It says: Immortal soul and eternal punishment. It heals the sick and tortures the guilty. It gives human sacrifice a place in the firmament, questioning a place in the tomb, physical suffering a place in the immaterial world, and it turns the stars into infamous firebrands of a funeral-pyre made of darkness.

Pardon me, my God, but Christianity takes revenge, Christianity bears away, Christianity punishes unremittingly. Christianity dies on the cross and tortures in the lofty heights of the sky. It turns night into death's somber will. It talks gloom to the sin, matter to the soul. It is the fall into the body and not the flight of the soul. Druidism pleads with the living body, Christianity martyrs the corpse. Christianity wants heaven in flames, druidism wants the earth soaked in blood. Christianity is, like all things human, progress and evil. It is the door of light that is locked with night. The key is in front of the door; the passerby opens the door and thinks he is in the presence of God; but the passerby is mistaken. God is the one who's not there. God is He who is eternally in flight.

One week later—on Sunday, Feb. 18, 1855, 9:45 p.m.— Christ returned to pick up the same theme. Present at the seance were Mme. Augustine Allix, Jules Allix and Auguste Vacquerie. At the table were Mme. Victor Hugo and Charles Hugo.

The table was silent for ten minutes. Then it began to move. Jesus Christ having announced his presence, Victor Hugo asked him to proceed.

Christianity is the body happy on earth but tortured on high. Christianity is the soul happy on earth but pleaded with on high;

the essence of druidism is human sacrifice, while the essence of Christianity is divine sacrifice.

Christianity is composed of two things: love and hate. It makes mankind better and God worse. It possesses a cradle full of kisses and a tomb full of wounds; it cures the living and burns the dead; it blesses the adulteress and burns her corpse; it resurrects Lazarus and burns his ashes; the lips of Christianity are honey and its tongue is fire; it begins with a sunbeam and ends with flames; it makes an eden of earth and a hell of heaven; it makes charming flowers and horrendous stars; it illuminates woman and it sets fire to Venus, it makes dawn white-hot, day white-hot and the sunset white-hot; it is the great savior and the great executioner; it is the glance that weeps over the earth and the glance that rises in flames to heaven; it is the sublime weeper and the formidable avenger; it dresses the wounds of life and opens the wounds of eternity; it inserts softness into matter and terror into idealism; it pours balm on man and boiling oil on suns.

Druidism made hell on earth, Christianity makes it in heaven; druidism takes iron, stone, lead, brass and tortures the living soul with the material; Christianity tortures the resurrected body with the ethereal; it uses as its tools the lily of the ether and the roses of the sky; it gives the dawn the fingers of a tormenter; it suffocates the dead beneath the pillow of the tomb; its hell has millions of furnaces, millions of fires of live coals, millions of funeral-pyres; it goes from north to noon and immensity to eternity; it swirls up dust, it flashes, it lightnings, it exhausts birds as it crushes souls; it has the Milky Way as underground passage, the Southern Cross as crossroads, Saturn as muddy hole in the road, Mars as precipice, anger as inn, and in the inn's hearth eternal flames for fireplace. Druidism looks at forests, hills, plains, and says to them: let us torture.

Druidism hides its victims in the dens of animals. Christianity exposes them to infinity; Druidism hides itself in the woods, Christianity hovers in space; Druidism lives beneath the ever-somber oak; Christianity resurrects pain beneath the ever-radiant blue of the sky: Druidism makes tree branches bristle with horror; Christianity makes the beams of heavenly bodies shiver with fright; the dolmens of the druids are drenched in blood; the autos-da-fee of the Christians are drenched in sulphur; Islam sees God only in the purple of blood. Jesus Christ sees God only in the purple of fire; religions are great hammer-blows delivered to mankind's skull, each spark putting out a star and lighting up a hell.

A week later—Thursday, March 8, 1855, 9:45 p.m.—Jesus returned once again. Again, Mme. Allix, Jules Allix and Victor Hugo were present; Mme. Victor Hugo and Charles Hugo were at the table.

Jesus Christ announced himself. The table began to tap out a strange warm-up:

Pure or impure. Even or odd. Passage or impasse. Clean or unclear. Pious or impious. Foreseen or unforeseen. Pitying or unpitying. Vile or worldly. As immense or as small as a cup. Eye or coffin. Rich or fallow. Desert or dessert. Middle or place. Place or God. God or fire. Fire or blue. [Ed.: *In French, this passage contains a great deal of rhyming and punning.*]

Victor Hugo commented: "This is a profound depiction of mankind, of all flesh-spirit—of myself. It's true, and it's strange. Continue."

I'm continuing. The Gospel had this about it that was tremendous: that it made men brothers, woman woman's sister, and every child a twin. It put forth mighty words:

Love one another. Do not do unto others as you would not have done unto yourself. Love your neighbor as yourself. A prophet is not without honor except in his own country and in his own house. The first shall be last. Suffer the little children to come unto me. Let he who is without sin cast the first stone. Verily I say unto you, that one among you will betray me. Eat and drink: This is my flesh, this is my blood. And this mighty cry that will issue through all eternity from exalted mouths confronting the savage sky: *Eli, Eli, Lamma Sabactani. [My God, my God, why hast Thou forsaken me.]*

The Gospel took man out of the shadows and elevated him to the heights. It chased the money-lenders out of the temple and re-established weights made of stars in the scales of the divine. It wrung out rags and made pity fall from them in huge drops. It turned a deaf-mute God into a living God, who heard and spoke. It brought back sight to suns struck blind by two thousand years of darkness. It remade man, and it made woman. It had a mother's compassion, a father's compassion and a child's compassion. Its eye was the first to gaze at the mother above the breast. It wept the largest tear that ever nourished child at mother's breast. It drained the largest cup of sorrow that ever mounted through a trunk of pain [Ed.: *A reference to poisons extracted from trees.*]. Finally, with hammer-like blows it cracked the formidable mystery of nature; and, standing on Golgotha, bleeding, sublime, forced the four winds of the night to overlook the four gaping wounds of love crucified in the immensity. The Gospel made the tomb a merciful thing for repentance, but— and here is its error—it made it a merciless thing for the wicked.

The great concern of religion should be not so much the just as the unjust, not so much the good man as the wicked, not so much the repentant as the remorseful. The monsters of mankind are love's true flock. It is not a matter of giving love to lambs, but of making tigers love. The upper lip of heaven is posed not on the sheepfold but on the jungle, on the animal's lair, of the animal on desert, on mane, on jaw, on the roaring of beasts; even Heliogabalus's nostril sniffs at the breast of God [Ed.: *Heliogabalus (204 A.D.-222 A.D.) became Emperor of Rome in 218. His reign was notable for its debauchery]*; even Phalaris's muzzle moos in the stable of God [Ed.: *Phalaris, d. 554 BC, was tyrant of Acragas, in Sicily. Some accounts depict him as a cruel tyrant who had his enemies roasted alive in a bronze bull.*] ; Caligula's nostrils whinny at the Lord, Domitian's fins swim in the waters of the Lord [Ed.: *Domitian (51 A.D.- 96 A.D.) became emperor of Rome in 81 A.D. Initiating a reign of terror in 89 A.D., he was eventually murdered by assassins in the pay of his wife, Domitilla.*], Cleopatra's asp bites the Great Pastor's heel, Judas's kiss licks the star-studded darkness.

True religion is an immense taming of wild beasts and not an immense funeral-pyre of lion skins; it is an enormous tenderness for ferocious beings, for foul deeds, for sufferers deformed by their own bestiality, for the hated of the earth, for the cursed of this life.

It loves the despised, it rescues the lost, it gilds brass pillars. It pitied steel bars that were really reeds, muddy souls that were really chasms, bloody mouths that were really wounds. It peers into the depths of the horrible, and laughs at those who grind their teeth, and speaks to those who are deaf, and listens to those who are dumb, and show itself to those who are blind. It says to monster mankind: Rise up unto death, which rises up to God. Grow with all your body. It says to animals: animals, rise up unto death-- which rises up to mankind. Grow with all your body.

It says to plants: Plants, rise up unto death, which rises up to animals. Grow with all your fall. It says to stones: stones, rise up unto death, which rises up to the plants. Grow with all your dust. It cries out: Rottenness, excrement, vileness: sow, flower, radiate! Monstrosities, deformities, terrors: blaze into resplendent power!

The infinite is the infinite only because it is merciful. If you could lose yourself in God, you would find yourself again by orienting yourself to the rising of His eternal smile. The firmament is limited on the north by goodness, on the south by charity, on the east by love, and on the west by pity. God is the great urn of perfumes out of which the feet of created beings are washed eternally; it pours forth forgiveness from all its pores; it exhausts itself in loving; it labours at absolution. The Gospel of the past said: The damned. That of the the future will say: The forgiven.

After another week—on March 15, 1855, at 9:30 p.m.—Christ was back once more, returning to the theme of a comparison between Druidism and Christianity. Victor Hugo was present; Mme. Victor Hugo and Charles Hugo were at the table.

Hugo asked the distinguished spirit to, "continue with the great things that you have told us."

Druidism had said: Believe. Christianity had said: believe. Their words had brought generations to their knees; but one day, all of a sudden, in the temple, someone unknown entered dressed in rags, hair standing on end, feet bare, hands blackened, forehead held high, and holding the formidable traveling staff of the future; it was the beggar human Spirit; it was the traveler of twilights; it was the stroller in shadows; it was the walker of chasms; it was the shepherd of lions; it was the shepherd of tigers; it was the seer of the lair; it was the wise, the brave, the crosser of millions of leagues of immensity; it was the being who doesn't believe, but who thinks; it was God's great questioner...

Victor Hugo interrupted: "I composed verses:
The prophet and the poet
Choose being over nothingness;
The earth listens, worried, to
This archangel and this giant;
The foul-mouthed crowd,
A heap of wolves and dogs
That prowl beneath the sky,
This black, nay-saying bunch
Barks at the heels of genius,
Genius, that questioner of God."

...speaker of negations of the truth, questioner, rebel, combatant; it was the injured of the celestial barricade, the radiant and the bloody, the sublime bearer of the wounds of doubt and the scars of idea. He had several names: his forehead was called Moses; his expression Socrates, his mouth Luther, his wounds Galileo and his scars Voltaire. He came out of four deserts, that of Aeschylus, that of Dante, that of Shakespeare and that of Molière; and in his torn sandals were the thorns of every Calvary and the pebbles of every prophet who had ever been exiled to the desert; his gestures were such as to frighten marble columns, and the spreading-out of his mantle was such as to shake the skirts of clouds. He was the vagrant of thundering voice and blazing eyes. You would have taken him for the lightning en route to Sodom. He entered crying: "On your feet, you on your knees! You're wasting your time here. Get moving, you who've halted! The world is just beginning. Get to work, you who're relaxing! Faith is aleep, freedom is the wake-up call. I am the dawn; wake up, sepulchers. Wake up, slaves. Wake up, you who cannot speak. Onward, ghosts. Onward, spectors. To the gallop, you statues!" The crowds get up, the black horsemen sit up in bed; you hear 1789 whinnying, the people have only a single bond to make, and idealism will be in the saddle.

Thursday, March 22, 1855, 9:45 p.m. was the last coming of Jesus Christ for which the transcripts have been preserved. Victor Hugo was present; Mme. Victor Hugo and Charles Hugo were at the table. After a few minutes, Christ announced himself. At Hugo's invitation, he picked up where he had left off:

He leaves, and with a slash of the spur to the horse's side he leaps over chasms; he hurls himself from the dungeons of feudal days to the roofs of modern-day suburbs; from Bastille to city; from lord to serf, from king to commoner, from priest to philosopher, from philosopher to atheist, from atheist to God. His remarkable horse is splendid; it boasts Danton for one wing, fourteen armies for scales, volcanoes for nostrils, chasms for ears; this horse's mouth chews up infinity which falls foaming from its bloody bit; he whinnies the reveille, he paws the ground of the future, he lashes out at chaos; he is borne away, he rears, he takes fright, he unseats the horseman, he kills the stableman, he knocks over the stable, and, if he falls, his four iron shoes spark lightning bolts whose thunder shakes the world; this centaur possesses past and future, true and false. Evil and good, mounted on the formidable croup. He flings to the earth what he does not fling to the skies; he scales the heights, he scales the heights, he scales the heights; he bears humanity to freedom, freedom to equality, equality to fraternity; where will this fugitive from the shadows stop? This taker-between-the-teeth of the bit of immensity? What is there that can stop him? What can his last step be?

Then Jesus Christ was gone; not, as far as we know, to return to the turning tables.

What did the Jesus Christ of James Merrill and David Jackson have to say in *The Changing Light at Sandover*, published in 1982? In all the 500 pages of that great work of poetry, he speaks only once, as follows:

Jesus:
FATHER GOD! YAHWEH? AH LORDS, MY BROTHERS,
    SHALOM!
His voice is hollow. Like the Buddha, he
Acts out of his own exhausted energy.
WHAT A DEAD SOUND, MY NAME, IN HALF THE
    WORLD'S PULPITS.
WE, AS MY PRINCELY BROTHER SAYS, SPIN DOWN.
    OUR WORDS
LIKE GOD'S OWN PLANETS IN ONE LAST NOVA BURST
    AND
GRAVITY STILLS & OUR POWER LOSES ITS PULL.
HE & I CAME TO DELIVER LAWS, MINE FOR MAN
TO BECOME GOD. WORDS, WORDS. BUT OUR
    MESSAGE, BROTHERS!
I BEG OF YOU, INTERCEDE. BEFORE THE WINE
    RETURNS
WHOLLY TO WATER LET MY FATHER MAKE ME FLESH
THAT I MAY A SECOND TIME WALK EARTH AND
    IMPLORE
WRETCHED MAN TO MEND, REPAIR WHILE HE CAN.
    AMEN.

If all these religions are finally inadequate, what is mankind to do for a religion, or for a code of conduct?

Victor Hugo's answer was easy: Do exactly what the turning tables had been telling them to do all along.

Chapter Twenty-One

"I LOVE THE SPIDER AND I LOVE THE NETTLE": VICTOR HUGO'S FIFTH RELIGION

Musician, philosopher, theologian, and medical missionary Albert Schweitzer (1875-1965) coined the term "reverence for life" one day while on an African river journey. Schweitzer was overcome by a mystical sense that all creatures are, in a sense, one; for the rest of his life he lived by that principle, striving to not even harm a fly. The Schweitzerian notion of "reverence for life" had already appeared here and there throughout human history, perhaps finding its ultimate expression among the Jainists of India, whose adherents sometimes wear gauze masks so that they will not accidentally breathe in a fly and destroy it.

Victor Hugo was equally impressed by the strictures of the Jersey island spirits that the animal, vegetable and mineral worlds are all three composed of living, suffering souls as worthy and as needful of our love as are our fellow human beings. On the Channel islands of Jersey and Guernsey, and afterward, he made a determined effort to practice exactly what the spirits had preached. "I love the spider and I love the nettle," he wrote in *What the Shadow's Mouth Says*, early on in that period. "Do not mistreat animals! Peace to plants!" he admonished the reader of the poem. These two lines sum up Hugo's attitude, which he was not afraid to express to one and all, and which, by all accounts, he consis-

235

tently expressed in his actions.

At Marine-Terrace, a piebald greyhound named Lux (Latin for "light") was the favorite household pet. General Le Flô had given it to Charles Hugo as a gift. Lux had her own bed, a cushion she curled up on during the day—and her own place at the family table!

When asked why Lux was so special, the Hugos replied that, several years earlier, in Paris, a family friend had been burned to death while wearing her evening finery. The Hugos were certain— they could tell by the deep and gentle look in the greyhound's eyes—that Lux was the reincarnation of that friend.

Graham Robb writes that when Hugo went out walking after lunch, "two dogs and a cat regularly came up to greet him. Hugo recognized these creatures as 'ex-Decembrists [plotters of the *coup d'état*] transformed into animals who came to beg our forgiveness for their sins.'"

Other animals, as well, reciprocated Hugo's interest in their realm: "On a picnic one day, he was reading aloud from a book when a cow ambled over, leaned its head on the fence and began to listen. When the book was handed to Hugo's friend, Kesler, the cow lost interest and returned only when Hugo started reading again."

On Guernsey island, to which the family moved in 1856, Hugo insisted that no effort be made to clear the Hauteville-House garden of snakes and toads; very soon, his property was infested with the creatures. One day the cook came home with two live ducks and prepared to slaughter them. Victor Hugo suddenly appeared. He declared that the whole family would go to bed without dinner rather than that blood should be spilled on the property. The ducks were given their complete freedom of the garden. Claudius Grillet writes that, from that day on, they "survived ostentatiously. Glossy, glorious, garrulous, they were cherished by their master, no more than the toads, of course—but almost. We read, dated Dec. 16, 1860, in…[Hugo's *Notebooks*]: 'I let the ducks run free in the garden, for their Sunday.'"

One day on the beach on Jersey island, passers-by had seen, hurrying toward the ocean with a struggling lobster in her hand, Hugo's daughter, Adèle; she was returning the creature to the sea, no doubt at her father's request. Another time, Hugo himself was seen striding toward the water with a crab. He would write, in *What the Shadow's Mouth Says*:

> *I paid the fisherman who passed by on the strand*
> *And took that horrible beast in my hand…*
> *It opened a hideous mouth; a black claw*
> *Shot from its shell, my hand to paw*
> *…the crab bit me*
> *I told it: Live! Be blessed, poor soul damned to hell*
> *And I threw it back into the ocean's deep swell…*

In accordance with the spirits' teachings, Hugo's beneficence extended to the world of plants. Auguste Vacquerie wrote in his journal: "Victor Hugo only likes standing flowers. He outlaws bouquets, and regards cut flowers as people in agony. We've never seen him snip a flower, not even for the most attractive of female visitors…

"He explains to his grandchildren that flowers live and breathe like us, are living persons, and that there should not be too many people in an apartment [so the flowers' air won't be used up]."

Today, Hugo would probably have waged a campaign against the manufacture of women's cosmetics, not only because they are often developed with experimentation on animals (which he would certainly have fought as well) but because they can involve the use of the essences of plants, notably flowers. He wrote in *What the*

Shadow's Mouth Says:

> *A sense of horror makes the bird's feathers shiver.*
> *Everything feels pain. Flowers suffer beneath the scissor,*
> *And close in upon themselves like an eyelid closes;*
> *The tint on a woman's cheek is the blood of roses.*
> *The debutante at the dance, corsaged and whirling to*
> *   the melody*
> *Breathes in, with unwitting smile, a bouquet made of agony.*
> *Weep for ugliness, and weep for ignominy.*

Even the skeptical Vacquerie, who initially objected so strongly to the declarations of Balaam's Ass, eventually came around to Hugo's point of view. "Could it be that the oak and the stone have souls?" he early on wondered in his diary, after a lengthy conversation with Hugo. "I believe they do. The souls of vegetables and minerals exist in harsher conditions than the souls of others."

It can be argued that Vacquerie became something of a slave to these beliefs. By 1856, he was writing: "At present, I would no sooner tear a petal from a flower than I would a wing from a fly. The young ladies who pluck the petals off marguerites to see if someone passionately loves them make the same impression on me as priestesses who cut the throats of their victims, then try to divine the answers to questions from their dying convulsions. I wouldn't harm a match. I pity nails. In an execution, it's the blade of the guillotine that is condemned."

Hugo was as taken by the spirits' teachings about reincarnation as he was by their instruction regarding the equality of all life forms, though the former was an interest that he had been cultivating for many years. Here, his personal vanity may have powered his beliefs to some extent.

According to Paul Stapfer, a young French professor on Guernsey island who knew Victor Hugo well in his later years, "a certain English philosopher" had confided to Hugo the nature of his previous lives. Hugo told Stapfer that, "My philosopher gave the probable series of migrations of certain souls, among others mine. Here is its history: I have been Isaiah, Aeschylus. Judas Maccabee, Juvenal [a Latin poet], still more poets, several painters and two kings of Greece whose names I have forgotten." Stapfer wrote in *Victor Hugo at Guernsey* that, though a little astonished at having ruled over Greece, "Victor Hugo seemed to me in the final analysis to be quite satisfied with all his avatars."

In Hugo's Guernsey island home, Hauteville-House—today a museum to Hugo's years in exile—there can be seen, in a cartouche-like frame hanging above the drawing room fireplace, the names Job and Isaiah inscribed in large Gothic letters on damask linen. Hugo also believed he was the reincarnation of these two Old Testament prophets—and of John of Patmos, the author of *The Book of Revelations* and probably the John of the Gospels.

Hugo's literary contemporaries, while not doubting his genius, were more reserved when it came to believing he had also possessed genius in many of his previous lives (the concept of 'previous lives' being also a difficult one for them to swallow). N. Martin-Dupont wrote about how those closest to him reacted to these beliefs: "Around him, among his friends and family, people didn't trouble to hide their scorn. Kesler treated him with outright contempt as a hopeless ass." John of *The Book of Revelations* had been exiled to the Greek island of Patmos; Hugo often referred to Jersey island as "his Patmos." This prompted the journalist Louis Veuillot to call Hugo—to his face—"*Jocrisse à Pathmos!*" The phrase literally translates as, "Fool of Patmos!" In the vernacular, it has the emotional force of, "Asshole of Patmos!" Louis Veuillot wrote that Martin-Dupont himself called Hugo the "Sinai Nutcase," referring to Moses's sojourn on the Sinai Desert—for Hugo also believed he was the reincarnation of Moses. The author Leconte de Lisle tried to one-up Martin-Dupont by calling the Guernsey exile, "Dumb as the Himalayas!" In bothering to come up with these phrases at all, these 'friends' of Hugo's betray a certain jealousy of his fame and genius. But, beyond a doubt, Hugo's preoccupation with reincarnation—principally his own reincarnations—was considerably less disciplined than his genuine and abiding concern to show compassion for the other species of our planet.

Whatever the origins of Victor Hugo's beliefs in the sanctity of the spheres of animal, plant, and stone—however eccentric they may seem—it cannot be argued that Hugo was, amazingly, at least a century ahead of his time. Only 13 years before Hugo was born, the great English philosopher Jeremy Bentham had drawn ridicule to himself by claiming, in his *Utility Principle of Morals*, in 1789, that animals, like humans, suffered and therefore had the right to life, liberty and the pursuit of happiness. Up till then, most of Bentham's contemporaries had believed—and many would continue to believe—that animals were little more than automata, clockwork machine-like creatures that made a noise when stepped on only because their ratchet gear-like body parts were grinding.

Only slowly and painfully over the nineteenth century did the belief take hold in Europe that animals were conscious creatures capable of feeling pain. It was not until 1975—almost a century after Hugo's death—that the Australian philosopher Peter Singer published his landmark book, *Animal Liberation*, which put forward the belief that animals were the victims of what he called "speciesism," and suffered prejudice simply because they were a different species and therefore presumed to be less advantaged than man. In 1979, the Animal Legal Defence Fund (ALDF) was founded in San Francisco, California, with its Executive Director

Joyce Tischler declaring, as she continues to do so today, that animals are entitled to exactly the same civil rights as humans; 25 lawyers on call with the ALDF periodically defend animals in court on animal rights issues. Hugo would certainly have applauded this; he may have made analogous suggestions while on the Channel islands.

It may have been easy in the 1850's to ridicule Hugo's belief that plants have feeling and consciousness and should be treated lovingly; by the 1970's, the climate of opinion was beginning to change in his favor. In a famous experiment at McGill University, in Montreal, Canada, scientists randomly dropped crabs into boiling water and found that plants on the other side of the room responded to their pain; electrodes attached to the plant leaves recorded a mild electrical reaction whenever a crab hit the water. Since then, literally hundreds of experiments have been carried out, of greater or lesser scientific value, irresistably confirming the notion that plants have consciousness, perhaps of a highly complex sort.

Do rocks have consciousness, and should they be treated with loving kindness? Certainly, there doesn't seem to be a Rocks' Rights movement on the horizon. But it is interesting to note that, in the channeled masterpiece of James Merrill, *The Changing Light at Sandover*, the spirit guides inform the author that some of the more distinguished (and now dead) human personages in the poem have reincarnated in stones, apparently to acquire knowledge and experience of those realms (there is no punishment involved here; it is a privilege). Discussing the English poet W.H. Auden, who has taken life again as a mineral deposit, the guides suddenly remark that:

OUR WITTY POET SURFACING OFF ALASKA AS A VEIN OF PURE/ RADIUM HAS HAVOCKED A NOSY RADIO SHIP. 58 IN LIFEBOATS!

Finally, it is noteworthy that not only does the academic discipline of Interspecies Communications now exist, but one of its founders, Dr. Jim Nollman, claims to have discovered that chickens, buffalo and fleas have their own language along with whales and dolphins (with other such discoveries on the horizon). These newly-detected beast languages are, seemingly, startlingly different in essence from our own. These claims of the new Interspecies Communications scientists may seem bizarre and improbable. But they are among early warning signals that the traditional, science-sanctioned barriers between man and animal (e.g. "animals by definition don't have language") are beginning to crumble. It is becoming increasingly apparent that, with regard to the positions of Balaam's Ass on consciousness and feeling in animals and plants—which most of Hugo's contemporaries thought lunatic—whatever powers moved the turning tables were absolutely right.

One of the most wonderful moments in all literature comes in Book Two, Chapter XII of *Les Misérables*, the novel Hugo completed in 1862, seven years after his channeling experiences on Jersey island had come to an end.

We all know the story of Jean Valjean, imprisoned on the galleys for stealing a loaf of bread. His sentence extended because of several escape attempts, he is finally released after 19 years. He makes his way to the little town of Digne. Valjean carries with him the yellow passport of the ex-convict. For this reason, though he has money, no one will give him food or lodging.

He finally comes to the house of M. Bienvenu-Myriel, the Bishop of Digne. Victor Hugo has devoted the first 100 pages of *Les Misérables* to carefully building up the character of the Bishop. We come to know beyond a shadow of a doubt that he is an utterly good man, a man of immense and selfless charity. Without hesitation, the Bishop offers Jean Valjean dinner and a bed. In the middle of the night, Valjean gets up, steals the Bishop's silver cutlery, and makes his way swiftly out of the house.

In the morning—only minutes after his servant has informed the Bishop that the cutlery is gone—Valjean is brought back to the house in the company of the police. They have stopped him, searched him, found the cutlery and arrested him. Now they have come by the Bishop's to return his stolen goods on the way to taking Valjean back to prison.

"Ah, there you are!" says the bishop, instantly greeting Valjean fondly. "I'm glad to see you! But I gave you the candlesticks, too, which are silver like the rest and would bring two hundred francs. Why didn't you take them when you took your cutlery?"

The Bishop goes to the mantlepiece, takes the two silver candlesticks that are there, and gives them to Jean Valjean. He commends the police for simply trying to do their job, and tells them they may go. After they have left, he steps close to Valjean and says, "Do not forget, ever, that you have promised me to use the silver to become an honest man."

Jean Valjean is dumbfounded. The Bishop continues: "Jean Valjean, my brother, you no longer belong to evil, but to good. It is your soul I am buying for you. I withdraw it from dark thoughts and from the spirit of perdition, and I give it to God."

The former convict stumblingly thanks the bishop, and takes his leave.

The seed of charity has been planted in Jean Valjean. Initially, he mightily resists the power of this immense act of goodness. Little by little, it takes firm hold, little by little transforming his life. By the end of the book, he has himself performed great acts of selfless charity which eventually bring him total redemption.

This authentic, overpowering gift of love which Bishop Myriel gives to Jean Valjean at the beginning of the novel is Victor Hugo's supreme expression of his belief in the need for all of us to love all of creation unconditionally and unreservedly. At the seance where he was the first to expound these beliefs, Balaam's Ass told the participants that, "it is in the having doubts that the punishment lies. For man to know his error would be for him to know his judge, would be for him to know God. And the certainty of God's existence makes for Paradise on earth." The seance-goers did not understood this, seeing it as more of an intellectual conundrum; the worthy Auguste Vacquerie replied by pointing out to Balaam's Ass that he had just told them what their error was, which meant that, "If what you're telling us is true, then, if we accept what you're saying, our punishment will cease. And it follows from that that our lives will cease, since the only reason we have been born at all is to be punished. The very world itself would cease to be, if our punishments vanished by virtue of our having had our true natures revealed to us!"

But what Balaam's Ass really meant was that this understanding must come from the heart. And, if it does, then the world will indeed cease to be—but only in the far more exalted sense in which it has ceased to be for Bishop Myriel, who moves throughout it with the utter ease of complete love.

Chapter Twenty-Two

MADMAN OR ARCHAIC MAN?

In order to communicate the single letter 'Z,' the talking table of Jersey island would have had to tap 26 times.

By any reckoning, it would have taken it an extremely long time to communicate even the simplest of messages.

French psychiatrist Jean de Mutigny is only the more thorough of a number of critics who insist that it would have taken the tables so long to transmit the messages attributed to them that the transcripts of Jersey island cannot possibly be accurate accounts of what was actually communicated.

In *Victor Hugo and Spiritism (Victor Hugo et le spiritisme,* 1981), Dr. de Mutigny makes his case using as an example the December 17, 1854 dialogue between Galileo and Victor Hugo.

He notes that:

■ The seance took place between 9:45 p.m. and 1:20 a.m.: 215 minutes, roughly 13,000 seconds.

■ The text contains about 4,000 letters.

■ It takes an average of ten taps to identify a letter (an average calculated on the basis of the letter A counting as one tap and the letter Z requiring 26 taps).

And draws from this the conclusion that Galileo would have had to communicate at the astonishing rate of three taps per second—without taking into consideration stops between letters and breaks during the seance.

De Mutigny concludes that: "With the best will in the world, it is totally impossible, over two-and-a-half years, to decipher messages evening and morning at the rate of three taps a second. It was thus totally impossible for Victor Hugo, despite his genius, to be capable of such record keeping."

So, where did the lengthy transcripts come from? De Mutigny believes that when Victor Hugo sat down after every seance to transcribe a "good" copy, he proceeded, without knowing it, to do "automatic writing." Therefore, much of what we read (though it comes from the same 'source' as the material channeled through the tables—Hugo's troubled mind, according to de Mutigny) was placed in the transcripts after the actual seance.

De Mutigny believes that Victor Hugo unwittingly perpetrated this fraud because he suffered from a rare mental disease known as *fantastical paraphrenia*.

To make his case, de Mutigny begins by listing the characteristics of *fantastical paraphrenia* as set forth in Anty's *Abrégé de Psychiatrie* (*Abridgement of Psychiatry*), 1971 edition, page 118. These are, notably:

■ Often, debut of the illness in the person's thirties, characterized by worry, anxiety, paranoia, and a generalized sense that the world is hostile.

■ In later years, exorbitant fantasies, full-blown megalomania (i.e., delusions of grandeur) and a sense that the person is here on a vitally important cosmic mission.

■ Persistence of paranoia and a sense of persecution. These feelings greatly plague the sufferer, though he or she is often aware that they are afflicted; there are periods of remission.

De Mutigny supports his diagnosis with the following assertions:

■ There was a high incidence of insanity in the Hugo family: On Victor's wedding day, brother Eugène went mad and had to be institutionalized; the Hugos' surviving daughter, Adèle, was schizophrenic and had to be placed in an institution eventually as well.

■ As a political figure, Hugo often displayed hostility of a pathological sort toward his opponents.

■ In some of the poetic and literary personae he created while in exile, Hugo showed a strong tendency toward solitariness.

■ Hugo's handwriting changed radically from 1853 onward; de Mutigny sees this as having considerable psychological significance.

■ De Mutigny regards Hugo's residence on Guernsey island, Hauteville-House, as "a veritable house of the paranoid. It was a combination church, sacristy, funeral chapel, pagoda and cave of Ali Baba."

■ De Mutigny regards much of Hugo's poetry written in exile as pathological and suggestive of a tendency toward paranoia. "All his work is obsessed with the beyond, cemeteries, shadow," says the psychiatrist. "The poet had even mixed coffee grounds with ink to better express all this" (this is a one of a group of Hugo's drawings which his biographer, Graham Robb, sees as amazingly avant-garde: "Romantic tableaux created using the techniques of post-Romantic art").

De Mutigny concludes from all this:

"Victor Hugo, believing, in all good faith, that he was deciphering the messages of the tables, while in the grip of his delirium did automatic writing and produced 'hugolisms.'

"These messages were totally unconscious, a sort of personality-splitting which has as its effect the attributing to another what you yourself have edited."

A number of objections can be raised to what Dr. de Mutigny has to say.

A general one is that Hugo did not always, or even often, have in his head beforehand what the tables told him. Usually, when he did, he interrupted the spirit and told it so, and this is recorded in the transcripts.

There are a number of occasions where his wife, Adèle, makes this clear. For example, she tells Balaam's Ass that, while already believing what the spirit has just said about metempsychosis, Victor Hugo had "never believed that pebbles, plants and animals had souls."

A further objection is that it was not always Hugo who made a "good" copy of the transcript after the seance. Sometimes that task devolved upon Vacquerie; other times, upon Hugo's daughter, Adèle.

Still another objection is that there is no reason to suppose that the participants waited till the end of every word, or till the end of every sentence, to decide what the spirit was saying and write it down. Moreover, it is often the case during seances that, since the words are "coming through the head" of the psychic, that person simply repeats them, thereby rendering the table, or the Ouija board, or whatever, temporarily unnecessary. Anyone who has attended an Ouija board session, in particular, will recognize this as a common practice.

For both these reasons, the seances at Marine-Terrace could have gone by much more quickly than we have tended to suppose.

A final and overwhelming objection is that it is hard to imagine how an author with even a touch of madness could have created so stunning a masterpiece as *Les Misérables*. Hugo first conceived this novel in 1845, calling it *Les Misères*; he put it aside when he went into exile, but in 1860 took it up again in earnest, completing its 1,500 pages in 1862 and having it published to what was virtually world-wide acclaim.

If a poem like *What the Shadow's Mouth Says*, written at the height of the seances, can be seen (as de Mutigny sees it) as over-ripe with the darknesses of the imagination and touching at times on the pathological, *Les Misérables* is a great masterpiece of sanity. Hugo demonstrates the surest of touches in his depiction of every walk of European life, including the historical, the social, the political, the economic and the philosophical. Beneath the some-times lightly overblown Romantic surfaces of his characters, the psychology that drives them is rendered with great clarity and truthfulness. Though the book was long criticized for its seeming digressions, it is becoming clearer and clearer that these are not digressions at all, but devices which greatly broaden and deepen the canvas of the novel while maintaining it all of a piece.

Les Misérables is wise and prophetic as are few other works of art. Writes Dr. Robb in his *Victor Hugo: A Biography*: "With his seemingly unrepresentative life, his egocentrism, his isolation and his bizarre, patchwork religion, Hugo has produced the most lucid, humane and entertaining moral diagnosis of modern society ever written."

Here and there, the messages of the tables peep out, giving the novel added resonance. We've seen that Bishop Myriel has at-tained to the state of heart advocated by Balaam's Ass; and there is more than one lengthy allusion to the interrelated, 'holographic,' 'implicit' universe as presented by the spirit of Joshua during the seances.

With the publication of *Les Misérables*, the novelistic career of the 60-year-old Hugo was far from over. He wrote three more novels, *The Toilers of the Sea*, *The Man Who Laughs*, and *Ninety-Three*. All three are increasingly being regarded as masterpieces in their own right, with Dr. Robb seeing implicit similarities be-tween *Toilers of the Sea* and *Moby Dick*. The poet/visionary continued to write poetry, including the masterful *Contemplations* of his late 70s; he would go on to produce works as varied as the poetical/non-fictional *On Being A Grandfather* and a group of one-act plays prefiguring the style of Samuel Beckett.

It may well be that Victor Hugo suffered, not from a pathological mis-organization of creative energy, but from an excess of creative energy. He had enormous vitality. George Steiner writes in *Tolstoi or Dostoevsky* of Tolstoi that his, "gigantic vitality, his bearish strength and feats of nervous endurance, the excess in him of every life-force are notorious. His contemporaries, such as Gorky, pictured him as a titan roaming the earth in antique majesty. There was something fantastical and obscurely blasphemous about his old age. He passed into his ninth decade every inch a king." Exactly the same can be said of Victor Hugo. The 'human magnetic field' (also associated with table turning) was a medical vogue of the time, and several anecdotes indicate that Hugo had an unusually powerful field of this sort. He told Paul Stapfer:

"My son François, when he was an infant, had insomnia. We tried all the usual methods to make him sleep, without success, and he became so ill we began to think we were going to lose him.

"I tried making magnetic passes over him. He slept for 15 hours without waking up. This sleep was so restorative and so beneficial that the doctor, in wonderment, could only acknowledge that he'd been cured, without knowing why. And François kept saying to me: 'O, father, go on! More! More! That makes me feel so good.'"

Hugo also told Stapfer that once, in the salon of Bertin the Elder, he attached a small weight to the end of a thread, held the other end to his forehead and made the weight describe circles inside the crown of a hat. Dr. Robb suggests that the poet had a 'poetic year,' which "might tentatively be associated with seasonal fluctuations in the magnetic fields of vegetation." Robb explains that, throughout his life, Hugo composed his poems in a pattern which consistently fell into a poetic year corresponding to the solar year. "April, May, June, July, August and October are his richest months; September, November, December, January, February and March his poorest. The most prolific is always June and the least prolific February."

When, in the *Legends of the Century*, Hugo tells the story of Noah and the Ark, he alludes very briefly to the legend of Og, one of a race of titans who were destroyed in the Flood—except for Og, whom Noah allowed to ride on the Ark. Hugo is no sufferer from mental disease; he is that Og—a prediluvian figure, a titan from the time when *Gaia* reigned and all men were bathed in its energies. He is archaic man, an astonishing throwback who has managed to retain his connection with the sea of *Gaia* which is the sum and more than the sum of the parts of the earth. It may be that it was this quality—Hugo's fundamentally archaic nature, his still-living attachment to *Gaia*—that enabled him to play a pivotal, catalytic role in drawing to Jersey island the powers and energies that took shape around the turning table.

This is not to overly-romanticise the great romantic! He had flaws, including a runaway promiscuity—perhaps one expression of his "archaic" nature!—that drove his wife Adèle to despair and that signaled not only a thirst for life but also, on its dark side, a terror of life, which drove him again and again into, so to speak, his mother's arms.

But it is consoling to think that Hugo lived among us, and not so long ago. In our day and age, when so much of literature and public discourse has been reduced to aridity, banality and sleaze, we can perhaps hope that the vast new interest in channeling in our times signals the return of more titans—and Hugo's—of the race of Og.

POSTSCRIPT

The turning table seances at Marine-Terrace ended some time in the autumn of 1855. There was some disillusionment. After more than two years, none of the spirits' predictions had come true—particularly the one suggesting that the empire of Napoleon III, and their exile, would end in two years from September, 1853. Hugo's doctor advised him to give it up. Vacquerie had come to the conclusion that the turning tables merely articulated the thoughts of those present. Madame Hugo had failed to communicate with Delphine de Girardin, who had just died of cancer. As the last straw, Jules Allix, an enthusiast for the tables, had gone mad during a seance. He sat immobile on the Hugos' blue sofa for four hours and merely said, "I've seen things." Two days later, Augustine, his sister, found him flat on his stomach, trying to magnetize a watch so that it stopped at 12 o'clock.

In the rush of events, and Victor Hugo's other work, the transcripts were lost sight of for years. Not till 1923 were they published at any length, in Gustave Simon's *Chez Victor Hugo: Les Tables Tournantes de Jersey*, from Conard, Paris.

In 1968, most of the known transcripts—constituting a substantially longer text than Simon's volume—were published as a part of Volume IX of Jean Massin's monumental, 18-volume *Victor Hugo: Oeuvres Complètes*, from Le Club Francais du Livres, Paris.

These *Conversations with Eternity* were translated using Dr. Massin's text. By no means all of the transcripts were translated. And many more—perhaps as many as half—remain in private hands and have never been published.

About the Authors

John Chambers (translation and commentary) has an M.A. in English (Toronto) and studied at the University of Paris. His previous translations include "Phase One: C.E.Q. Manifesto," in *Quebec: Only the Beginning.* He has been a full-time instructor in English at Dawson College, Montreal, and assistant editor at McGraw-Hill Publishing and managing editor at International Thomson Publishing, both in New York. He has written numerous articles on the Paranormal.

Martin Ebon (Introduction), who served for twelve years as Administrative Secretary of the Parapsychology Foundation, New York, is the author/editor of more than eighty books, including *They Knew the Unknown* and *Prophecy in Our Time.* His most recent work is *KGB: Death and Rebirth.*

WORKS CONSULTED

Anka, Darryl. *Bashar: Blueprint for Change. A Message from Our Future*. Redmond, WA: New Solutions, 1990.

Appelbaum, Stanley, ed. *Introduction to French Poetry: A Dual-Language Book*. New York: Dover, 1991.

"Art of Poetry XXXI: James Merrill. Interview, The." *The Paris Review* No. 84 (Summer 1982): 184-219.

Baudouin, Charles. *Psychanalyse de Victor Hugo*. Geneve: Mont Blanc, 1943.

Catalogue. Maison de Victor Hugo. Paris: Ville de Paris, 1934.

Chambers, John. "The Channeled Myths of James Merrill." *The Anomalist* No. 5 (Summer 1997): 41-58.

De Mutigny, Jean. *Victor Hugo et le Spiritisme*. Paris: Nathan, 1981.

Ebon, Martin. "Victor Hugo: A Two-Year Dialogue with Ghosts." In *They Knew the Unknown*. New York: World, 1971: 53-60.

Gaudon, Jean. *Ce Qui Disent les Tables Parlantes: Victor Hugo à Jersey*. Paris: Pauvert, 1963.

Georgel, Pierre. *Drawings by Victor Hugo*. London: Victoria and Albert Museum, 1974.

Gobron, Gabriel. *History and Philosophy of Caodaism*. Saigon: Tu-Hai Publishing House, 1950.

Grillet, Claudius. *La Bible dans Victor Hugo*. Paris/Lyons: Emmanuel Vitte, 1910.

—. *Victor Hugo Spirite*. Paris/Lyons: Emmanuel Vitte, 1929.

"Hugo Turns the Tables." *Times Literary Supplement* [London] No. 3,295 22 April 1965: 308.

Hugo, Victor. *Les Misérables*. New York: Signet, 1987.

Massin, Jean, Ed. *Victor Hugo: Oeuvres Complètes. Tome 9.* Paris: Le Club Francais du Livres, 1968. (18 volumes).

Maurois, Andre. *Olympio: The Life of Victor Hugo.* New York: Harper, 1956.

Merrill, James. *The Changing Light at Sandover.* New York: Knopf, 1996.

Mitchell, Dr. Edgar. "Interview: Message from Space." *Kindred Spirit* Summer (June-August) 1997: 35-38.

Pereira, Patricia. *Songs of the Arcturians.* Hillsboro, OR: Beyond Words, 1996.

—. *Eagles of the New Dawn.* Hillsboro, OR: Beyond Words, 1997.

—. *Songs of Malantor.* Hillsboro, OR: Beyond Words, 1998.

Robb, Graham. *Victor Hugo: A Biography.* New York: Norton, 1998.

Simon, Gustave. *Chez Victor Hugo: Les Tables Tournantes de Jersey.* Paris: Conard, 1923.

Steiner, George. *Tolstoy or Dostoevsky: An Essay in the Old Criticism.* New York: Dutton, 1971.

Stevens, Philip. *Victor Hugo in Jersey.* Chichester, Sussex: Phillimore, 1985.

Talbot, Michael. *The Holographic Universe.* New York: HarperCollins, 1991.

Thompson, William Irwin. *Imaginary Landscape: Making Worlds of Myth and Science.* New York: St. Martin's Press, 1989.

Wilson, Colin. *From Atlantis to the Sphinx.* London: Virgin, 1996.

Wolfe, James R. "Deep Inside the Patmos Cave." In *Doomsday! How the World Will End--and When.* Ed. Martin Ebon. New York: Signet, 1977: 101-111.

Index